Quod scriptura, non iubet vetat

The Latin translates, "What is not commanded in scripture, is forbidden:'

On the Cover: Baptists rejoice to hold in common with other evangelicals the main principles of the orthodox Christian faith. However, there are points of difference and these differences are significant. In fact, because these differences arise out of God's revealed will, they are of vital importance. Hence, the barriers of separation between Baptists and others can hardly be considered a trifling matter. To suppose that Baptists are kept apart solely by their views on Baptism or the Lord's Supper is a regrettable misunderstanding. Baptists hold views which distinguish them from Catholics, Congregationalists, Episcopalians, Lutherans, Methodists, Pentecostals, and Presbyterians, and the differences are so great as not only to justify, but to demand, the separate denominational existence of Baptists. Some people think Baptists ought not teach and emphasize their differences but as E.J. Forrester stated in 1893, "Any denomination that has views which justify its separate existence, is bound to promulgate those views. If those views are of sufficient importance to justify a separate existence, they are important enough to create a duty for their promulgation ... the very same reasons which justify the separate existence of any denomination make it the duty of that denomination to teach the distinctive doctrines upon which its separate existence rests." If Baptists have a right to a separate denominational life, it is their duty to propagate their distinctive principles, without which their separate life cannot be justified or maintained.

Many among today's professing Baptists have an agenda to revise the Baptist distinctives and redefine what it means to be a Baptist. Others don't understand why it even matters. The books being reproduced in the *Baptist Distinctives Series* are republished in order that Baptists from the past may state, explain and defend the primary Baptist distinctives as they understood them. It is hoped that this Series will provide a more thorough historical perspective on what it means to be distinctively Baptist.

The Lord Jesus Christ asked, *"And why call ye me, Lord, Lord, and do not the things which I say?"* (Luke 6:46). The immediate context surrounding this question explains what it means to be a true disciple of Christ. Addressing the same issue, Christ's question is meant to show that a confession of discipleship to the Lord Jesus Christ is inconsistent and untrue if it is not accompanied with a corresponding submission to His authoritative commands. Christ's question teaches us that a true recognition of His authority as Lord inevitably includes a submission to the authority of His Word. Hence, with this question Christ has made it forever impossible to separate His authority as King from the authority of His Word. These two principles—the authority of Christ as King and the authority of His Word—are the two most fundamental Baptist distinctives. The first gives rise to the second and out of these two all the other Baptist distinctives emanate. As F.M. lams wrote in 1894, "Loyalty to Christ as King, manifesting itself in a constant and unswerving obedience to His will as revealed in His written Word, is the real source of all the Baptist distinctives:' In the search for the *primary* Baptist distinctive many have settled on the Lordship of Christ as the most basic distinctive. Strangely, in doing this, some have attempted to separate Christ's Lordship from the authority of Scripture, as if you could embrace Christ's authority without submitting to what He commanded. However, while Christ's Lordship and Kingly authority can be isolated and considered essentially for discussion's sake, we see from Christ's own words in Luke 6:46 that His Lordship is really inseparable from His Word and, with regard to real Christian discipleship, there can be no practical submission to the one without a practical submission to the other.

In the symbol above the Kingly Crown and the Open Bible represent the inseparable truths of Christ's Kingly and Biblical authority. The Crown and Bible graphics are supplemented by three Bible verses (Ecclesiastes 8:4, Matthew 28:18-20, and Luke 6:46) that reiterate and reinforce the inextricable connection between the authority of Christ as King and the authority of His Word. The truths symbolized by these components are further emphasized by the Latin quotation - *quod scriptura, non iubet vetat*— i.e., "What is not commanded in scripture, is forbidden:' This Latin quote has been considered historically as a summary statement of the regulative principle of Scripture. Together these various symbolic components converge to exhibit the two most foundational Baptist Distinctives out of which all the other Baptist Distinctives arise. Consequently, we have chosen this composite symbol as a logo to represent the primary truths set forth in the *Baptist Distinctives Series.*

LETTERS
ON
CHRISTIAN BAPTISM

LETTERS ON
CHRISTIAN BAPTISM,

AS THE

INITIATING ORDINANCE INTO THE REAL KINGDOM OF CHRIST.

ALSO,

On the CONTRAST between the Kingdom as organized by Christ, and the present Sectarian state of the Christian World.

BY JOHN FLAVEL BLISS, A.M.

Late Pastor of several Congregational and Presbyterian Churches, in Western New York.

With a Biographical Sketch of the Author by John Franklin Jones

Addressed to all his Christian Friends and Acquaintance.

HIGH TREASON is the crime of injured majesty.

High treason against the King of Zion, is where the crime is against either the Person of the King—his Kingdom—his dominion—his laws—the oath of allegiance to Him, against proper persons taking it, against the union of all his people under him, within his own Fold, or against his exclusive jurisdiction over them.

To build up other Folds, under other Rulers, is High Treason.

Whosoever either aids, abets, or in any way assists in a crime, is as really guilty as a principal, and is equally liable to the penalty.

LEXINGTON, N.Y.
PUBLISHED BY LEVI L. HILL
1841

he Baptist Standard Bearer, Inc.

NUMBER ONE IRON OAKS DRIVE • PARIS, ARKANSAS 72855

Thou hast given a *standard* to them that fear thee;
that it may be displayed because of the truth.
– *Psalm 60:4*

Reprinted 2006

by

THE BAPTIST STANDARD BEARER, INC.
No. 1 Iron Oaks Drive
Paris, Arkansas 72855
(479) 963-3831

THE WALDENSIAN EMBLEM
lux lucet in tenebris
"The Light Shineth in the Darkness"

ISBN# 1579786383

LETTERS

On CHRISTIAN BAPTISM, as the initiating ordinance into the real Kingdom of Christ:

On the alterations of it, by Despotic Powers, in principle and in form, and the misapplication of Baptism, and the substitute, to improper subjects, enforced by the same powers, for sectarian purposes, and the delusions accompanying:

On the REAL KINGDOM OF CHRIST, exclusively under his own jurisdiction, into which Christian Baptism introduces the Convert:

On the extent to which that Kingdom has been BROKEN DOWN, by the formation of rival folds, under rival rulers, accomplishing their ends by stratagem, and the substitute for Baptism:

On the CONTRAST between that Kingdom, so organized, by Christ himself, and the present scatterd state of the sheep, into folds the devices of men, and under rival and competing Rulers:

On the ORIGIN and ILLEGITIMACY of those folds contrived by men, and confining the Sheep away from the rightful Shepherd's jurisdiction, and under the jurisdiction of those who have no right to control them; and the treasonable position of such folds, as rivals against the Fold of Christ, and as obstacles in the way of its prevalence:

On the CRUELTY of that use of the substitute for Baptism which makes unconscious and helpless babes, Church members, in such folds as are the inventions of men, and ruled by men, and at antipodes against the One Fold of Christ; thus hindering them, when converted, from Christian Baptism, and from going into the Fold of Christ, under his exclusive jurisdiction, and thus inclining the babe, through delusion, deception, and stratagem, to remain in a treasonable state of rivalship against the Fold of Christ during all his life, breeding and perpetuating divisions, "not knowing what he does:"

And on the DIVISIONS in the Zion of God, traced to their true origin; and the true scriptural basis of CHRISTIAN UNION, to which Christians must necessarilly come, before they can ever be ONE again, as they were during the first and second centuries of the Christian era.

RECOMMENDATIONS.

UTICA, October 26, 1840.

DEAR BROTHER HILL.—I have been highly gratified with the lucid, scriptural view of the Kingdom of Christ, presented in the Letters of brother Bliss; and in this, as well as in many other particulars, I deem them an invaluable acquisition to Baptist literature and the cause of truth. On no subject do the Christian community need instruction more than on this: and brother Bliss has been peculiarly happy and discriminating in the discussion. Some of our own brethren may be greatly helped by a close attention to brother Bliss' expose.

Yours truly, A. M. BEEBEE.

From Gerrit Smith, Esq., to the Author, after reading part of these Letters.

"You have certainly furnished no small amount of evidence that *infant baptism*, and *sprinkling*, are but *human inventions*. *I have long suspected that they were no better.* I should like to know for a certainty, '*what is truth*' on the subject, that I might act accordingly. If immersion be necessary to constitute valid scriptural baptism, then do I earnestly desire to be immersed myself. But I seem never to have had sufficient leisure for the due examination of this subject; or rather, perhaps, I have never attached sufficient importance to it. I admit that it is important to know the Saviour's own mode; and that knowing it, it is *sin to refuse to conform to it.*"

From the Editor of the New-York Baptist Register, July 10.

"The applications for the republication of these letters, have been such, that the author will probably be induced to consider them, and give to the public his labors in a more permanent shape. No doubt there will be a careful revision. ———Individuals who have been liberated from the power of tradition, after a long period of thraldom—when their eyes are fully opened, and God gives them to see the delusion, the utter absurdity of it fills them with amazement; and they are surprised their former associates do not see as well as themselves. When we consider the almost indescribable interest such persons feel in behalf of their brethren they have left in error, Br. Bliss' plainness will no doubt be pardoned. In regard to redundancy, Br. Bliss had his object. He knew that many required the subject to be presented in a great variety of points of light —and he cared not if he sometimes seemed repetitious, so he effected his object, in making the truth irresistable.

"In these letters, we must say, with hundreds of our brethren who will unite with us, there is a distinctness and definiteness of position given to the Church of Jesus Christ, and a contrast drawn with illegitimate associations rarely to be met with; and some who have indulged in the charge of redundancy here, we have no doubt might go over them again to great advantage, and learn still more of the nature and Kingdom of Christ. Even Baptists, in many instances, have but muddy views of the nature of this kingdom, and are too often disposed to jumble it up with anything and everything that has in it a moral biending. A multitude of contentions and difficulties have arisen from such confused and imperfect apprehensions, which a clear perception of its character would have prevented. If there was nothing in the work but this, we would give it wings to speed its flight in every region."

From the same, of October 16, 1840.

"These letters must be an invaluable addition to any Library. They exhibit the whole subject of the contrast between the original Kingdom of Christ, and the present scattered state of the sheep into human folds, in a clear, concise and forcible light."

From the same, of October 23, 1840.

"We are indeed highly gratified to receive the intelligence of the prospect of their publication. Many of our readers also, who have been so anxious for their re-publication, in a revised form, will be no less gratified. There is no publication that we have on the subject of the ordinances of Christ's house that can supply their place."

From the Livingston Baptist Ministerial Conference, prepared by Rev. E. Stone.

"Every man is under moral obligation to vindicate the cause of truth.—— We seem afraid to attempt the removal of the scales from the eyes of others, lest we lose their friendship. While errors have been flooding churches, now and then a bold champion, like Luther, has ventured forth to stem the torrent of error, for which they have been fined, imprisoned, and burnt at the stake. Brother Bliss, it is true, is not terrified at the fires of Smithfield; still, it needs some moral courage to step forth before the world to say what he has. The subject has been handled without gloves. It needed handling with a fearless pen. It may be asked, Has not the Editor of the Register spoken the minds of the denomination generally with regard to the Letters? If so, why say any more? Has not Brother Bliss written "the truth, the whole truth, and nothing but the truth?" Grant this: but does brother Bliss *know* that the people to whom he belongs will bear him out in *publishing* what he has written? The approbation of his own conscience is his best security—still, he must desire to know the feelings of his brethren. For ourselves, we feel under obligations to the author of those Letters, and wish to contribute our mite towards discharging the debt. He must desire to know, in addition to what the Editor has well said, that what he has fearlessly written ought to be spread before the Christian public.——We believe Brother Beebee has expressed the views of our denomination, &c.

From the Rev. William Sands, Editor of the Religious Herald, Richmond, Virginia.

"Brother Bliss has entered into a full and thorough investigation of this subject, especially on infant baptism. He has, we think, overthrown the arguments usually adduced in favor of this tradition of the fathers. These letters have already undeceived several as to this delusion. The re-publication of them has been strongly urged, and we are glad the request has been acceded to. We hope they will yet do more good, in opening the eyes of the supporters of infant sprinkling, and cause them to renounce their unscriptural theory.

PREPARATORY STATEMENT.

The writer aims solely at usefulness, in defending the rights of Jesus Christ, against the invaders of his prerogative, and in defending the best interests of all his people. In ordering them all to be "gathered together in one," within "one Fold," and under "one Shepherd," by "one baptism"—to have but "one Lord," and "no divisions," and in praying so earnestly; "that they all might be one," the Saviour himself displayed the most benevolent design.

The building up of illegitimate folds, under human rulers, is certainly waging war with this most benevolent arrangement of the Redeemer.

The writer was deluded when a youth, by what was falsely called infant *baptism*—his confidence secured in the usual way; his reading was entirely on one side till he was 45 years of age. He took unwearied pains to become master of all the published arguments on that side; and, (as he now believes,) because of an unconquerable anxiety to obtain more satisfactory and sound arguments, and not because he began, even during all that time, to suspect that system.

His confidence in the sprinkling of babes was first shaken in an effort to defend it, against the attack of it, by an intelligent Baptist Minister, within his parish.

His mind was uneasy for nearly a year, and was searching for scriptural and historical proof: but in vain. At length he gave up to a determination to follow truth, let it lead where it would, and let it cost what it might. Soon the bubble burst. Yet, it was not till he had carefully written out a literal translation from the Greek Testament of every passage that relates to baptism, and collected them, so as to have a clear view of the mind of the Spirit. It was six months more before his mind became adjusted, against the influence of all his former prejudices, in relation to Baptism.

Most gladly would he have kept quiet, if he dared. But as he saw, through this his delusion, he had exerted a wrong influence in the Kingdom of Christ, he felt that he must counteract it, let it cost what it might.

It was a costly transaction. To feel obliged to condemn one's former principles, so often and so publicly defended—to cease all further services with the churches, and feel obli- to refuse all invitations—to remain ostensibly *laid up* for one or two years, in private studies—to feel obliged, by convictions of truth, to join the "sect which is every where spoken against"—and to turn the back upon all one's former associates and spiritual interests, and to expose one's self to all the obloquy or persecution that *might* follow, and to contravene the tenderest feelings of one's own dear family, is one of the greatest trials in the world. Reader, infant sprinkling, and the accompanying delusions, which turn us into a fold the device of men, instead of the One Fold of Christ, is the cause of all this trouble, as well as of most of the divisions in the Zion of God.

Regard for truth—for the rights of Jesus Christ—for his exclusive jurisdiction, and for his regulations for the best interests of his people, constrained the author to take the course he has.

As the subject matter of the one fold of Christ, his title to all the sheep, and to exclusive jurisdiction, and the tendency of infant sprinkling to build up and continue the competing folds of men, and thus to breed and perpetuate divisions, and keep the dear friends of Christ in separate folds, in future ages, and prevent them from ever being One under Christ, rose to view in a clearer and more forcible light, he felt constrained to write a few friendly letters on the subject, to Christian friends, his former associates. As he continued to write, the subject swelled and enlarged to the present size.

He is happy to say that he has certainly no less friendship

for his former associates, but an increase—and he knows not that there is any diminution on the part of his former associates, unless it be in a few cases.

As friends insisted the letters should be published, he has finally consented, in the hope they may be of use to the bleeding cause of Christ, and to those minds that are anxious to know the truth. Perfection in thought or expression cannot be expected. He will cheerfully correct errors, as soon as convinced of them.

A generous public are requested candidly to reflect on the *scope* of the thoughts and arguments, and not to be fastidious on little points; and to recollect it is the rights of Jesus Christ, the great Redeemer, that we wish to defend.

To the influence of the Holy Spirit, who will *always* accompany his own truth, to the consciences and hearts of those to whom it is presented, unless through prejudice and rebellious hearts, they grieve him away, this work is devoutly commended, praying that he will guide all who read in the right ways of the Lord.

If the writer in any thing seems pointedly severe, it is not because of any lack of tenderness to those who differ, but because he feels for the bleeding cause of Christ, and feels a holy indignancy against the propagation of those delusions that are breeding so many divisions, and are are so perfectly unfounded in the word of God, and mislead so many excellent minds, during all their lives, and often lead them to do more hurt than good, notwithstanding they have good intentions.

If a Minister or a Christian support, during all his life, either the treasonable jurisdiction of the Pope over Christianity—or that of the National Governments—or that of the Civil and Episcopal Government of England—or that of the Episcopal Government in the United States, or that of the Presbyterian Aristocracies—or that of the Methodist Episcopal Bishops, and subordinate rulers, or that of any other competing fold, or jurisdiction, that hinders the unlimited, unrivalled, and exclusive jurisdiction of Jesus Christ, over his own cause, and supports the great feeder, or supply, of all this treason, the making of babes Church members, within these folds, by stratagem, when helpless; and if he supports the deluding of parents, by false pretences, and the making of them the blind and cruel agents in enslaving their own children, in this way; it is a matter of serious doubt whether he does not perform more evil than good, during his life, notwithstanding he may have good intentions, and may actually accomplish a great deal of good. The author now looks back upon his own misguided course, in this mirror, with serious regret. Minister of the Gospel! if you continue this course, even though you now, through delusion, refuse to look at it, yet you will be *obliged* to look at it in the great reckoning day. How will it then appear to you, in the light of eternity! Professed Christian! if you support this evil, how will you meet it at the bar of God! Whether the benevolent institutions of the day that stand connected with such treason against Heaven, will be of more benefit than injury to the world, is certainly very questionable. Such rulers always display such crooked management and give such a sectarian turn and selfish direction to every thing under their control, that the general movement becomes a state of absolute rivalship against the jurisdiction of Christ.

Sir Isaac Newton, after examining the History of the Baptists, from the apostolic times downward, declared of them, (as Whiston informs us,) that they were the only community that had never symbolized with antichrist, (alluding to their uniform recognition of the exclusive jurisdiction of Jesus Christ,) and that "he was inclined to consider them as one of the two Witnesses of the Apocalypse.

LETTER I.

JANUARY 1, 1840.

To my Numerous Christian Friends and acquaintance:

The recurrence of a new year's day reminds us of time past, the rapidity of its flight, our rapid approach to the judgment, and that whatever we do for the prosperity of Zion must be done soon.

A subject has rested with great weight upon my mind, during three or four years past, which, to me, appears to be of great importance. Taking one side of the question involved, tends, in my view, to continue and increase divisions among Christians, to divide and weaken their influence, to establish more firmly sectarian jars, with all its horrors, to increase and foment divisions in the cause of benevolence, at home and abroad, and thus to be instrumental in the ruin of souls, and greatly to retard the millenial day. But taking the right side of the question, to me seems necessary, in order to unite the influence of Christians in those noble objects, to remove divisions, to stop the mouth of gainsayers and infidels, and to "*prepare the way of the Lord.*"

It is now about two hundred years since Christian Baptism, a *positive* ordinance of Jesus Christ, was actually cashiered and pushed away by a whole kingdom, in ecclesiastical council, at Westminister, and something substituted in its place, of mere human invention. The circumstances, I am sure, are not generally understood. A portion of Christendom still honestly and conscientiously cleave to Christian baptism as an ordinance of Christ, and can not, dare not, exchange it for a mere human invention. They feel that thus to alter the laws of Christ by human legislation, would be high treason against Heaven; that to alter the laws of Christ in the least, is to establish a principle which would admit of unlimited alterations; that to discard one ordinance or law, is to establish a principle that is unlimited in its tendency to add *others.* We are strictly forbidden by the Saviour from adding any thing to, or taking any thing from, his laws, under the severest penalty. (Rev. xxii, 18, 19.) We believe that a portion of Christendom have been blinded, misled, and seduced from the truth by the inventions of men, and been made by predecessors, from infancy up, the unconscious and unintentional agents in promoting a systematic delusion, which has been appended to the Christian system: I mean the system of church organization that stands connected with the sprinkling of babes and of adults, and thereby discarding entirely, as it does, Christian baptism.

Is Christ divided? Who ever authorized the formation of churches except they consist of professed believers, and except they profess Christ themselves, by baptism, in its true sense, after conversion? Surely not the Lord Jesus Christ. Infant baptism is among the many errors that crept into the church in a few very rare cases, somewhere near the middle of the third century. But it was *baptism*, not *sprinkling*, until the last part of the sixteenth century, or the beginning of the seventeenth. The system, since that time, of organizing churches, chiefly by the mere sprinkling of unconscious babes, a totally unauthorized ceremony, and when in the Bible there is not the least shadow of any authority for applying baptism at all to such sujects, and the human constitutions, necessary to hold such churches together, has a totally disorganizing tendency upon Jesus Christ's kingdom, establishes a rival competition between the organizations,—establishes a precedent unlimited in its tendency of forming another and another organization, according to human caprice, and therefore leads to endless jars and broils among the friends of Christ. Who can think of the evils that have followed from such rival organizations, during the whole period, the unkind misrepresentations, the criminations, and recriminations, the mutual jealousies, the obstacles thrown in the way of *Christ's* organization, defeating as it does the efforts and success of those who cleave to it, the evils of a separate train of expences in building separate houses of worship, supporting a separate and rival ministry,—the hostility of all this against the heart and soul of the dear Saviour, who prayed that all his people might be one; the weakening of Christian influence; the discouragements thus thrown in the way of those on both sides who would *wish* to do right, if they only understood the cause and cure of the troubles, and the tendency of this whole state of things, to feast the infidel, to ruin souls, and to retard the millenium, without being sick and distressed beyond measure?

And what is peculiarly wounding, is, that these rival organizations are carried by the dear, well-meaning missionaries among the poor, blind heathen, with the certain prospect of a similar train of evils to be introduced, together with

Christianity, among *them*, and perhaps to be of long duration. Infidels, among the heathen, are already fortifying *their* minds against the gospel on account of the sectarianism that accompanies it. And with us at home the greatest obstacles in the way of extending the cause of Christ grow out of these *rival* organizations. Behold, how the hearts of the dear ministers and Christians in these organizations are discouraged, how the scoffers and infidels embolden each other, how jealous the unconverted are that we possess a selfish and sectarian spirit, and how exceedingly difficult it has become to get near them, or them near us, that we may do them good, on account of this state of things. It is, in my opinion, chiefly owing to these sectarian organizations and their effects, that efforts in promoting revivals have become so unsuccessful of late.

In the apostolic time it was not so. Then revivals accompanied the ministers and churches everywhere. God is now just as ready to give his Spirit as then. The reason of the superior success then, more than now, must be because *then* "*the multitude of them that believed* were *of one heart* and *one soul:*" then, in one spirit were they all baptized into one body." Then the apostles nipt every division in the bud, and a rival fold would not have been endured for a moment.

The question arises, what inventions of men, and delusive systems, what human constitution of a delusive tendency, empowering the few to govern the many, and keep them under,—what change of ordinances, what lording over God's heritage, by *spiritual wickedness* in high places, and what organizations, adapted to perpetuate these evils, have been oppented to the Christian system? If I can start some points, give some hints, and afford some relief, even to one mind, and correct some of my past teaching, and help even one out of trouble, I shall have done something.

The eight hundred million of our race on the globe die about as fast as to include that whole number during every thirty-two years. This will be, on an average, about twenty-five million each year, two million and more each month, five hundred and twenty-one thousand each week, sixty-eight thousand each day, nearly three thousand each hour, and forty-eight each minute. During the two hundred years that these rival and contending church organizations have existed, about five *billion*, or *five thousand million of souls* have passed into eternity. The subject swells in magnitude be-

B

yond description. It is not a little petty question about *how much water?* or a question where every man may follow his own blind feelings, and *falsely call them conscience.* It is a question involving the greatest and most important principles conceivable, all of them having a direct bearing upon the conversion of the world. They relate to the rival and contending systems of church organization. Whichever side is in the wrong has a vast load of responsibility in holding up a system productive of all these evils, as well as each individual under it, who aids in its support.

Must things remain so? *Can* they never be adjusted and settled? Souls are fast perishing. The subject is too great to lie neglected. We *must* know *how*, and *when*, and *where*, these divisions, and rivalships, and jars *began*, and how they have been *continued*, in order to know the remedy. For one so insignificant as myself to attempt any thing of the kind may be thought foolish. Nothing but a fear that more *able* persons will neglect it, and a desire to do what I can, before I go to the judgment, and a consciousness that I was blinded and in the wrong a great many years, could induce me to it. I know that the delusions connected with infant sprinkling, and that whole way of church organization, (for I must speak out,) are of a peculiarly blinding, darkening, deluding nature; and in my opinion this delusion, as a system of church organization, is stronger than any delusion with which I have ever been acquainted. Another strong *delusion* once cost me much effort; but *this* has cost me far more. I know that thousands of honest minds are willing to do right, if they only understood the subject. Conviction with those whose minds are made up is not to be expected; because delusion is so evasive there is no reasoning with it. All I can hope is to help some few honest minds.

LETTER II.

THE LAW ON BAPTISM.

When Jesus Christ commands all true believers to be baptized, and his ministers to baptize them, what does he mean by that law?

Baptizo is the Greek word used by our Savior, in the law and it has become *anglicised* within the last three centuries, by those who did not wish the people to understand its real meaning. If there had been any other ordinance equally disagreeable to human nature, and one they wished to alter, they probably would have transferred also the Greek of that. Common people can not know its meaning only from Greek dictionaries, and from the use of it, also, before the ordinance of baptism was *changed*. Because, the common rule with lexicographers is to define words, in English. and other dictionartes, first according to their primary meaning, and then, if any considerable portion of people, at the time, use the word in a *new* sense, to add that also. Dr. Webster somewhere says, we may use a word in any sense we please, if we only define what we really *do* mean by it. Ever since the ordinance of baptism was *changed*, some two hundred years ago, by the British Parliament,* and by the Westminster Assembly by a majority of ONE,† and a new ceremony, invented by men, to supply its place, efforts have been constantly made to have *baptizo* so construed as to favor that treasonable crime against heaven. But the Lord in his providence has laughed all these efforts to scorn.

To use the word baptizo, according to the sense of those who have *done* this deed, is by no means ascertaining the mind of Christ. Its modern use by the sprinklers is by no means the test. Its use before that treasonable crime, is the *only* true test. We might just as well construe the word "*pay*," in a civil law, and say it means to *run away*—to *evade*, because some in modern times use the word in that sense; as to define *baptizo* according to the use of it by those during the last two hundred years, who have in fact totaly evaded its force. Our question is,—What did *Christ* mean? not what *alterations* of it have these made.

In Wilson's Christian Dictionary, 1678, baptizo is rendered to dip into the water, or plunge one into the water.

In Dr. William Young's Dictionary it is rendered to dip, all over, to wash, to baptize.

In the Greek Dictionary of Schleusner it is rendered, to immerse, to plunge, to sink into water.

In the Greek Dictionary of Charles Richardson, justly esteemed the most valuable one ever published, it is renderd, to dip, or merge in water, to sink, to plunge, to immerse.

In the Greek Dictionary of the learned John Jones, it is rendered, in the first person, I plunge, I plunge in water, I bury, I overwhelm.

---

* At 1644. † At 1643

In Pickerings Greek Dictionary, it is rendered, to dip, immerse, submerge, plunge, sink.

In Donnegan's Greek Dictionary,* it is rendered, to immerse, submerge, saturate, drench, &c.

In Grove's Greek Dictionary, and also in that of Robertson, it is rendered substantially in the same way, unless one of them has added a modern use of it, as a sixth or seventh definition.

In Schrevilius' Lexicon, 17th edition, improved by Hill, Boyer, and Entick, it is rendered into Latin, by mergo, abluo, lavo — that is, to immerse, to baptize, to wash away, to wash.

In the twelfth edition, however, London 1738, Baptizo has in the same lexicon, but *two* definitions, to wit, mergo, and lavo,—to immerse, to wash. Four new definitions have been added then, in that same author's Lexicon, since his death, and since 1738. This demonstrates intentional corruption somewhere.

One or two of the above authors, have added *sprinkle* as a seventh or eighth definition also, within some ten years past, but with an asterisk, thereby apprising us that it is a very modern definition. Many of the other remote definitions, after the primary, have also been added in modern times. It is certain Jesus Christ in his law could have had no allusion to any of these secondary or remote definitions, added within the last fifty years, and so many centuries since the law was made. By having Baptizo in some lexicons rendered into Latin, and of late by six Latin words, each of which, of itself, has often some six or eight definitions, and by assuming that Baptizo has all the various meanings of all these six Latin words, many, through the impulse of their delusion, helping along the mistake, have been grossly misled and deceived, and been led in this way to deceive thousands of others, not knowing what they did.

The Dictionary of the learned Bailey, justly esteemed one of the most accurate of any ever published, gives immerse as the definition of Baptizo.

Butterworth renders Baptize to dip, immerse, or plunge.

In the Dictionay of the very learned and celebrated John Ash, London, 1775, Baptize is rendered to dip, to plunge, to overwhelm, to administer Baptism.

---

* Small edition.

Baptism he renders an immersion in water, a washing by immersion, a Christian ordinance, whereby a person "puts *on Christ*," or, makes a public profession of the Christian religion.

Baptizo : "In its primary and radical sense, I cover with water."—*Ewing's Dict.*

To the same effect are Stourdza, Greenfield, Junius, Calmet, Bucheners, and many others.

The Greek Church unanimously give the same meaning to the word baptizo, and have always unanimously practised immersion. They certainly know the meaning of their own language.

It is those who hold that the rulers over the Church had a right to alter the ordinances, and make new laws for the Church, that have, since 1556, introduced another custom, and falsely caled it baptism, and procured it to be established, in the year 1644, by Parliamentary law. Of this we are informed by Dr. Gill and John Floyer. The original law of 1534, enforced immersion, and those who were not baptized were to betreated as outlaws. The act of Parliament of 1644, repealed so much of the old law as enforced immersion, and enforced sprinkling in its stead, and left the original penalty annexed to sprinkling. After this, those who were not sprinkled were treated as outlaws.

After my investigations, I affirm with boldness, that not a Lexican can be found, published previous to 1644, that gives any other definition to baptizo than immerse; all other definitions have been added since by designing men.

By perverting the translation of the Scriptures, by infusing delusion, and the strong love of our own party, into the youthful mind—by excluding the true History of what has been done in the way of alterations, from all the schools and colleges, thereby keeping the youth, in all his studies, in a state of ignorance of these facts—by introducing such Lexicons only for a long time among the youth as mislead—by teaching the youth that baptizo has as many meanings as all the Latin words put together by which it is defined, (many of which have been corruply added, within the last 75 years,) thus making baptizo mean almost any thing and every thing—by the strong co-operation of the force of habit, and of respect for parents and associates, with the help of the pride of consistency—and by the strong delusions thus engendered, through party feelings, and a sort of determination, like party feelings in politics, to sustain the sect, at all hazards, many minds, otherwise enlightened, have become as blind on this subject as though they were covered over with thick Egyptian darkness. I speak all this from experience, and from a review of myself and former associates.

In the first formation of language, words were arbitrary sounds, and no word had more than one meaning. That meaning, with every word, is now called its *primary;* and is usually given in dictionaries, as the first definition. In all the dictionaries in the world, *immerse* is given as this *primary* meaning of Baptizo, and *immersion* of *baptisma.*

The effect of the action contained in verbs is often improperly given as a secondary or remote definition of those words. To shew how this is adapted to mislead from the truth, let us notice the effects of this way of defining verbs, as in the word Dip. Every one knows what is the real meaning of this word. But the effect of dipping in dye is to color, of dipping in clean water, is to cleanse or wash, of dipping in filth, is to besmear, of dipping a hot iron in water is to boil the water and cool the iron, of dipping an animal into strong ley is to take off the skin, and of dipping a vessel into a neighbor's grain, is to steal. Some lexicographers after rendering dip by *immerse,* as the primary meaning, are just as unphilosophical in giving multitudinous definitions as if they were to add, to color, to cleanse or wash, to besmear, to boil, to cool, to skin, or to steal, as definitions of this word. If a law existed, and *dip* were the primary action enforced in that law, how absurd it would be to take those remote definitions, and by boiling, cooling, skinning, or stealing, hold out the pretence that the law had been obeyed. This shows how words acquire secondary and remote definitions which do not, on any philosophical principle, fairly belong to them. Every body can see that these remote definitions do not express the real legitimate meaning of the word, but only the effects of the action implied in that verb, and exceedingly contradictory under different circumstances.

Now Baptizo is perfectly parallel to the English word dip, and the necessity of taking the *primary,* as the *real* meaning of the law expressed by Baptizo, is just as plain as it is in the above instance of dip. And it would be perfectly absurd to construe the law by the second, third, fourth, fifth, or sixth, or any other remote or contradictory definitions, or by any modern definition tacked on for sectarian purposes, 1700 years after the law was made, or by any modern definition tacked on to the word in a lexicon an hundred years after the death of the author, by persons who wished to avoid the real law, and to bring a substitute for it into general use.

The word *pay* signifies the discharge of a debt. But when an insolvent dies or absconds, it is often said he has paid his debts. How perfectly iniquitous it would be to construe a law, of which *pay* is the prominent word, and to say the intent of the law is fulfilled by dying or absconding. But this is no more iniquitous than it is to pretend that the law in which Baptizo is the prominent word, is fulfilled by conforming to any remote, modern, or corrupt and unphilosophical definitions.

The man who insists that the law of Christ is fulfilled by pouring or sprinkling, acts on the same principle that would justify another in saying that boiling, cooling, skinning, or stealing, are the fulfilment of that law, and that Christ meant to enforce stealing.

The man who insists that baptizo signifies to *cleanse*, has just as good ground for his assertion, as another has who asserts that it signifies to besmear, or to color,* Such trifling with the law of Christ, were it not for the delusions from infancy up in those minds who are guilty of it, would be treasonable, profane, rebellious and wicked beyond description. As to the amount of mitigation on account of this delusion, the Searcher of hearts will judge, as well as the extent of the guilt for neglecting, or refusing to know the law.

Dr. Campbell, of Aberdeen College, says, baptizo, both in sacred authors and classical, signifies, to dip, to plunge, to immerse.

John Calvin says, to baptize, signifies to immerse, and it is certain that immersion was the practice of the ancient church.

Grotius says, that baptism used to be performed by immersion, and not pouring, as appears from the proper signification of the word, and the places chosen," &c.

The very learned Joseph Mede says, there was no such thing as sprinkling for a great many centuries after Christ.

---

* I was conversing, not long since, with a very candid Presbyterian minister, Rev. Mr. Goodell, of Clarkson, a thorough linguist, and a teacher in the Academy in that place, who perfectly coincided in all these views. "Facio," he said, "to which some twenty definitions are tacked in the dictionaries, after all, in fact, has but one real, primary meaning, to wit, to do or make. All the others," he said, "are either an expression of the effects of the legitimate action belonging to the word, or are some modern definitions added." What then, said I to him, is the real meaning of the word Baptizo? "To immerse," was his reply. "To dye, and to wash, or cleanse, are only the effects of the legitimate action belonging to the word, and are not, strictly, a definition of it." A brother sitting by inquired, "Is there any other Greek word that will as well express immerse as Baptizo? Mr. G. replied, "No. Dupto and Duno signify to dive, and do not as well express immerse as Baptizo."

Beza says, Christ commanded us to be baptized, by which word it is certain immersion is signified.

Luther says, baptism may be rendered a dipping, when we dip something in water, that it may be entirely covered with water.

Venema says, the word *baptizo* is no where used in the scripture for sprinkling.

Buddeus says, the words baptizo and baptismos are *never* to be interpreted of aspersions, but always of immersions.

Salmasius says, baptism is *immersion*, and was administered in former times according to the *force* and *meaning* of the word.

Vitringa says, the act of baptizing is the immersion of believers in water.

Gustlerius says, to *baptize* is undoubtedly to immerse, to *dip*.

Dr. Daniel Rogers, a learned Episcopalian, says, "that the minister is to *dip* in water, the word *baptizo* notes it. None of old were wont to be *sprinkled*."

The twelve last, are learned and standard pædobaptist authors, and many of them teachers in Pædobaptist Seminaries. The authors of the above lexicons, are all supposed to be pædobaptists, except Butterworth.

"It cannot be denied that the native signification of the word *baptizien* is to plunge to dip." Witsius, Econ. of Gov. Lib. 4 Chap. 16. Sec. 13.

"The original and natural signification of the word *Baptizo* imports to dip." Ridgely's Body of Divinity.

"The very word Baptizo, signifies to immerse. Calvin.

With such testimony from so many of the most learned and standard authors, and scarce one of them a Baptist, and not a single standard author in the world bearing a contrary testamony, and especially with such unity of definition from Greek dictionaries, how clear is its meaning. We might as well dispute the meaning of the word pay, in a law requiring a man to pay his debts, as to dispute the meaning of the words baptize and baptism, in the law of Christ, where he commands all believers to be baptized, and all ministers to baptize them.

Our saviour knew what he said, and he meant what he said, when he commanded baptism. He knew all the objections which pride would raise, and all the inconveniences attending it; and that it had nothing in it that was fashionable, or gratifying, or inviting, to a single feeling of the natural heart. But for each of these reasons it is so much the better, as it tests the entire acquiescence of the soul in his will, far more than the anxious seat, or anything else with which we have ever been acquainted; and being public, this submission to him is publicly made before the world. The public act of leaving the world–of going into his kingdom, and of yielding to his authority, and in this self-denying way, is just what he requires of every one that is born again. " Except a man be born of water, &c., John iii. 5, (An expression, which Wall tells us, was always construed to mean Baptism, until John Calvin's time,) as well as " of the Spirit he cannot enter into the Kingdom of God;" i. e. his kingdom on earth. John, iii. 2.

If the Saviour had commanded *sprinkling* in the the law, pouring and immersion would be wrong—a total failure to obey, an addition to or a taking from the law of Christ, a crime which is expressly prohibited under the severest penalties. Rev. 18—22.

If he had commanded *pouring*, then immersion and sprinkling, for the same reasons, would be a failure to obey the law, and an exposure to the same penalty for the same reasons.

But as he has commanded *immersion*, sprinkling and pouring, for the same reasons, are a total failure to fulfil the law, and the observance of them, is *adding to*, and *taking from* that law, a crime which is threatened with that awful penalty.

As well might a person at the Sacramental table, by putting a crumb of the bread in his pocket, pretend he had fulfilled the law requiring him to *eat* it, and by putting a drop of the wine on his face, pretend he had obeyed the law requiring him to drink it, as for a person by sprinkling or pouring to pretend he has fulfilled the law of Christ, enforcing baptism.

Sprinkling and pouring are not baptism, are not the things commanded, and therefore to observe them is adding to, and taking from the law of God, a crime, to which an awful penalty is annexed in the passage above referred to.

It results from all this that when we were sprinkled ourselves, we were not baptized. The *mode of baptism* is the *mode of immersion*. Sprikling and pouring are not the thing which Christ commands, and are not even the mimicry of it, but the evasion. The man who evades the payment of a debt may as well think he has paid it, as the man who is sprinkled think he has been baptized. It results, also, that when we, as ministers, used to wet the face, and say, " *I baptize thee*," &c., we did not tell the truth in *fact*; but it was a *falsehood* in *fact*. We were not then conscious, that it was a falsehood, and were as honest as people are in any other delusion. But we could not do it again, after thus having the subject demonstrated to us, without " *lying to the Holy Ghost*." We are not excusable for any delusion, because we are bound to know the truth. For the dear ministers of the gospel publicly to falsify the truth, in fact, however earnest in heart they may be, and to do it in the name of the sacred Trinity, is extremely to be regretted. Who hath required this at your hand? Baptism is that which Christ requires; but the other *ceremony*, falsely called baptism, adapted as it is to change and evade the real ordinance, to alter the laws of Christ, to perpetuate delusion; and adapted as it is, if universally practiced, totally to *annihilate* and remove from the world, the real ordinance of Christ, is what I dare not do; and I believe the time is not far distant when no *enlightened minister* will *dare* to do it. For me to do it, after my examination of the subject, would be *conscious profanity.* When I used to do it I was under a delusion, fixed upon me in my childhood, by others.

It results especially that those who were sprinkled in infancy, and had this false declaration uttered with the ceremony, were no more *baptized* in *reality*, than the child where the Roman Catholic held up his hand, and said the words, "I baptize," &c., without any water; or the other case where another Roman Catholic sprinkled sand, and profanely said the words. Who ever required this at the hands of those who do it? "If any man shall add—to him shall be added all the plagues." Carrying a babe to the anxious seat, that he may excuse himself when he grows up, would be just as rational as to sprinkle him in infancy, that he may *evade* Christian baptism, after he grows up, and becomes converted.

It results also that those churches that are organized merely on infant sprinkling, are organized *without Christian baptism.* They depend upon a constitution which is the invention of men in order to keep them together. And those who remain connected with this way of organizing churches, are responsible for all the evils and all the divisions that result from it.

If Jesus Christ's way of organizing churches presents Himself as sole lawgiver and Ruler, his own revealed constitution as the foundation, His jurisdiction over christians as exclusive, baptism after believing as the public transaction whereby members are admitted, and excludes unconscious babes, as well as all the unconverted; and if he commands every convert forthwith to join his church in His way, as soon as converted, then the *former* way is at variance with *Christ's* way, defeats and hinders it and keeps back a great many of Christ's redeemed ones from joining his kingdom, a new constitution to Christ's laws, contrary to Revelation, xxii. 18, 19. Stands forth in bold competition against Christ's organization, with separate houses of worship, a separate ministry, and separate expenses, (which if not properly applied are wasted,) and it stands forth chargeable with all the sectarianism, and evils, and injuries, to the cause of Christ which result. It is certainly high time for us to look into these things, and search deep for the root of these evils, and that all return to primitive gospel order.

LETTER III.

HOW IT HAS BEEN VIEWED IN ALL AGES.

Are my Christian friends, and former associates aware, (I know they generally are not,) how many of the most learned authors confirm the same definition of baptizo, which we have given, and of baptism as being *immersion only*, and confirm the fact thst *immersion* has always been considered by the church of Christ as being indispensably requisite to the ordinance of baptism, from the days of the apostles until now, and still is by all Christians in all parts of the world, except those who have inherited their views from the *alterations* of the ordinance in England, or have grown up in nations that have derived their *alteration of the ordinance* from the church of Rome?

Rev. Moses Stuart, Professor of the Andover Pædobaptist Theological Seminary, says, "The man that denies that immersion was practiced in the primitive church, for several centuries after the apostles, must possess grest want of candor or be unacquainted with church history. It is a thing made out. So indeed, all the writers who have thoroughly investigated this subject conclude. I know of no one usage of ancient times, which seems to be more clearly and certainly made out. I can not see how it is possible for any candid man who examines the subject to *deny* this." This is candid. When he still practices and countenances the *alteration* of Christ's ordinance after all, and thus by his great influence sanctions a divided state of the church, is a subject which he must meet at the tremendous bar of God Himself.

Moshiem, one of the most candid, and learned, and faithful historians, as all admit, says, concerning the ceremonies of the *first* century, (Vol. 1. p. 108) " The sacrament of *baptism* was administered in this century apart from the public assemblies, in places appointed and prepared for that purpose, and was performed by *immersion of the whole body in the baptismal font.*" The same author in describing the ceremonies of the second century, (Vol. 1. p. 170,) also says, "The persons that were to be baptized after they had repeated the creed, &c., were *immersed under water*, and received into Christ's Kingdom by a solemn invocation of *Father, Son*, and *Holy Ghost*, according to the *express command of our blessed Lord.*" This last clause shows us very clearly what was the opinion of this learned man concerning the import of the command of Christ on this subject.

Bishop Smith of the episcopal church, Kentucky, in a recent Sermon, at the immersion of his own babe, says.

"We have only to go back 6 or 800 years, and immersion was the ONLY mode, except in the case of the few baptized on their beds, when death was near. And with regard to such cases, it disqualified its recipient for holy orders, in case he recovered. Immersion was not only UNIVERSAL, 6 or 800 years ago, but it was PRIMITIVE, and APOSTOLIC, no case of baptism standing on record by *any* other mode for the first three hundred years, except the few cases of those baptized *clinically*, i. e. lying in bed. The place of baptism in most cases, the significance of baptism, the washing of the soul in the blood of the atonement, as 'our bodies are washed in pure water,' Heb. x. 22. the allusion of baptism to the death and reusrrection of Christ, 'buried with him in baptism,' all continue to render the fact, as early ascertained, far more reconcileable with scripture than any contrary theory can possibly be. If any one practice of the early church is clearly ascertainable, it is immersion.

He also asserts, that "The BOWL and SPRINKLING are strictly Genevan in their origin, i. e. were introduced by Calvin at Geneva, as the Empedopidins also assert."

In relation to the phrase, Rom. vi. 4, and Col. ii. 12, "Buried with him by baptism," &c., the learned Dr. Cave, Locke, Poole, Burkitt, Samuel Clark, the Assembly of Divines, John Calvin, and also the two great founders of Methodism, John Wesley, and Adam Clark, all a*gree and affirm* that allusion is here made to immersion as the baptism of those times. John Calvin expressly tells us that immersion was always the baptism practiced previous to this time, Inst. Chr. Relig. Dr. Whitby, a very learned Episcopalian, on the place says, "It being so expressly declared here (Rom. vi. 4, and Col. ii. 12,) that we were buried with Christ in baptism, *by being* *buried under water*, and the argument to oblige us to a conformity to his death, by dying to sin, being taken thence; and this IMMERSION being religiously observed by all christians for *thirteen* centuries, and approved by our church; and the CHANGE of it into sprinkling even without any allowance from the Author of its institution, or any licence from any council of the church; it were to be wished that this custom (immersion) might be again of general use." We notice here the substance of this learned Bishops opinion of the passage, viz. that the fact here stands by the apostle, is, that in baptism, we turn our backs upon the ways of the world, and die to sin, and we are buried in the act of baptism, and then are raised to a spiritual life in the church, in which we are thus *planted* or placed; and that all this is a striking parallel to the *death burial,* and *resurrection* of Christ; and that these facts were notorious to those churches; and that the apostle states these notorious facts, in order to press the argument thence derived. to wit, that for these very reasons, professors ought "to walk in newness of life." As Christ after his resurrection lives in heaven, so we after our resurrection, at our baptism, should live in the church, a holy life. Now, those who sprinkle blot out the whole of this pungent argument, and the whole foundation of it from God's book, and destroy its meaning. Is there no danger in thus taking away from God's book? If we may take away this argument and deny the fact, from which the duty enforced is drawn, we establish a principle that will lead us to take away another, and another' argument, penned by the Spirit of God, and another, and another fact, though stated by the same authority. How deeply does this learned Bishop regret this course, and how earnestly does he desire the restoration of the original ordinance.

He incidentally states here two great facts, well known in his time, to wit,☞That immersion had been religously observed by all Christians for THIRTEEN centuries, and that somewhere between the beginning of the fourteenth century and his time, the ordinance of baptism had been CHANGED. We have a proof before our own eyes, in these passages, and in what we see in our land, that this ordinance of Christ has been CHANGED. The Rantism (sprinkling,) and the Perichysm (pouring) in this country, are radically different from the Baptism, (immersion), enforced by Christ. In sprinkling and pouring there is no burial: no resemblance to the death, burial, and resurrection, of Christ. The reason is, they are not baptism, but something else. The ordinance has been

C

CHANGED, or rather EXCHANGED. Baptism has been discarded, and substitutes been adopted. How silly would the apostle have appeared, if he had said, We are buried with Christ by sprinkling or by pouring. It is a falsehood on the face of it. Pouring and sprinkling are not, then, the baptism which the apostles and early Christians observed, and which Jesus Christ enforced. They are only a substitute and cheat played off upon the community by popery, by the British Parliament, and by the persecuting bishops of England, during the 16th and 17th centuries, and by other coercive authority. Afterwards, the practice was handed along from generation to generation, parents applying it to their babes for a long time with a superstitious belief that it was necessary to their salvation and with tame submission to the rulers over them. So strong has the superstition and delusion finally become, that it is now almost impossible to break the spell. Even Free-masonry and Mormonism are not stronger delusions and superstitions than the baby-sprinkling of our land. Sprinkling and pouring were not the ceremony which our Saviour observed. He was baptized, and in Jordan; and we have proved beyond the shadow of a doubt, that to be baptized was to be immersed.* And Jesus being immersed, ascended immediately out of the water." This is the literal tranalation. So also Philip and the eunuch descended both into the water, and he (in Greek baptized,) in English immersed him. Sprinkling and pouring then, are not baptism. Baptism has been exchanged for something else. Those churches who simply sprinkle and pour water, have no baptism. They have substituted rantism, and perichysm, and discarded baptism.

All the learned authors agree that *baptism* (in the Greek,) i. e. *immersion* in the English, was the uniform practice with all christians during the first century, which century terminated with the death of Christ's beloved disciple John. There is not the possibility of a mistake. Not a single author can be found, who contradicts this historical fact. But hundreds, of all denominations bear testimony to it. If you ask why so many blindly take the side of the SPRINKLERS, I will ask you why people adopt and blindly defend so many *other delusions, superstitions*, and *traditions?* and *your* answer will be the answer to your own question. And if you ask why I blindly

---

* " The travellers rested on the banks of the Jordan, at the spot where, tradition says, the Lord was baptized. They bathed in the stream, the water was about eight feet deep."

This is from the N. Y. Evangelist, a Presbyterian paper. We commend it to the attention of such as doubt that the Saviour was immersed

defended the wrong side of this question *so long*, I will ask you why you, and many thousands of others, *still* blindly defend it, and you will answer your own question. The real reason is, that our early impressions, all our early reading, feelings, associations and interests, were on that side, and we were blinded. If you ask what difference it makes, I ask you again, what difference does it make whether we obey Christ in *anything*? Naaman, the leper, must not only *wash*, but must wash in *Jordan*, and must wash *seven times*. *Wetting a little*, would not have answered; washing even *six* times in Jordan would not have answered; and washing even *seven* times in the *waters of Damascus*, would not have answered. And for the best of all reasons—the *principle of disobedience* to the will of heaven would have been in it. The form is good for nothing without the heart. We love to have our own will gratified. This is the reason why implicit obedience to the will of God is required; to wit, because without entire obedience we have our own will, and do not submit to the will of God. And there is no such thing as doing right unless our wills are subjected to his. This is the reason why sprinkling can not possibly be right, and why immersion is indispensable; the one is having our own blind will, or with a blind impulse called conscience, to make a good enough law for ourselves. The other is taking the will of *another* already expressed, to wit, the will of God.

Dr. Wall says, "the Presbyterian church in Geneva, is the first church on earth that ever *enjoined* sprinkling." The new Edinburgh Encyclopædia says, sprinkling was first introduced into the kirk of Scotland, and into England, in 1559 —that John Calvin was the first man among Protestants that *changed* the ordinance. It intimates that a popish council at Ravenna, in 1311, had said that sprinkling or pouring would do among papists, but yet scarce any adopted it. The very learned Dr. Gale, in 1707, writes, (Reflections on Wall, p. 153,) "Baptism which *all men* know was used to be administered in England by dipping, or immersion, till Queen Elizabeth's time, 1558; since which time that *pure primitive* MANNER, is grown into a *total disuse*, within a little more than one hundred years; and *sprinkling*, the *most opposite* to it imaginable, introduced in its stead. The fact is notorious," &c. Grotius, on Mat. iii. 6, asserts also, that the "ordinance has been CHANGED from immersion to sprinkling." The learned Dionysius Petavius, refers to the same *alteration*. "Immersion, he says, is properly styled *baptism*, though at present we content ourselves with pouring water on the head which in Greek in Greek is called perichusis, i. e. *perychism* if I may so Anglicise, but *not* baptism." The learned antiquary, archdeacon Nicholson, bishop of Carlisle, in 1707, in speaking of the baptismal font at Bridekirk, says, " There is fairly represented on the font, a person in a sacerdotal habit, dipping a child into the water," and adds, " I need not acquaint you that the sacrament of baptism was anciently administered by *plunging into the water* in the western, as well as the eastern part of the church, and that the Gothic word (Mark i. 8. Luke iii. 7, 12.) the German word *tauffen*, the Danish word *dobe*, and the Belgic *doopen*, do as clearly make out *that practice*, as the Greek word *baptizo*. Dr. Wall says, " all those nations of Christians, that do now or formerly *did submit to the authority of the Bishop of Rome*, do ordinarily baptize (we should have said, *rantize*) their infants by pouring or sprinkling :—☞The English received not this custom, (sprinkling) till after the decay of popery. But all other Christians in the world, who never owned the Pope's usurped power, DO and EVER DID DIP." He particularly informs us that all the Greek church, all Christians in Asia, all in Africa, and about one third part of Europe, to wit, all Gracia, Thracia, Servia, Bulgaria, Roscia, Wallachia, Moldavia, Russia, Nigra, and so on, and even the Muscovites, who, if coldness of country will excuse, might plead for a dispensation with the most reason of any, still most conscientiously cleave to the ordinance of IMMERSION." The fact is, then, most amply and fully made out, as an historical fact, that Popery, the British Parliament, and the Westminster Assembly, are all the authority there is for *sprinkling* or *pouring ;* and that ALL Christians in all parts of the world, except the descendants of such as have been tinctured with popery, or with these other authorities, do now, and always have, agreed in the fact, that baptism is immersion, and that nothing else is baptism.

Those, then, who practice sprinkling and pouring have been misled by their youthful impressions on the subject, by taking it for granted, that what they see with their eyes is baptism, by refusing to examine the subject, by following the "traditions of the elders," by satisfying themselves with specious arguments that are untrue in fact, by being deluded, by following in many instances, a blind superstition, or an honest mistake, or the influence of others, or by yielding to the force of education, or by following the popish principle, that 'tradition, is of equal force with the word of God.' Nearly all the delusions in the world have been propagated and continued in the same way. Free-masonry, Mormonism, and even no small part of popery itself, have been propagated and continued in this way.

I write these things in the fear of God, expecting to meet what I say in the judgment, and my sole object is to recover the ordinances of Christ from the perversion which has been made of them, in order to help my fellow Chrirtians to return to a course of implicit obedience to the will of our common Lord, and that they may take a right stand, and exert a right influence on his bleeding, divided, distracted, cause. If those who *baptize* are *right in fact*, they will of course continue to do it. Those who take the other course, then, will in that case be responsible for continuing to promote and perpetuate divisions.

How exceedingly evident it is that those who sprinkle or pour in the name of the sacred trinity, have no authority for it further back than the sixteenth century, fifteen hundred and more years too late to be of divine authority; and that it is, and must be, from the nature of the case, an invention of men, and that in taking this substitute they have unawares dashed away a positive ordinance of Jesus Christ. How exceedingly dangerous it is to cleave to a human ceremony, when in doing it we discard an ordinance divine. Naaman was no more wrong in fact, than those are who discard Christ's ordinance, and cleave to the substitute.

LETTER IV.

CHANGE OF THE ORDINANCE.

In my last I was proving that the divine ordinance of baptism had been, during the latter part of the sixteenth, and the first part of the seventeenth centuries, totally discarded by the popish, the Episcopalian, the Congregational, and the Presbyterian organizations, and a human ceremony, totally unlike it, been *substituted* in its place. The Methodist organization was not formed till between 1739, and 1784, and was not completed till the latter period, and was, therefore, about 140 years after the profane exchange was made; and Wesley, its founder, aimed to have this resemble the Episcopalian form of church organization. Of course he took the substitute, in lieu of the divine ordinance, just as it stood at that time in the Episcopal church. Still, he baptized many Welsh, as he says in his journal to Georgia, by immersion, "according to the custom of the ancient church." He also immersed E. K., as Toplady gives it, in England, and was strongly predisposed, even to a fault, (in Toplady's view,) to practice immersion. This the rather honors his conscience, as being strongly inclined to obey the divine command when he could. Benedict informs us, that he refused to sprinkle children, until, according to the Rubrics of the English Church, it was certified that the child was incapable of being immersed without endangering life. Had it not been, then, that he was inured to believe that the civil government had the right to make laws, and regulate the things of religion, HE certainly would have practised immersion. This certainly honors his heart, as displaying a respect for the divine ordinance.

He says, "We believe it would not be lawful for us to baptize, if we had not a commission from the bishops, whom we apprehend to be in succession from the Apostles." (Journal, vol. i. p. 514. Ed. 1827.) It was feeling such allegiance to human rulers, then, that misled him into sprinkling, according to the then usages of the civil and Episcopal government, and contrary to his own honest preference of the real ordinance of Christ.

[Query. What if all our civil rulers should modestly claim the right of appointing successors in office, *ad infinitum*, and the people were to feel thus servile under it?]

I was proving in my last, from the most scientific and standard authors, the historical fact above stated; and also that all the Christian world, besides the above organizations, ever have, from the time of Christ, and do now, every where, most conscientiously cleave to the original divine ordinance, and discard the SUBSTITUTE as a profane exchange. The bohan upas of sectarianism with all its desolations, rending and tearing as it does the church of Christ, has resulted almost entirely from the profane exchange, and from trampling down the initiating ordinance into Christ's kingdom, and initiating men into the sects by a SUBSTITUTE, and from the delusion of infant baptism or infant sprinkling, as it stood connected with these things. It is this fact which gives so much importance to the subject. You will therefore bear with me for presenting at this time the plain facts in the case.

With the papists the exchange, it is certain, never *began* till after the year 1311.* The exchange with them was also very slow, and but very few adopted it for more than two hundred years.† For at the time of the Reformation it is cer-

---

* New Edinburgh Encyclopædia, Art. Bap.   † Ibid.

tain they generally immersed. It is true a small council of papists at Ravenna, in 1311, were inquired of, whether sprinkling or pouring, in case the child was sick, would do; and that small council seemed to think it would answer the purposes of papacy well enough, especially in such extraordinary cases.*
It is certain that the church of England, first formed and organized out of popery, as their own authors abundantly assert, and in 1534, adopted immersion, at their first organization.† This fact is confirmed by all history, and by all their rituals, by the Parliamentary act of 1534, *enforcing immersion*, and by their great reluctance, during one hundred years' struggle, to take the substitute. It is equally certain that the Congregational and Presbyterian organizations, which first came into existence about the same time, also then adopted immersion. This fact is confirmed by the concentrated testimony of all history, by their writings during those times, and by the fact that even as late as 1643, the Westminster Assembly were exceedingly reluctant to adopt the substitute; and the vote was ultimately carried by the efforts of Dr. Lightfoot, and finally obtained by a majority of only ONE. The honest part of the Episcopal church even as far down as 1640, are found to be exceedingly reluctant to give up the divine ordinance, and to adopt the substitute: and to their honor be it remembered, they never did do it, as a body, till an act of Parliament enforced it in 1644. As a religious body they have never, in England, altered their rituals from immersion, whatever may be the state of the prayer book, and whatever alterations it may have undergone in the United States.

These things demonstrate that all these denominations originally had a conscience in favor of the divine ordinance, and against the profane EXCHANGE.

Bishop Smith, in his recent charge to the clergy of Kentucky, as well as in his Sermons, conveys fully, the idea, that immersion was the practice of the primitive churches. Mather, in his Magnalia, more than intimates that in New England, from 1620, to 1648, immersion was continued by many at least.

The fact is, that John Calvin stands at the head of the profane exchange among Protestants, and is the father of it. He first began it in 1556, at Geneva. The number of baptisms there become so much increased, that he first, in that year, in-

---

* Ibid. See also British Encyclopædia, and Encyclopædia Americana.
† Lowth.

vented the practice of *drenching* the candidate by pouring a pail full of water, as being more convenient than immersion, afterwards of pouring a less quantity, and finally of mere sprinkling. Dr. Wall, vicar of Shoreham, in describing the fact, says, that "pouring was the substitute for baptism, which Calvin first adopted, and that his sprinkling was only the substitute of a *substitute*, and was the most scandalous thing ever adopted for baptism, The sprinkling of our country, then, the Episcopal Wall being witness, is only the scandalous "*substitute of a substitute;*"—quite another thing, than the divine ordinance itself. During the persecutions under Queen Mary,* and the bloody bishop Bonner, many persons had fled to the continent, and visited Geneva. On the death of Queen Mary in 1558, and the accession of Elizabeth, they returned, and in Scotland and England reported how " the famous godly man, John Calvin, (as he was called,)had improved on baptism; and this substitute was not half so troublesome." From this, a small beginning of the use of the substitute commenced in Scotland, and in England. The proud persecuting bishops of the time, seeing its convenience, immediately set themselves at work to *establish* it as a *good enough baptism* for their purposes; and it was so much more convenient! They commenced and continued an excitement in its favor, with which the worldly and unprincipled part of the Episcopalians fell in; but the honest part opposed. The bishops preached before the Parliament, attempting to incite them to pass a law enforcing it; and used language like this, that the " devil of immersion ought to be l*egislated* out of the realm, it was so troublesome." Under this state of feeling and excitement, so much of our present translation of the Bible as relates to baptism, was made by these bishops in 1568, copied from the Bishop's Bible." All the perversions we find in it, on baptism, were made by them as the result of that state of feeling. For when King James, in 1604, authorised a new translation, (completed in 1611,) James ordered the translators to leave baptism just as it had been rendered by the bishops. When we read it on baptism, therefore, let us remember who were the translators on that subject, and the spirit they had in view, and then cease to wonder at the perversions. Let us, however, remember that we can never preach, and send the gospel to every creature, without a *literal* trsnsla-

---

† Queen Mary caused 300 Martyrs, mostly Baptists, to be put to death, in he short space of only five years; solely because they had the rebellious spirit of being honest and conscientious in obeying God, in his laws and ordinances.

tion of God's word; and that we sin if we indirectly cover over the mind of the Holy Spirit on any subject, by neglecting to have it literally translated, and sent every where. It is these bishops and the sprinklers, who have the new Bible. *We plead for the old-fashioned Bible, that has an honest and literal translation, such as has always translated the Greek word baptizo and baptisma, and not left them in Greek, to blind the people, and had no perversions on the subject; and such as the bishops gathered up and destroyed, at the time of their new translation, in 1568.*

To return; the bishops persisted in their efforts to exchange away the divine ordinance of immersion, while Wall and others wrote in defence of it, as having always been the ordinance from the days of John the Baptist till then. Still the bishop's party gained ground—so large a portion of the national church being void of christian principle.

It was not till about 1640, to 1644, that a Parliamentary act was finally passed, requiring all the children born in the realm, and all the people, to be sprinkled, under the old penalty of being treated as outlaws, and of being deprived of the right of inheritance of estate, the right of burial; and in short of all the rights secured to the other SPRINKLED citizens of the realm. From 1534, the beginning of the Episcopal organization, the immersion of all the babes in the kingdom, and of all the people, had been enforced by law, under the same penalty. After 1648, immersion was prohibited, and for many years made *penal.* * Thus *might* makes right, and

---

* The Ana-Baptists (an opprobrious epithet, given to those who baptized according to the command of Christ, regardless of the stratagem played upon babes,) were always objects of persecution, by the Parliament, the Episcopalians, and the Presbyterians. I have not the means of gathering all the Parliamentary Acts against them, and against the ordinance of Baptism, and establishing the substitute by the arm of civil power. As early as 1640, we find Edward Barber, a Baptist minister in London, imprisoned for a year, for baptizing converts according to the command of Christ, and contrary to the laws of the Parliament. Many others shared the some fate. In what year the law was passed, I cannot tell: it was not till 1644, that an ordinance of Parliament was finally obtained, establishing *sprinkling* as the national baptism. An ordinance, dated May 2, 1648, reads thus: " Whosoever shall say that the baptism [sprinkling, it had then become,] of infants is unlawful and void, or that such persons ought to be baptized again, shall, upon conviction, by the oath of two witnesses, or by his own confession, be ORDERED to renounce his said error, in the public congregation of the parish, where the offence was committed. And, in case of refusal, he shall be committed to prison, till he find sureties that he shall not publish or maintain said error any more." Much persecution was carried on against the Baptists, under this statute. The laws making immersion penal, were, some of them, somewhat indirect in language, but intended to be direct in their application. Soon after this, we find *four-hundred* Baptists crowded into New.

makes right to become wrong, at pleasure; alters the laws of God, and lords it over God's heritage, and over the consciences of men, and changes or annihilates divine ordinances.

The principles of republicanism, and the rights of conscience, were not in those days understood by any. Lording it by some, in matters of religion, and subjection by the rest, was the only government known. Accordingly, Calvin, who evidently loved to lord it, invented the Presbyterian form of church government, empowering the few to govern the many, and acceding to the aristocracies he established above the church, legislative, judicial, and executive, powers; the very powers that in fact belong solely to Jesus Christ. This aristocratic Presbyterian body soon passed a law, at Geneva, (about 1560) enforcing sprinkling as baptism. This usurpation of power is a fair specimen of Presbyterianism. Calvin alludes to this when he says, " The church (i, e. Presbyterianism,) hath granted to herself the privilege of somewhat altering the form of baptism, retaining the substance ; i. e. the words."† What a jewel this, and similar Presbyterianisms!!

John Calvin, then, is the father of this exchange of a divine ordinance, as well as the father of Presbyterianism. His Presbyterian aristocracy, acting under the constitution he had formed, and powers he had given them, passed the first law of all, enforcing this profane exchange, and enforcing the sprinkling of babes. (New Edinburgh Encyclopædia, Walls Hist. Bish. Smith's Serm., Dr. Gill, John Floyer, Gale's Reply to Wall.) It was about the year 1560. Here is the first beginning of baby-sprinkling, and the ceremony is the child of John Calvin. Baby immersion into popery had beed enforced during all the dark ages, and as long as popery had existed; and a little of it had been practiced, in some rare cases, from the year 255 along down to the days of popery, under different pretensions. It was however more than two hundred years too late to be of divine origin. It originated in

---

gate (*Rites and Ceremonies*, p. 593,) for no other crime only for teaching, in relation to baptism, obedience to the law of Christ, and practising accordingly; but contrary to Parliamentary laws. The cruel Act of Uniformity, is notorious to the world. Delaune was imprisoned, and literally starved to death, for writing on this subject, his Plea for Non-Conformists. Not long after the above Acts, a national proclamation was issued, ordering all the Baptists to depart out of the Realm, whether natives or foreigners. The Presbyterians, who had just decided by a majority of one, in favor of sprinkling, were the most active in informing against the Baptists, and in bringing about these persecutions. (See Crosby's History of Religion.) The imprisonment of the above 400, was almost entirely produced by their activity in these persecutions.

† Institut. Christ. Relig. Lib. 4, chap. 15, § 19. See also his Commentary on John 3, 23, and Acts 8, 38.

the time of the pious frauds, baby-communion at the Lord's table, and a hundred other delusions. The case, then, stands thus: The exchange of the divine ordinance of baptism for a more human device, was invented by John Calvin, in 1556, was enforced at Geneva by Presbyterian law, about 1560, was first begun in Scotland and England in 1558, was embraced and determinately contended for by the proud persecuting bishops; (they perverting the translation of the Bible on Baptism, in 1568, in order to favor it,) was finally enforforced by parliamentary law, and was passed into a law for the Presbyterian community, by the Westminster assembly, in 1643, by a majority of one--24 voting against, and 25 for it.*
The puritans were then accustomed to receive the decisions of a Presbyterian council, or association, as law, and the end of all strife. Accordingly sprinkling became their law from that time forward, as much as the Book of Mormon became the law of the Mormons, in 1830, and as much as masonic rules became the law of free-masons after the institution

---

* Some different accounts given of the vote of the Westminster Assembly, are these: "In the Westminster Assembly, it was decided that dipping of the person in water, is not necessary: but baptism is rightly administered by pouring or sprinkling water upon the person. This decision, was, however, carried by a majority of ONE, there being 25 for it, and 24 against it."—*Alex. Haldame, De Bap. p.* 17

"This Directory, adopted at Westminster, is the first in the world that pre scribes aspersion. Sprinkling, properly so called, at 1645, was just BEGINNING, and used by very few. Then came the Presbyterian Directory, and says, "Baptism is to be administered in the public assemblies," not in the places of fonts, &c. So they reformed the FONT into a BASIN. This Assembly could not re-. member, that fonts, to baptize in, had been *always* used by the primitive Christians, long before the beginning of Popery, &c. It is only where the usurped power of the Pope is, that they have left off dipping. Basins, (except in case of necessity) were never used, till used by Presbyterians."—*Wall's Hist. Inf. Bap.* P. II. chap. ix., p. 463, 477.

"Dr. Lightfoot was the man who caused dipping to be excluded, and sprinkling to be declared sufficient, in the Assembly of Divines, 1643. On the motion 'The minister shall take water and sprinkle or pour it, with his hand, upon the face or forehead,' the vote came to an equality, within ONE."—*Robinson's Hist. Bap.* p. 463.

Some account of this, will be found in Neale's History of the Puritans, vol. ii. p. 106, 107; also in the life of Lightfoot, by Styrpe, in Pref. to Lightfoot's works, vol. i. p. 4.

Because the Directory was ultimately carried, with a good degree of unanimity, some, through the influence of strong delusion, have supposed the consciences of these twenty-four were pacified. But, the greater probability is, that they only gave it the go-bye, because they were the minority. If ten thousand Presbyterians, however, had been agreed in this alteration of the law of Christ, it would make it no nearer to being right.

The pitiful evasions of Samuel Miller, and of Edwin Hall, of this *alteration of the law of Christ,* would be truly disgraceful to those men, were it not that they are under the influence of "*a strong delusion.*"

of free-masonry was contrived by Elias Ashmole, in June 1717. The delusion of sprinkling, and of infant sprinkling, falsely called baptism, have been propagated on precisely the same principle as these and other delusions, to wit, by assuming the popish maxim, that "the traditions of mother-church, and the laws of her rulers, are of equal force as 'proofs of holy writ,' and also by wresting holy writ to favour him." This is the secret of the whole delusion. Any person wishing to investigate the subject will do well to consult Booth's Pedobaptism Examined, the New Edinburgh Encyclopædia, art. Baptism, the British Encyclopædia, Pengilly's Scrpture Guide, Robinson' History of Baptism, Frey's Essay, Gale's Reflections on Walls's History of Infant Baptism, Floyer's Essay to restore dipping, Dr. Gills Infant Baptism a part and pillar of popery, Benedict's Hist. of the Baptists, &c.

The puritants settled New England and after this brought their sprinkling principles, and taught them to their children, and we took up with the tradition, of mother-church.

The danger of taking a human substitute for a divine ordinance is seen in the tendency of such a principle. If we may take a substitute for baptism, we may take a substitute for the Lord's supper, the sorrow of the world for gospel repentance, eternal mortality for piety, disobedience for the love of God, sin, for holiness, our own imaginations for the doctrine of the Trinity, free masonry or the Book of Mormon, for the Bible, the constitutions of the sects for Jesus Christ's constitution of his Church, and infidelity for Christianity. There is no limit to the principle, when once adopted; and if we may apply the substitute for baptism to babes, why not apply a substitute for the Lord's supper also to babes? What if a delusion of mixing a teaspoon-full of milk and wine, and calling it the Lord's supper, and administering it to babes, accompanied with the prayers and services incident to the supper, had been generally observed in the above churches since the days of John Calvin, accompained with the traditions that if it is once administered to the babe it will become wrong ever to partake of the real sacrament after it grows up because it would destroy this tradition; and this milk and wine in infancy is all the observance of the supper that is *ever* required. Who can say there might not have been by this time as much superstitious pertinacity in its observance, and piety mixed with delusion in applying this insignificant substitute to babes, as we now see in relation to infant sprinkling. Would this be any more profane than infant sprinkling?

When we see what a strong hold the delusions of popery

have acquired over thousands, what a hold the delusions of Mormonism has acquired over the minds of hundreds, even during its ten years' continuance, and that the delusion of free-masonry, even within an hundred and ten years from the time Ashmole contrived it, had duped and deluded two hundred thousand of our citizens, and was leading them to expend millions of dollars annually, and was leading many of them to believe it *divine*, that it came from heaven, was coeval with the world, &c., the wonder ceaces how John Calvin's baby-sprinkling, and his sprinkling substitute for a divine ordinance have deluded and misled so many. The secret of it consists in yielding the same confidence in a delusion, being a tradition of mother church which we have witnessed, and been inured by parents to revere from our infancy, as we do in the plain written truths of God's holy word.

LETTER V.

CHANGE OF THE ORDINANCE.

The New Edinburgh Encyclopædia, edited by Sir David Brewster, a Presbyterian, gives the following account, after stating that immersion was the ancient baptism, he proceeds, " The first law for *sprinkling* was obtained in the following manner: Pope Stephen II., being driven from Rome, fled to the usurper of the crown of France, in 753. While there certain monks inquired of him whether baptism, performed by pouring water on the head of the infant, would be lawful. The Pope replied that it would. But though the truth of this fact should be allowed, which, however, many Catholics deny, yet pouring or sprinkling was admitted *only in cases of necessity*. It was not till the year 1311, that the Legislature, in a council held at Ravenna, declared immersion or sprinkling, to be indifferent. In this country (Scotland) however, sprinkling was never practised in ordinary cases, till after this Reformation, (the date we have given,) and in England, even in the reign of Edward VI., (from 1547, to 1553.) trine immersion was commonly observed. But during the persecution of many (from 1553, to 1558,) many persons, most of whom were Scotsmen, fled from England to Geneva, and there greedily imbibed the opinions of that (Presbyterian) church. In 1556, a book was published at that place (Geneva) contain-

D

ing "The FORM of PRAYERS and MINISTRATION of SACRAMENTS. APPROVED by the FAMOUS, GODLY, LEARNED MAN, JOHN CALVIN," in which the administrator is ENJOINED to take water in his hand, and lay it on the child's forehead. These Scottish exiles, who had renounced the authority of the Pope, implicitly *acknowledged* the authority of Calvin: and returning to their own country with Knox at their head, in 1559, established sprinkling (by authority of the famous, godly, learned man, John Calvin,) in Scotland. From Scotland, this practice made its way into England, in the reign of Elizabeth, (which began in 1558,) but was not authorized by the established Church."—See *Art. Bap.* Thus far the New Edinburgh Encyclopædia.

Sir John Floyer, an eminent physician, in an address to the high officers of the Episcopal Church, in Lichfield, England, says, "I do appeal to you, as persons well versed in the ancient history, canons, and ceremonies of the Church of England; and therefore, are sufficient witnesses of the matter of fact, which I design to prove, viz., That immersion continued in the church of England, till about the year 1600. And, from hence I shall infer, that if God and the Church thought that practice innocent for 1600 years, it must be considered an unreasonable nicety, in this present age, to scruple either immersion or cold bathing, as dangerous practices. We must always acknowledge, that He that made our bodies, would never command any practice prejudicial to our healths; but, on the contrary, He best knows what will be most for the preservation of our healths, and does, frequently, take care both of our bodies and souls in the same command," In another place, he says, "The church of Rome use only the wafer, (for the supper,) and instead of immersion, *they* introduced *aspersion.*" "I have now," he adds, "given testimony from our English authors, to prove the practice of immersion, from the time the Britons and Saxons were first baptized, till King James' days, about 1600: when the people grew peevish with *all* ancient ceremonies, and then the love of novelty, the niceness of parents, and on the *pretence of modesty*, they laid aside immersion."—*Hist. of Cold Bathing*, p. 11, 15. 51, 61.

Dr. R. Wetham says, "Not only the Catholic church, but also the *pretended* reformed Churches have ALTERED this primitive custom, in Baptism, and now allow of baptism, by pouring or sprinkling water on the person baptized. Nay, many of their ministers do it, now a'days, by filliping a wet finger and thumb over a child's head, or by shaking a wet finger or two over the child; which is hard enough to call baptizing in ANY SENSE."—*Annot. on Matt.* iii. 6.

In the year 251, at Rome, one Novatian was elected bishop, by one party. His baptism had occurred when he was sick. He had been *drenched* in water, all over, on his bed, as well as the nature of the case would admit. He was rejected from the office of bishop, on the ground, that no one, unless regularly baptized, and so made a member of the church, could be admitted to any office. See Wall's Hist. chap. 9, p. 563. See also Eusebius' Hist. b. vi. chap. 43.

Wall tells us, it was in 1643, that sprinkling was just beginning, and used by very few among the Presbyterians; at which time, they reformed the font into a basin, and that France (Ravenna,) first began the exchange of baptism, for the substitute (sprinkling,) and then it was followed by other popish countries.

Brenner, a Roman Catholic writer, in a late work on Baptism, says, for "thirteen hundred years was baptism generally and ordinarily performed by immersion under the water; and only in extraordinary cases, was sprinkling, or effusion *permitted*, (by the Catholics even.) These latter methods of baptism were called in question, and even prohibited."

Hermas, (second century,) speaks of the water of baptism "into which men go down bound unto death, but come up appointed unto life."—*Simil.* 9, § 16.

Justin Martyr, who was converted about the year 130, and suffered martyrdom about the year 150, of converted persons says, "They are led out to a place where there is water, and there are washed or bathed in the name of of the Father of the Universe, and of the Saviour, Jesus Christ, and of the Holy Ghost."—*Apolog*.

Tertullian, writing about the year 200, (*De Cov. Millitis.* § 2.) speaks of the person as "let down into the water, and dipped, during the utterance of the words, "I baptize, &c." In sec. 4, he says, " It is a matter of indifference whether one is washed in a pool, in a fountain, in a lake, or in a bath; nor is there any difference between those whom John immersed in the Jordan, or Peter in the Tiber."

Barnabas, (second century,) says, "We go down into the water, &c., but come up again bringing forth fruit," &c.

The first liturgy of the Church of England, drawn up in 1547, enjoins trine immersion, "unless the childe be sickly. The childe is to be dipped in the water, so it be discreetly and warily don." The Presbyterians and Congregationalists used this confession of faith, till 1643. As is asserted by Mather,

T. Lawson, the Quaker, observes, "To sprinkle young or old, and call it baptism, is very incongruous; yea, as improper as to call a horse, a cow: for *baptisma* signifies dipping." Also, G. Whitehead, another learned Quaker, says, "Sprinkling infants, I deny to be baptism, either in a proper or scriptural sense. For sprinkling is rantism and not baptism."

The very learned Bailey, in his Dictionary, says, Baptism in strictness of speech, is that kind of washing which consists in dipping; and when applied to the Christian institution, so called, it was used by the primitive Christians in *no other* sense than that of *dipping*, as the learned Grotius and Causabon well observe."

Witsius, on the Covenant, says, "It cannot be denied, that the native signification of the word baptizo, is, to dip."

Venema says, "the word baptizo is no where used in the scripture, for sprinkling."

Bp. Hoadley says of Rom. vi. 4, and Col. ii. 12. "If baptism had been then (in the days of the apostles,) performed as it was now among us, (by sprinkling,) we should have never so much as heard of this form of expression—of dying—being buried—and rising again, in this ordinance."

John Wesley, on Rom vi. 4, says, "Alluding to the ancient manner of baptizing by immersion."

Richard Baxter, author of Saints Rest, says, "It is commonly confessed by us, that in the Apostles' times, the baptized were dipped over head in the water," &c.

Calvin, on Acts viii. 38, says, "Here we perceive how baptism was administered among the ancients For they immersed the whole body in water. Now, it is the prevailing practice (at Geneva, and as far as his influence then extended;) for a minister only to sprinkle the body or the head."

To contend against immersion, and in favor of sprinkling, as the divine ordinance, in view of all this, is as ridiculous as it would be to contend against the fact of the full blaze of the sun at mid-day. There can be no mistake; sprinkling is not a divine ordinance, but is only an ordinance of men—a mere "*substitute* of a substitute" for God's ordinance; and to contend for a moment, that the sprinkling of unconscious babes is a divine ordinance, is more ridiculous still. It is palpable, and unquestionable, that such have never been baptized at all, much less in pursuance of any divine law. They have only been rantized; and that according to the sectarian laws and usages of the rulers of the sect wherever it is done.

As farther proofs of the exchange of the divine ordinance, for a substitute, at the time specified, we add,

1 The Greeks, who, of course, understand the meaning of the Greek words, *baptizo* and *baptismos*, do now, and ever have immersed; and they all declare, that pouring or sprinkling is not baptism. One recently came to America, and was astonished at our ceremony of sprinkling, and said, it had no more resemblance to baptism, than hanging on a tree has to decapitation on a block. The fact that they always immerse, is notorious to every person having any information on the subject.

2 All the ancient Chapels in England, still contain the Baptisteries, prepared for the exclusive purpose of immersion, except where they have, since the exchange of the ordinance been destroyed. In one place, they have still, a silver baptistery.

3 All the rituals of the Church of England, still enforce immersion.

4 Emigrants from England, in many instances, are able to detail all the circumstances of the change of the ordinance, in England, as handed down by tradition from their progenitors.

5 Booth has collected the frank admissions of more than a hundred Pædobaptist writers of those times. As it was then notorious, all admitted it, and no author thought of denying the fact. Those who have grown up, in these later times, under the stratagem of baby-sprinkling, have truly been *managed* into a state of ignorance of these things, by the withdrawal of the books containing the facts, from their train of education; and by the alteration of the definition of the words in the Greek Lexicons. But these things only show the desperate state to which the cause of the sprinklers is reduced, by the fact of their resorting to such measures.

6 The contrast between the opinions of all Christendom, down to 1556, and the present practice of the sprinklers, is an overwhelming demonstration against the practice of the latter, as well as the total failure, since the time of the exchange, to show, that baptizo has any other meaning than immerse, notwithstanding the great efforts that have been made to that effect.

The French minister, Bossuet, says, "We are able to make it appear, that for *thirteen hundred years* baptism was administered by immersion throughout the *whole church*," i. e. the whole of Christendom. He admits a little variation with a few Catholics after 1311. Stackhouse says, "Several authors have shown and proved, that immersion continued to be used for thirteen hundred years." Bp. Stillingfleet says, "Rites and customs apostolical are altered—as dipping in baptism." Dr. Doddridge, on Rom. vi. 4, says, "It seems the part of candor to confess that here is an allusion to the ancient manner of baptizing by immersion." How exceedingly reluctant the good doctor seems to be in this confession. The very learned Joseph Mede says, " In the ancient church there was no such thing as *rantism* or sprinkling." Bp. Pearce says of the apostolic times, "The person baptized, went down under the water, and was buried under it." The Assembly of Divines, on Rom. vi. 4, say, " The Apostle alludes to the ancient manner of baptism, which was to dip the parties baptized, and bury them under the water." Sir John Floyer aserts the change, and regrets it very much. Calvin says, the rite of immersion was observed by the ancient church." Dr. Gale, in 1707, writes, "It is notorious to every body, that the divine ordinance, within less than a hundred years, has been discarded, and something totally unlike it, has been substituted." Dr. Chalmers, on Rom. vi. 4, says, "The original meaning of the word baptism, is immersion. We doubt not, that the prevalent style of the administration, in the apostles' days, was by an actual submersion of the whole body under water." The learned Dr. Samuel Johnson, who could read Greek, and write and converse in Greek as readily as in English, in speaking of the popish practice of withholding the cup from the laity, says, " I think they are as well warranted to make this alteration in that ordinance, as we are to substitute sprinkling in the room of ancient baptism." Dr. Whitby, in his endeavors to reconcile the Dissenters to the Church of England, says, " If, notwithstanding the evidence that *immersion* is the *apostolic baptism*, they, (the Dissenters) do agree, after all, now to *sprinkle*, why may they not *as well* submit to the *other* ceremonies of our church?" Dr Cheyne, " I cannot sufficiently admire how cold bathing should ever have come into such disuse, especially among Christians, when commanded by the greatest lawgiver that ever was."

I further say to my former associates, that authors have grossly misled us. Notwithstanding Mosheim, the faithful historian, tells us, that the origin of the Baptists is lost in the remotest depths of antiquity—that John the Baptist immersed, and that the sacrament of baptism was performed in the first century by the immersion of the whole body in the baptismal font, (vol. i. p. 126.) and that the persons, during the second century, to be baptized, after they had repeated the creed, and confessed and renounced their sins, (an act of adults alone,) were immersed under water, and received into Christ's kingdom, by a solemn invocation of Father, Son, and Holy Ghost; (vol. i. p. 170.) and tells us about the rise of infant-baptism, *after* this century, and that the papists always persecuted those who held the sentiments of the present Baptists, whether Albigenses, Waldenses, Petrobrusians, Henricians, or of any other names; evidently admitting, as he is forced to do, their continuation regularly from the Apostles: yet other authors of sectarian feelings, deluded and blinded by the influence of baby-sprinkling, who have copied after him, have thrown all these things into the shade. Rev. T. Haweis, L. L. D., who has written a History of the Church, and copied much from Mosheim, could not copy these facts, but unjustly and falsely ascribes the origin of the Baptists, to the affair of Munster, some 300 years ago. Rev. John Marsh, of Connecticut, in his Ecclesiastical History, a popular work, used much in schools, falsely, and doubtless, through the influence of his delusion, takes the same ground. It was generally taught in the New England Colleges, that the origin of the Baptists, was in the affair of Munster. Even free-masonry itself might laugh such delusion to scorn. Mosheim, though a Lutheran, gives us all the Christians of the first two centuries, as Baptists. We will now give the learned Curcellæns, Professor of Divinity in the Pædobaptist seminary at Amsterdam, in the 17th century. He says, " Pædobaptism (baby baptism,) was *unknown* in the first two ages after Christ. In the third and fourth, it was approved by a *few*; at length in the fifth, and following ages, it *began* to obtain in divers places. Therefore, this rite is, indeed, observed by us as an *ancient custom*, but *not* as an *apostolic* tradition." If by ages, centuries are here meant, he here teaches that encroachments upon Baptist sentiments, were very slow, even until the fifth century. These other authors we have quoted, teach us the continuance of Baptist sentiments, so far as the nature of baptism is concerned, for SIXTEEN HUNDRED years.

The Baptist principle, that Christ has the right to the exclusive jurisdiction over all his people, within his One Fold, is clearly taught in the Bible; and even those whose practice is to go into the other, and modern folds, and to be subject to other rulers, still, will not often venture to defend themselves in these points. We have only to show more clearly, therefore, and to prove that baby-baptism, and baby-sprinkling*

---

† Some friends complain, because we call it by that name. But what shall we call it? Infant (from *in* and *fans*,) is a word including minors, all under twenty-one years of age. Baptism is immersion. The immersion of minors is too comprehensive. Therefore, I cannot tell the truth, and call it *infant-baptism*.

are innovations and inventions of men? having gradually encroached upon the original organization, and we shall have shown how the Kingdom of Christ was originally organized. By showing, in a short sketch, who have enforced these stratagems upon babes — who have been persecuted for not observing them, and who were the persecutors, we shall readily perceive that the kingdom of Christ originally was organized without any such thing; and that these stratagems have been instrumental in aiding other lords, in making encroachments upon the real kingdom of Christ, and thus divided the Zion of God. Was it ever known that people were persecuted for not obeying the commands of God? Never. It was only for disregarding the dogmas of men, that they have been persecuted. The Donatists, in the fifth century, were cruelly persecuted for refusing to baptize babes, and for holding they could be saved without it.

Christianity was planted in Britain, by the Apostles, in A. D. 63. The Saxons conquered the Britons, and drove them into Wales. Austin, the monk, was sent, in 596, to convert them to popery and to the Romish rites. He demanded of them, 1. To keep Easter, 2. To baptize their babes, as did the papists. 3. That they join in teaching the Saxons in the same way. But they refused. Whereupon Austin brought on a cruel war against them, and well nigh exterminated them.

In the year 610, baby-baptism being much neglected, the pope ordained, concluded and published, that young children *must* be baptized, as being necessary to salvation, and upon penalty of damnation. One of the kings of the West Saxons, A. D. 700, prescribed a heavy penalty for deferring the baptism of babes, beyond thirty days from their birth. Charlemagne required from 20 to 60 and 120 shillings fine of every parent who deferred the baptism of a child, more than twelve months. In the year 1050, Pope Leo III, commanded that young children be baptized. In the year 1070, Pope Gregory VII, deemed that those children whose parents were absent or unknown, should be baptized. So in Massachusetts, in the year 1653, ministers decreed, that if parents die, before the babes were sprinkled, they must still be sprinkled;

Pædo is a babe; *Pædo*-baptism, is the immersion of babes. The sprinkling of these, then, is not Pædo-*baptism*. *Infant*-sprinkling, is the sprinkling of minors. The sprinkling of *babes*, or *baby-sprinkling*, then, are the only names we can give to the transaction, and speak the truth. We have a conscience against calling it what it is not. The Bible requires us always to speak the truth. We cannot follow others, and call it by a false name.

and the General Court passed it into law. In the eleventh century, it was deemed, if parents neglect to have their children baptized, they shall be torn from them—be baptized, and then be returned. In the year 1022, fourteen persons, in Orleans in France, were burnt, for opposing the baptism of babes. In the time of Henry III, several persons were put to death, for opposing the baptism of babes. In 1095, many were put to death in Italy, for opposing it. In 1105, many persons were banished out of the bishoprick of Tryers, for opposing it. Peter de Bruys, from whom is named the Petrobrusians, was burnt at St. Giles', in 1130, for preaching the Bible principles, as to the kingdom of Christ, and opposing baby baptism. Henry, his successor, from whom the Henricians were named, after preaching a long time in various places, similar sentiments, was, in 1148, seized and imprisoned, where he died; and chiefly because he opposed the baptism of babes. The Albigenses, and Waldenses generally, (as we are taught in Twisk's Chron. in the Dutch Martyrology, and in Cassander's Hist.) opposed infant baptism. Pope Alexander III, in 1179, anathematized them for opposing it. In the year 1200, many of them were burnt in Germany, for the same reason. In 1230, many of them suffered death at Tryers, for opposing it. In 1232, nineteen persons were burnt at Thoulouse, for opposing baby baptism. In 1336, four baptized persons were imprisoned—placed upon the rack—tortured—and finally beheaded, for the same offence. In 1315, many Waldenses were burnt in Austria, for opposing the baptism of babes. In 1522, two guilders was the fine, at Zurich, set upon all those who neglected the baptism of their children. In 1529, nine persons, who had had this stratagem played off upon them, when babes, becoming converted, were baptized according to the command of Christ, and for this reason were put to death at Gant. In 1527, a Baptist minister was beheaded, with seventy of his associates, for opposing baby baptism. About 1527, three persons were roasted to death by a slow fire, for no other offence.

These are only specimens of what was continually practised. The Episcopalian, Congregational, and Presbyterian organizations, all springing up between 1534, and 1545, enforced the baptism of babes on all they could control, under the penalty of excommunication. Baby-sprinkling, which must have commenced after 1556, has been since enforced, under similar penalties. After 1648, the Baptists were cruelly persecuted in New England. The eight hundred martyrs murdered in England, between 1553, and 1558, were mostly Baptists.

All this proves, first, that there have been Baptists in all ages, who have endured these persecutions. And secondly, that suspicion rests upon baby baptism, from the fact of its being enforced by the arm of despotism, and been accompanied with such cruel persecutions.

LETTER VI.

PERVERSIONS OF SCRIPTURE.

I my first letter I alluded to some perversions of scripture, made by the bishops in 1568, nine or ten years after the excitement in favor of Calvin's substitute for baptism began. And as these perversions, by the express command of King James' were to be retained in his version of 1611, and are still continued in America, their connexion with this point of history gives them fresh interest.

The first perversion I will name is the transfer of the Greek words baptize and baptism and refusing to translate them. While the bishops who had killed so many martyrs were so eager to introduce sprinkling; if the words could possibly have been twisted into such a version, they would surely have rendered them *sprinkle*. The fact that they did not, is, of itself full proof that they knew they could not. Their other perversions are a clear proof that they would have done this if they possibly could.

Dr. Campbell, principal of the Marischal College, Aberdeen, a Presbyterian minister, of great candor, and one of the most learned men in the world, (Dissert. on Gospels,) says: " The Greek word *peritome*, the Latins translate *circumcisio*; (circumcision,) which exactly corresponds in etymology. But the Greek word *baptisma*, (baptism,) they have retained, changing only the letters from Greek to Roman. Yet the latter was just as susceptible of a literal translation into Latin as the former. Immersio (immersion) answers as *exact'y* in the one case as circumcisio (circumcision) in the other. When the language furnishes us with materials for a version *so exact*, such a version conveys the sense more perspicuously than a *foreign* (i. e. Greek) name. For this reason, I should think the word immersion a better English name (for the ordinance,) than baptism,*were we now at liberty to make a choice* ;"

e. were there no civil law or civil government against it,

Also in his note on Matt. iii. 11, he says: "The word bap-tizo, both in sacred authors and classical, signifies *to dip, to plunge, to immerse.*"

The bishops saw it would be too barefaced a falsehood to have translated it sprinkle. But they did all they dared. They transferred the Greek words, thus giving those who were in their views the power to deceive the multitude who were ignorant of the Greek language. King James, in 1604, expressly enjoind upon his translators the retention of "*these old ecclesiastical words,*" and the whole subject-matter con-nected with them. This is the reason the perversions are transmitted to us in the present version. His reason was the same as that which influenced the bishops. The parliamen-tary act of 1644, enforcing sprinkling as the law of the land, and excluding immersion, was based upon the same princi-ples, and on the retention of the same perversions. The peo-ple, after these events, in the emphatic language of Campbell, were "*not now at liberty to make a choice.*" The object in the whole transaction evidently was to cast mist upon the subject, to cover up the ordinance of Christ, and to countenance a substitute; to bury in perpetual oblivion the doctrine of be-lievers' baptism, whereby Christians were subjected to Christ, and to establish a sprinkling operation, that should subject all the people and all the babes in the realm to the civil gov-ernment, in all matters of religion. This, then, is a bare-faced perversion, in its practical operation, and intended to subserve a heaven-daring invasion of the prerogative and ju-risdiction of Christ. Whatever intrigues the Catholics might have previously practiced on the same point, served only to show these how this perversion could be effected. The Cath-olics only led the way. The whole transaction is a studied intrigueing fraudulent perversion of the ordinance, in its de-sign. It is impossible, any person can avoid arriving at that conclusion, who candidly reflects on the time and the circum-stances connected with this transfer of these Greek words.

It is objected, that the bishop's Bible merely followed Tyn-dale's of 1526; Coverdales of 1585; Matthew's of 1537; Cran-mers, and Travenner's of 1539; and the Genevan, of 1557.

We reply, if it precisely followed those, why did they call it the "Bishops Version." Why burn up all the others, that this might prevail? There was palpable iniquity in this. We admit the Genevan Bible of 1557, and probably some oth-ers, had transferred the word baptizo. But we do not admit, that they had the other perversions we have named below. And further, we reject the principle, that any demonstrable guilt in the above, is any palliation for those bishops. The bishops knew better than to give such perversions, as according with truth, and therefore, the charge of conscious and intentional corruption, is demonstrably true. Those bishops, that ten years before, could be employed in killing so many martyrs, would do the latter deed, and they did it, mauger all the efforts to screen their guilt; and they burnt the other versions, so that none but the Bishops' Bible, thus perverted, could be had.

The *second* perversion I will name, is I Cor. 12, 13. The literal translation is, "Because in one spirit were we all baptized into one Body, whether Jews or Greeks, whether bond or free; and have all drank in one spirit." The particular thoughts "in one spirit (i. e. in the same spirit of piety) *all* of every nation were baptized," and "*into one body* i. e. into one kingdom, and "all drank in one spirit" (i. e. cultivated the same christian spirit, through the influence of the Holy Ghost.) This teaches that baptism introduces into the church or kingdom—that all the members were adults, and supposed to be pious," drinking in the same spirit," that none were then members but such, and that there was of course no such thing as infant baptism, or infant sprinkling, or infant membership, then in the church. These views were so repugnant to the Episcopal national organization, that it became necessary for the bishops to cover it all over, by perverting some words, and totally changing the whole scope and train of thought. It is all effected by translating *en* falsely by the preposition *by*, and beginning the word spirit with a capital letter, as "by one Spirit."

This little perversion turns off the whole attention into a visionary field of falsely called *spiritual baptism*, and of a falsely called *spiritual* Kingdom; a form of thought which is never found in the New Testament. The literal translation confines the attention to the *real* Kingdom consisting of those, and those only, who in one spirit 'were baptized into it,' and were old enough to drink in one and the same spirit, or temper. This fact is asserted of all the members—of course no babes. This is another just such perversion as might be expected from those bishops at that time having such an object in view.

To show that this criticism is correct, it should be noticed that the apostle, from verse 1 to 11, is speaking, not of converting grace, but of the different *miraculous* gifts bestowed upon the different members "*as he wills*;" and yet, verses 12, to 27, that as a human body, having many members, is one, so is the church, the Kingdom of Christ one, though consisting (as in the literal translation of v. 27) "*of parts.*" What a gross perversion, and how evidently intentional, in thus changing the thought, and thus covering up this discription the Holy Ghost has left on record of the kingdom of Jesus Christ, and making the language describe something else!

A *third* perversion I will name is Matt. iii. 2. The literal translation is, "Repent, for the kingdom of heaven has come," or has come near. John's custom of immersing penitent believers, thus subjecting them to the King of heaven in his kingdom, and into which Jesus Christ was formally introduced in the same way, in order "to fulfil all righteousness," and John's exclusion of those who did not bring forth fruits meet for repentance, are facts clearly described by the Evangelists. On the imprisonment of John, Christ took the lead in that kingdom and baptized (by his disciples) into it more disciples than John," as we are taught John iv. 1, 2, and elsewhere. It is thus John prepared the way of the Lord, and was the messenger before his face.

But this immersion itself, as the initiating ordinance into the kingdom, and its limitation to the penitent, are so clearly described, and were so inconsistent with the national pædobaptism of England, and with the sprinkling they were at the time so eager to introduce, that it was necessary to do what they could to darken counsel, and cover up or pervert the whole passage. This they have done by perversely rendering it " the kingdom of heaven is *at hand.*" By this perversion, thus putting the labors of John over into the old dispensation, and intimating that the "kingdom of heaven" was not yet set up, they have by the perversion done what they could to destroy that argument against them.

A *fourth* perversion is of a class of passages. The Greek word εν (*en*) had been in the quiet and peaceful possession of one meaning for more than two thousand years, as baptism had been of immersion, and baptizo of *immerse.* The phrase "immerse *in* water," or " *in* Jordan," if literally translated, occurs in *ten* instances in the New Testament; and if it had so translated, would have rooted up the whole of their sprinkling project. Accordingly they have perversely translated it "*with water,*" in seven out of the ten instances. The instances of the perversion are Matt. iii. 11; Mark i. 8; Luke ii. 16; John i. 26, 31, 33; and Acts i. 5. The translation "*in* water," or " *in* Jordan," is given Matt. iii. 6; and Mark i. 5, 9.

Dr. Campbell remarks: " Nothing can be plainer than that if there be any incongruity in the expression, *in water,* this

E

in Jordan, must be equally incongruous." Mr. Hervey, in his second letter to Mr. Wesley, says; "I can prove that εν signifies *in*, and I can prove it to have been in the peaceable possession of that signification for more than *two thousand years.*" L'Enfant, on the phrases "in water." and "in the Holy Ghost," says, "These words do very well express the ceremony of baptism, which was at first performed by plunging the whole body into water, as also the copious effusion of the Holy Ghost on the day of Pentecost." The perversion of "immerse *in* water," to "*baptize with water*," in seven instances, and by the bishops in 1568, was evidently intended for the same general purpose they then had in view.

A *fifth* class of perversions is of such passages as Mark i. 8, and Luke iii. 16, literally rendered, would be, " He shall baptize you in the Holy Ghost," and " in the Holy Ghost and fire," The fulfilment is recorded in Acts ii. 2—4, when the Holy Ghost like a rushing mighty wind filled all the house, as well as cloven tongues like as of fire ; and when the disciples were endued with *miraculous powers.* They were then emphatically immersed in and surrounded by the miraculous displays of the Holy Ghost. The perversion, baptize *with* the Holy Ghost, was evidently intended totally to change the scope of thought into another different train of thoughts. It fixes the attention on the common effusions of the Holy Ghost, so as to make the expressions favor their sprinkling project, by its similarity to these effusions. It should here forever be remembered by those who in prayer use the expression, " baptize us with the Holy Ghost," that they use not the language which the Spirit teaches, but the corrupted and perverse phraseology of those corrupt and heaven daring bishops; and that they perversely gave this phraseology for the sake of wresting and perverting the truth. Converting and sanctifying grace, is never called baptism in God's word, except by perversion, and by corrupting the word of God.

A *sixth* perversion is in 1 Peter iii. 21. *Eperotema,* never signifies the *answer.* It always signifies the *question*, or the *test.* The Bible is a book of tests. Baptism tests the consciences of men whether they will subject themselves to the authority of Christ in his kingdom, or not. Here we are taught it is the " test of a good conscience." By perverting it as " the ANSWER *of a good eonscience,*" the bishops evidently intended to give unbounded latitude to every person to follow his own feelings in relation to baptism, and to call it the *answer* of a good conscience. This perversion makes each one's *feelings* (blindly called conscience) his own law-maker in relation to baptism. It virtually repeals the law of Christ, and leaves every one to his own notions and wishes.

Surely the delusions of a Bible Society must be as strong as ever were those of the free-masons, or those of the Mormons, in strenuously refusing to aid in the circulation of the Scriptures, unless all these heaven-daring perversions are retained. And the question rushes and presses upon the consciences of all Christians, and especially of those whose fundamental principle of organization is *entire obedience to Jesus Christ in all things:* how can we be said to obey Christ in causing his gospel to be preached to every creature under heaven, when parts of it, so vital in gathering together all his people in one, and in preventing sectarianism, are thus covered up and concealed; and when these perversions so evidently *intentional*, and so palpably adapted as they are to favor divisions and sectarianism, are palmed off upon the world as the real language of the living God.

A *seventh* perversion is Isaiah lii. 15. The literal translation is, "So shall he astonish many nations."* The visage and form being so marred, as expressed in the previous verse, is the cause of the astonishment. The bishops have perverted it "So shall he *sprinkle* many nations." They were at the time devoting all their energies to the defence of a national religion, and in laying the foundation for national sprinkling to become the initiating ordinance into the national establishment.

An *eighth* perversion is Heb. x. 22. It is expressed. "and our bodies washed *with* pure water." "With," is here put in roman letters, as if it were found in the original, thus expressing a falsehood.

It was the custom of the translators, when they supplied a word, to give it in *italics*. This passage is the only instance I know of, where they have not done it. They doubtless, had their reasons *mentally* for not doing it here. The people would infer that "with" was merely the opinion of the translators, and that "in water," was full as likely to be the meaning, and more so. As we have shown that immersion is the real Christian ordinance, this proves that "in water,"

---

* I follow the Septuagint, as the Saviour used it, quoted from it, and approved the version. *Thaumasei*—shall astonish.

The Hebrew *Nazah*, it is true, signifies to leap, to exult—to leap for joy. It is here in the Hiphical conjugation; implying a casual action, as "*cause to rejoice*"

Gesenius renders the Hebrew "So shall he cause many nations to rejoice." —*So shall he organize many national churches;* which would be a no more gross perversion than—*So shall he sprinkle many nations.*

is the only phrase that can express this real fact, and give the intention of the Holy Spirit.

By giving "with" and in roman characters, thereby teaching that "with" is found in the Greek Testament, as a part of inspiration, they have palmed off a falsehood upon the world. If they had given "with" in italics, we should have said this is merely their exposition. But as it is, they have practically said, this is a translation.

Bishop Smith, of Kentucky, in his recent sermon on baptism, has twice rendered this passage "having our bodies washed *in* pure water." Such testimony, from their own side of the house, cannot certainly be suspected of partiality for us. It is, and must be the testimony of candid criticism, and sound conviction.

These are only specimens out of many other passages. Whenever the Saviour is made to say, "Repent, for the kingdom of heaven is *at hand;*" the last words are also a perversion. "For the kingdom of heaven *has* come," or has come near;" implying that it is now in existence, and has actually come close to them, is the thought the Holy Ghost has recorded in the Greek Testament. So also Matt. x. 7. He commands the disciples to "preach, saying, The kingdom of heaven has come." The bishops perversion is "the kingdom of heaven is at hand,"—is about to be set up hereafter—not so cogent a reason for repentance, as the real reason, and a false statement is never as good a reason to urge for repentance, as the truth.

While I make these remarks, I must bear testimony to our version, as being generally very accurate; except simply, in the items of baptism; and there it is palpably sectarian, as the above specimens show, and I might show many others.

But notwithstanding these and all the other efforts, no direct Parliamentary law, enforcing sprinkling, could be obtained till 1644; notwithstanding many indirect laws, intended for a direct effect, were passed previous to that time.

LETTER VII.

MISAPPLICATION OF BAPTISM, AND THE SUBSTITUTE.

It should be steadily kept in view, that baptism is the initiating ordinance into a state of entire subjection to the exclusive jurisdiction of Christ, within his kingdom. As conversion is the private surrender of the whole soul to his will, through the internal workings of the Spirit, so baptism is the public subjection of self entirely to his will, within his kingdom. "Putting on Christ," "baptized into Christ," and similar phrases, fully express this truth. The person baptized is supposed voluntarily and freely so to subject himself publicly and fully to the will of Christ. But the use of the substitute is not taking the will of Christ as the rule, and therefore is not the thing. It is still cleaving to the will of man, or to our own selfish feelings. It must be the thing Christ requires, or the surrender of the heart to his will is not made. And further, the substitute is only used in other folds, and only misleads one away from the organized kingdom of Christ, into the wrong fold; i. e. some modern fold contrived by men, and ruled by men, thus dividing the kingdom of Christ. That all converts should subject themselves to Christ within his kingdom, and his jurisdiction, and by that transaction which is the initiating ordinance there, is as necessary as it is there should be but One Fold, and One Shepherd. And further, as another person cannot repent for us, so another cannot do this duty for us in infancy. It is premature if done, and therefore is nothing. Jesus Christ requires of all believers the personal subjection of themselves. The delusion of parents can never excuse us from this invariable claim of Christ upon our own personal obedience, his right to have us in a state of entire subjection to him and free from human lords, and within his kingdom.

Christ will not have any rival powers with him over the church, nor any rival folds. The existence of these is forbidden, and the ceremony which initiates them is forbidden, Rev. xxii. 18. Such a baptism, and into such a church as subjects us partly to the will of human rulers, and partly to the will of Christ, is vitiated in just so far as there is any subjection to human rulers. Because Christ will not have such competitors or partners in power. But it can be cured by leaving such rulers. As the ordinance must be right, so the purpose must be right, and the subjection to Christ complete, and within his kingdom. Such was evidently the apostolic practice.

The ordinance of Christ, right in external form, has been grossly misapplied to wicked and selfish purposes. In the mirror above given, we propose to point to the map of the history of baptism, and point out some of these misapplications.

The first misapplication is A. D. 206. The children in the schools, called catechumens, were hurried on to be immersed before conversion. Tertullian raises his voice against it. Robinson fully demonstrates from the original words used in the discussion, and from the fact that they asked to be immersed (as the description is,) that they could not possibly be babes. It was youths without conversion, to whom the ordinance was misapplied. The re-action against it clearly shows the general and universal opinion then prevalent, that none but believers were proper subjects of baptism.

The next misapplication of the real ordinance is A. D. 255. One Fidus, had a country parish in the interior of Africa. The heathen around for centuries had been accustomed to sacrifice their own babes to Saturn, a heated brazen statue, and to destroy them in the flames. So strong was the delusion, that no civil law could check it. They were accustomed also to steal and sacrifice the babes of Christians. Yet on account of the civil law, they did not meddle with Christians; i. e. baptized persons. Fidus' parish was in the midst of these depredations. His ingenuity devised the scheme of immersing the babes, in the name of the Trinity, whereby they took the name of Christians, and were thus protected. He soon laid the case before a council. Cyprian, who is described as an "ignorant fanatic, and a great tyrant, and a confused genius, ambitious for power," at the head of the council managed the question. After first deciding that a certain deacon should be put to death for treating his pastor with contumacy, according to Deut. xvii. 12, and secondly, that any person who should employ the clergy to do secular business, should be excommunicated, they decided in **favor** of Fidus' course, on two grounds: first, "God would be a respecter of persons, if he denied to infants that which he grants to adults;" secondly, "that Elisha lay upon a child, and put his mouth upon his mouth—the spiritual sense of which (they said) is, that babes are equal to men, and you destroy this equality if you refuse to baptize them." Bible logic this!!

This council of confused geniuses, and the church they represented, were full of ignorance and fanaticism, having a greater amount of Jewish and heathen, than of Christian notions.

This is the first case of the baptism of babes, that can be demonstrated. Perfect uncertainty, and the entire lack of proof, rests upon every pretended case anterior to this. I pronounce it impossible to demonstrate, from all history, the baptism of a babe previous to this case. The sheer possibility of alluding to such a thing is all that can possibly be said of any writers or of their language, previous to this. And the character of Cyprian, and of his council, the character of the other decisions, at the same meeting, and the grounds of this decision in favor of Fidus' practice, only prove that it was about as good as a hundred other decisions of councils in those times, too ridiculous to be mentioned, and which no person of common sense would think of following. Here is an instance of the misapplication of the real ordinance, immersion, to the humane purpose of saving babes from heathen depredations, and the flames.

The next misapplication of the ordinance, on the map of history, grew out of the interpretation given of John iii. 5. The fanatics of those times, in urging the people to be baptized, had told them that passage meant that no one could go to heaven without baptism. Hence sick persons and sick babes, were baptized. The ordinance was thus misapplied to the purpose of being an imaginary passport to heaven.

The next case is, the council of Mela, in Africa; sometimes called the council of Carthage, in 418. In this country, the heathen practice of lustration. i. e. using water at the naming of babes, which had been customary in all the heathen countries, for centuries, was continued by many half heathen Christians. Full as many heathen and Jewish practices had been intermingled in the church of Africa, as Christian, for more than two hundred years; and the government of the church had become exceedingly despotic. This despotic hierarchy contrived the stratagem of enforcing infant baptism, for the purpose of securing them under their control; being instigated by the love of rule. This is the *first* council, as Grotius and all historians affirm, that enforced infant baptism, i. e. the immersion of babes.

It was not till the government of men began thus to prevail over the church, that the baptism of babes began to be *enforced*. The object, no doubt, was, to secure numbers under their control. This council, at the same time, passed about twenty other laws equally disgraceful and tyrannic, all of them contrary to the express and fundamental principles of the word of God. One was, Whosoever shall deny that the Lord's supper is to be administered to new-born babes, let him be *accursed*. This law and the one for infant baptism stand on the same basis.

From this time until the establishment of popery in 606, a number of councils for a similar purpose, enacted a similar law, to be enforced as far as their several jurisdictions extended, to secure numbers.

In the year 606, popery became regularly organized, and infant immersion was enforced throughout the pope's dominions. The object was to enslave the rising generation, by taking advantage of their helpless state, and securing them under the pope. Immersion in form, and the name of the sacred Trinity were observed. But in fact it did not subject them to Christ, but it was perverted by others to the purpose of subjecting them to the pope. By his arbitrary power, the parents were forced to be the tools in this profane and cruel transaction. It was cruel because of the purpose; it was profane because the whole mockery was done in the name, and by pretended authority from the triune God.

Had it not been for the stratagem of infant baptism, whereby advantage was taken of the rising generation, popery could never have been established or continued as it has. For more than a thousand years, the ordinance instituted for the purpose named in the beginning of this letter, was perverted to this most cruel purpose. In the year 789, the cruel Charlemagne, King of France, and Emperor of the West, in his efforts to subdue the Saxons, reduced them to the dreadful alternative of either being assassinated by his troops, or of being baptized into subjection to his authority. He also required them to have all their children baptized, and thus subjected to him within a year from their birth, under the penalty of one hundred and twenty shillings, if of noble blood; sixty shillings, if free-born; and thirty shillings if peasants; to be enforced, collected, and paid into the King's treasury. The Greek church only practised infant baptism in case of prospective death, down to the time when human beings acquired the government over the church; and then infant baptism was enforced by law. As soon as church and state became connected, the immersion of all the babes in the nations, was enforced by the national governments. All the Eastern and other churches, as soon as they consented to be ruled by human beings, immediately had laws enforced upon them requiring babes by stratagem, to be subjected to them, in the external form of Christian baptism. The baptism of babes was effectually resisted in England, until the sixth century; and it was effectually resisted in Wales, so as to gain *no footing* there until the twelfth century. Tyranny over the church, has always enforced it, where it could, so as to secure and extend its dominion. But until human beings began to lord it over Christians, nothing of it was ever known, except in the above cases of delusion, beginning at A. D. 255.

When the Episcopal church was organized in 1534, it stopped midway, as Bishop Lowth expresses it, in the reformation from Popery. Its constitution was formed by the civil powers and was intended as a church and state organization; and to pattern very much after the popish church. Of these facts we are assured by Episcopal authors themselves. Of course they would take infant baptism as a main ground of support. It would be indispensable to their purposes in securing their own subjects, and in competing for numbers against the church of Rome, and against the kingdom of Christ. Here then the immersion of babes in the name of the Trinity, was also enforced and converted to secular purposes. After about one hundred years it was decided, as we have shown, that sprinkling would answer the same purposes. The Congregational church first assumed a form and consistency about the same time or a little later. Those who planned that organization, would, of course take along infant baptism, both to secure their own children within their own pale or fence; and to compete for numbers with other organization. The plan of the Presbyterian church, was invented and contrived by John Calvin; and the prominent feature of the few governing the many would of course be introduced by a man of his character and love of rule. He would also adopt infant baptism of course, to secure their own children within the pale—to subject as many others as possible to their government, and to prepare his ship to compete for numbers with all the other ships. In my fourth letter, I have shown how long these three last organizations retained baptism in form as Christ established it; and when they dashed it away and adopted the "substitute of a substitute." These three organizations and their successors, are the only ones so far as I know, that have totally discarded christian baptism, and established another ceremony as a *good enough* inititating ordinance into their folds. When we once begin the principle, that we may make laws for the church, and may rule, we know not how far the principle will carry us. And with these it has occurred in such a way, by tradition from parent to child that sprinkling is baptism, and they have so far imbibed their ideas from what they hear and see in their youth; and the books which contain the facts have been so entirely withdrawn from their Seminaries and course of education, and so many things in the Bible are falsely translated or covered over, that probably not one in a thousand now knows that the deed has been done. I am speaking of the wicked purposes to which baptism, as such, has been misapplied. These organizations, unconsciously make a profane use of the words connected with baptism, and of the name of the sacred Trinity. The use of water with them is not baptism, but is a very near resemblance to the *lustration* extensively practised before and since the Christian era, in heathen countries, in the naming of their children. It has no resemblance to *Christian* baptism at all, except the use of the words. Over this *fiction* we have unconsciously used the sacred name of God, in a very improper manner, not knowing what we did.

While it is true that these things are so, it is equally true, that in these organizations there are probably as many Christians of genuine piety and talents as can be found in any organization. I am thus plain in developing these things, because I see the evils of sectarianism, and I see clearly it will continue until Christians return to primitive gospel order. I see the importance of their union, in order to the conversion of the world; and I see how the cause bleeds, and how fast souls perish, and how fast infidelity increases because of these divisions, and I have searched deep a great many years for the root of the evil. I do not mean, and would not for my life, reproach a fellow-Christian; much less any whole denomination. But how can these things be reformed, unless they are proclaimed? And how can those who *know* they are on gospel ground, as to church organization, give it up for the organizations of the last three centuries, including the contrivances and mistakes of human beings? I add but one remark, Sectarianism and tyranny have always found the stratagem of baby baptism or its substitute *necessary;* and the people have been forced or deluded into it. But the kingdom of Christ, or his organization, needs no such thing.

LETTER VIII.

MISAPPLICATION—INJURIOUS TENDENCY, MONOMANIA.

The high handed and heaven-daring crime of annihilating the initiating ordinance of Jesus Christ into his kingdom, and of obtruding a contemptible substitute, as delineated in my fourth letter, is one which, if committed against an earthly government, would have exposed the offending party to the gallows, to banishment, or to imprisonment for life, and the confiscation of all his goods. An accessary to a crime is one who aids, abets, or in any way assists in its commission, either before or after the offence, and is held equally criminal as the principal. All are accessaries who countenance the act, or hold on to a substitute, which annihilates a law or connive at it.

An accessary, or an offender, who has the means of knowing the law, and yet neglects to acquaint himself with it, is held equally criminal, and liable to the same penalty, as if he knew it. Because his fault, in neglecting to know the law, is equal to all the consequences that result from that criminal negligence; and one fault can never be an excuse for another.

If the *immersion* of babes, as practised before 1556, be a divine ordinance, then the crime in dashing it away and obtruding the substitute, both with principals and accessaries, is a high-handed crime. On this supposition, baby sprinkling is a great crime; because the original law for baby immersion should have been obeyed, and not been annihilated by a substitute. If it is not a substitute for *that*, as a divine ordinance, then it is a *new ceremony*, begun in the year 1556, and hypocritically pretending to be divine. Take either horn of the dilemma, and this sprinkling of babes is a crime. It is either a crime in annihilating a divine law, or a crime as a *new pretender*. If this baby-sprinkling is right, then the apostles, the primitive church, and all Christendom for 1556 years, were exceedingly criminal in neglecting it. For not a trace of it is found during all that time, unless the Catholics, after the council of Ravenna, in 1311, had done a little of it. It is either wrong since it began, or they were all wrong for neglecting it during so many centuries.

The profane misapplication of the real ordinance of Christ to babes, as a pious fraud to entrap them in their helpless state, in order to build up aristocracy, despotism, and popery; and to subject them to such a cruel state, as we hinted in our last, will hardly be pretended to have accorded with the divine rule. If it did, then the apostles and primitive churches for 255 years, were grossly criminal for neglecting it. Before we get through, we shall demonstrate there was nothing of it for the first 255 years of the Christian era. The heaven daring atrocities of the bishops, and of King James, in transferring Greek words, in covering over and concealing the law of heaven, touching this ordinance, and the gross perversions of Scripture to which we have adverted, for the express purpose of starting and propagating this substitute, this baby sprinkling operation, does not argue very much in favor of its being a law of a holy God. The Parliamentary acts of 1644, or near that time, enforcing this baby sprinkling, and making immersion of believers penal, as well as the similar acts of

Calvin's Presbytery, near 1560, and those of the Westminster assembly, in 1643, obtained by a bare majority, do not argue very forcibly in favor of the law being divine. The late acts of the General Assembly of the Presbyterian church may just as well claim to be divine. They are scarcely more than two hundred years more remote from the Christian era. The reason these arguments have not been dilated upon by the English Baptists is, they live where it is treason to speak with disrespect of any acts of their own government, or of their King, who "can do no wrong." For this reason, the facts to which I alluded, are barely stated in a nude form, by many different English authors, and without any comment. And for this reason, their arguments have been confined chiefly to the definition of words. The facts I have collected stand scattered in different authors.

The fact is, that baby immersion, and baby sprinkling, have uniformly stood forth as traps by which to catch the helpless unawares. All the national organizations have adopted the one or the other, as such traps. All the aristocratic and despotic establishments in all ages—all the *church and state* establishments, and every founder of a new sect, and especially the founders of such sects as have been shaped after a national form, by joining churches together; and such as have been *ambitious* to become a national church, (as the Presbyterian, from the days of Calvin, to the days of Cromwell;) have uniformly resorted to one of these snares, by which to gain numbers. The most plausible things about its tendency to promote the child's salvation, have been said in order to beguile the parents. It has all served to build up sectarianism, and other jurisdictions, and in effect to compete for numbers against the real kingdom of Christ; to prevent anything like union among the people of God, and to ensnare and mislead hundreds of millions, in their helpless state: to blind those who were entrapped, and make them blind tools in entrapping others, and in extending the evil, and to prevent every thing like united effort on the part of Christians in the conversion of the world. Baby immersion, and baby sprinkling has built up more sectarianism, than every thing else. Millions and millions of souls have perished by neglect, in consequence of these things, and the real kingdom of Christ has become almost prostrated or lost in the fog. Christ is hardly seen as Ruler over Zion at all. Human despots, aristocrats, bishops, and other spiritual wickedness in high places, and human governments over the churches, have taken his seat, *usurped* his power, gathered sections of his people into sects, under themselves, and changed the whole government from *His* liberal jurisdiction and purpose, to *their own sectarian, selfish purposes.* The *love of rule*, is the beginning of all this offending, and the *ensnaring* of babes the means. A constitution and human laws by which to hold the people together under rulers, is resorted to: and this snare for catching babes and securing numbers, is the main dependance for success. And as the free-masons, when ensnared, were totally unconscious of any snare, and were made the blind and unconscious tools in extending that delusion; so it is with the delusion of baby sprinkling among the sects. The zealous and crafty propagators of the delusion, are as perfectly unconscious of the delusion as the free-masons were of their delusion. I know there is no foundation for the sprinkling or the baptism of babes in the Bible. I have carefully written out a literal translation of every passage on baptism, and carefully and prayerfully sought to know the mind of the Spirit. I know there is no more foundation for either in the Bible, than there is for free-masonry, or for Mormonism. And the position of baby immersion, as well as that of baby sprinkling, on the map of history, is as conclusive against the possibility of its being divine, as the position of any other modern delusion. And the arguments in support of the thing, as it exists in our country, and especially the circumcision argument, are as far back of the thing itself, and anterior to its real existence, as the pretended proofs of free-masonry are anterior to it. In each case the pretended proofs are two or three thousand years before the thing. Were it not that I have faithfully examined the subject, and know these things, I would not deal thus plainly with it. I verily believe, after looking over the whole map of church history, that the baptism of babes and the sprinkling of babes in building up sectarianism, have been snares which have occasioned greater injuries to the real kingdom of Christ, and subserved an end more cruel and tyrannic, and have done more to hinder the conversion of the world, and a united effort of Christians towards it, than any and every thing beside. Believing this, I must be plain: "the love of Christ constraineth me." His cause and kingdom, and the best good of the world are at stake.

I have reflected much since I awoke from this delusion, and will give my views of it. There is such a thing as *monomania;* i. e. derangement in *one thing,* while the mind is perfectly sound in every thing else. Medical books fully describe it, as one of the most common things in the world. Free-masons, after being *duped*, immediately partook of it. The Mormons and the papists partake of it. Anti-masonry partook of it. The wild speculations of late years have moved on that principle. The heathen, in sacrificing their children to Saturn, moved on the same principle. So *we* who were ensnared by baby sprinkling, were so moulded in the nature of things as to move on the same principle of MONOMANIA. People of the most sound judgment as to every thing else, are often entirely void of reason, and of all sound reasoning as to ONE thing. So our minds were *diseased* and *crazed* on this *one* subject by our early impressions. The fact that such men, and with truly pious feelings, cont'nue a ceremony so perfectly void of scriptural support, is clear demonstration of *monomania*. The baby immersion we described, as Hughes, and all the intelligent papists assert, is nothing but a popish tradition. It cannot possibly be anything else. It was a pious fraud to catch and secure and enslave babes. The baby sprinkling of our land according to Wall, is only the "*scandalous* substitute of a substitute" for that. It is only the mere substitute of the substitute of a *popish tradition*, and that a *pious fraud*. The conversion of the real ordinance into a pious fraud by misapplying it to babes was *profane*. What then is the substitute of the *substitute*? How pitiful, then, is the sight, when a man of talents, of sound mind in all other respects, defends and acts over this pitiful farce; falsely calls it baptism (a declaration was never more false in fact:) then calls the name of the Father, Son, and Holy Ghost, over it; as if it were done by authority of the great God; and then he prays, and that honestly too, and tells God he has done it according to the instructions of his holy word, when in fact the custom first began only 284 years ago. If the man was as crazy in all other respects as he is in this one thing, he would certainly be sent to the mad-house. And yet in all this mockery, there is usually as genuine piety of heart and honesty of purpose in the minister and the parents, as in anything whatever. And there is not even the *beginning* of a doubt of its being a *divine* ordinance. It is absolutely certain they are *deranged* in *this one* thing. Were it not for the fact of so many "strong delusions," and of monomania in so many things, we could not account for all this, while we know they are possessed of piety of heart, and good sense in other things. This mental aberration is begun in infancy; and is the result of the law of *influence*, a very common law of our natures. The filthy drunkard has very little influence. The moral and respectable citizen has much. The kind, intelligent, and pious parent, has *unbounded* influence over the child. Let that parent be diseased with *monomania*, and it will certainly be communicated to the child. Because the child, seeing the parent is right in every thing else, will conclude, of course, he is right also on the point where there is *monomania*. The pious minister, having the same mental *aberration*, will strengthen the same in the child. The child will form all of his ideas of baptism, from what he sees the *monomaniac* of a minister do and say. He does not even *begin to surmise* any mistake; much less does he see that his parents, his minister, and himself, are all monomaniacs. Instead of this, his delusion grows with his growth. Infant dedication, and this sprinkling farce (for I will call things by their right names,) are interchangeably used as being synonymous; and the real hearty dedication of children to God, all admit is proper. This confusion of the two thoughts, strengthens the mental disease. He is taught if there is no sprinkling ceremony there is *no dedication;* that if such children are afterwards converted, this *sprinkling* ceremony is a material link in the chain of causes; and that if they die, they will, if sprinkled, be saved.* Thus the child becomes perfectly spell-bound: so that a doubt cannot be wedged into his mind. He reads, as he advances, solely on one side; or if on the other, it is solely to oppose. If he becomes a minister, with one breath he rails against sectarianism, and with the next he blindly defends this sectarian scheme, not knowing it is such. He spreads the same monomania among thousands. The mind of the deluded victim dwells with so much ecstacy upon the charms of this hallucination, and becomes so perfectly spell-bound, that it would seem really cruel to break the charm were it not that this same little farce, enters into the very vitals of the kingdom of Christ, acts as an iron wedge to split it asunder, prevents the possibility of its union, prepares its dupes to be and remain at antipodes against the real organization of Christ's kingdom, blinds them to its outlines, prepares them to oppose those who do observe them; is a profane delusion, and it prepares its dupes to be the propagators of it during all their lives; and yet they know not what they do.

Was it not for the same monomania, converts would never

---

* Many Sects are taught by their rulers, that baby-sprinkling is necessary to salvation; and many creeds have taught the same. Popery teaches that babes *have no souls, and are annihilated if they die, unless they are* SPRINKLED into the popish jurisdiction.

hesitate as to the duty, as soon as converted, of being baptized into subjection to Christ. It therefore hinders their being gathered under his jurisdiction. The rights of conscience with many, seem to be nothing but the privilege of following their own feelings, in this blind monomania, at the expense of the divided, bleeding cause of Christ.

LETTER IX.

MONOMANIA A SNARE—ITS MODE OF SELF DEFENCE.

The monomania (described in my last,) with which the minds of children become infected by what they see, and through the same mental disease of their parents, and parents too, who are often hearty Christians, and often well informed on every other subject, except that pertaining to this mental aberration, according to the law of *influence*, and by taking for granted that the parents are right here, because they are right in all other things, leads such children when they grow up to do many wrong things when in fact " they know not what they do." They are caught in a snare and know it not. The parents and the minister have ensnared them, and knew it not. Progenitors for centuries have done the like, and knew it not. It is an unfortunate mental disease. It is an unfortunate case. Parents if they only knew it, could scarcely do any thing which would prepare the minds of their children to do greater injuries in the religous world, through delusion, not knowing what they do. They become the slaves to a sect, and to the self-created and usurped powers which control the sect, when they ought to be subjected to the exclusive power and jurisdiction of Christ, within his kingdom. If we show that the sect is in a state of rivalship, from the time it came into being, against the real organized kingdom of Christ; then the child is prepared to devote all his life in increasing and perpetuating the evil of such competitioa against the real kingdom of Christ. If the child becomes converted, he becomes prepared to have a conscience against personal obedience to Christ, in a plain and positive ordinance, wherein all converts are required by him who bought them with his own blood, to submit themselves exclusively to *His* authority and jurisdiction, in his kingdom. If the child becomes a minister, he becomes prepared by it to propagate the same mental aberration and to build *over against* the organized kingdom of Christ, into an organization where they will be subject to *human* lords. All such separations weaken the real kingdom, which ought and needs to be strengthened To say the least, all the sects can not be right, and therefore, this *may* be the wrong one. The bare possibility of this should lead every Christian, who is candid, to stop and think before he further goes. Delusions often lead people to commit atrocities, when they are not aware they are atrocities. Paul and others, when persecuting the church, are instances in point. The delusion of baby sprinkling, is doubtless one of the strongest delusions that ever prevailed. It may, therefore occasion some of the greatest injuries to to the church of Christ,when the deluded victims of the monomania, have no surmise that it is so. Every thing which crazes the mind either w*holly* or in *part*,or simply in *one thing*, is, or may be, a far greater injury than we imagine. A talented mind affected with monomania, in a point so vital to the cause of Christ, is prepared to do, unconsciously, immense injury in that particular train. That the mind contemplated, cannot be sound, is evident from the manner in which the delusion is produced, as well as the manner in which it is defended. It is produced by what the child sees in such churches, and by the mistaken instructions of honest but deluded parents. The history of the origin of the thing, is full proof that *that* which is so modern and so palpably a human device and stratagem, and which is so much reverenced by the deluded as divine, must be a deception. The mind, therefore, which cleaves to it as divine, cannot possibly be sound in that train of things.

Its manner of proving this delusion to be divine, shows the same crazy state of mind. It not unfrequently defends this profane delusion in connection with the dedication of children to God, as if it were absolutely essential to their salvation. Hence, also, the frequency of this ceremony upon children who are expected soon to die. Hence, also, the wounded hearts of parents are often soothed after bereavements in view of *their faithfulness in the observance of this* delusive *ceremony*, as a *passport* to heaven. As we know to a demonstration, when this ceremony originated, all these things demonstrate a mental derangement in that thing. It is pretended that God claims this modern ceremony, to be performed by parents on their children, as a divine ordinance ; and that it came down from heaven. This ceremony, which commenced two-hundred and eighty-four years ago, free-masonry, which commenced in 1717, and Mormonism, which commenced in 1830, all claim to have come down from heaven!! In each case, where people honestly believe the thing, the mind must be so far deranged.

The hearty and daily dedication of children to God, in prayer and faith by the parent, is right; but what has this modern delusion, this "substitute of a substitute," of a pious *fraud* of the Catholics, to do with such daily dedication, and such acts of faith? Does not this one dedication in connexion with this delusion tend to pacify the mind, by leading it to think the *chore* is done, and therefore to neglect these daily and continuous dedications. It shows derangement therefore, in relation to its own object.

It defends itself on the ground that children so dedicated and sprinkled, are very apt to be converted. It is admitted, that the piety, faithfulness, and daily dedication of children to God, by parents, in prayer and faith, have a most direct, and I might add, *sure* tendency to their conversion. But it is denied that this sprinkling delusion and stratagem has any more of a tendency to the child's conversion than free-masonry. On the contrary, if it tends to lead the parent to lean upon this delusion as an idol, or to feel as if the work was done up, it just so far tends to counteract the faithfulness and persevering effort of the parent towards the child's salvation.

It defends itself by assuming and taking for granted that the church organized on infant sprinkling is the truly apostolic church and organized kingdom of Christ, and that, therefore, the practice must be right. I have only to reply, that every reader of church history knows that no church organization based on infant sprinkling ever came into existence till the sixteenth or seventh centuries.* The influence of the assump-

---

* Miss Opie makes a distinction between *active* and *passive lying*: the former is conscious and intentional, the latter unconscious. The lies uttered at the rantism of babes, are usually unconscious; but they are no less lies in fact. "I baptize!"—it is a passive lie, the minister does not baptize; "in the name of the Father, Son, and Holy Ghost;"—thereby meaning by authority from &c. This is another passive lie, and an impeachment of the divine character, and an insult to Him. What! God authorise the utterance of such a falsehood? When the Master of the Lodge admitted the poor blind candidate into a room fitted out in imitation of the Holy of holies "*in the name of the Lord*," he did not utter a more barefaced or false pretence, or perform a more palpable farce, or minister to a mere profane delusion. As it was, however, *unconscious*, Miss Opie would call it a *passive lie*. Does the minister, by the words "In the name of" &c., mean into subjection to the jurisdiction of Father, Son, and Holy Ghost? This is another of Miss Opie's *passive lies*. The babe is always thus subjected in rival folds, under the rival usurpers of dominion. Where his jurisdiction prevails, this farce is not authorized at all. Seventy-five years ago, and previously, the common expression used about this transaction was, *giving them* (the babes)

tion, that this is the truly organized kingdom of Christ, when it is not, leads the deluded to think they are doing God service in opposing that which in fact is the truly organized kingdom of Christ, and in defending that which is not. If those under this delusion become ministers, they are prepared by it to devote all their energies and talents in building up a competition against the organized kingdom of Christ. Of course their whole drift and influence is to wound Christ in the house of his friends, to build against his kingdom, and to perpetuate distractions. It prepares them, in the time of revivals, to lead the unwary convert into the same delusion for life, and to throw into revivals a crooked, sectarian management, against the true interest of Christ's kingdom, without being aware of it. All this tends to dampen and counteract the revival, and to dishearten those friends of Christ, who have submitted to his real organization. My own candid opinion is, that as all the self-created authorities over the church are *obliged* to depend on some secret stratagem for success and continuance, this and similar stratagems indirectly become the producing cause of all the sectarianism which exists. This delusion defends itself on the ground that it has a right to do as it *pleases*. But has any one a right in the sight of God, to take the name of God in vain, or to perpetuate a barefaced delusion, and do it in the name of the Trinity, because he pleases! It defends itself because it is *the custom of the sect*. So the Jews defended themselves on the same principle against Christ. It pretends it is impossible so many great men should be in the wrong. Judaism and free-masonry, and every other delusion, can present the same argument. It pretends that it is benevolence to children to have parents *pledged* in this ceremony to be faithful. If such a pledge is needful, why not enter into it openly as a naked pledge, without this profane delusion? Such a pledge is certainly better without this delusion than with it. It pretends a sort of blind, vague notion that history defends it. We have shown what the real facts are. The bold assertion of fanatics under a monomania, are not to be accredited. There is no better defence of it in history than we have given. Every part, if disputed, can be proven from standard authors, to

---

to the church. By what logic giving and binding them out as church-members, in a rival fold invented by men, and under rulers who have usurped the jurisdiction, and by a ceremony too, which is palpably a modern invention of men, thereby building up a treasonable rivalship against the jurisdiction of Christ, can be giving them to the Lord, it is impossible to see. This is another of Miss Opie's *passive lies.* A great many such lies are always uttered in this farce.

be precisely what we have stated. "So shall he sprinkle many nations," Is. liii. 15, is adduced by the delusion in self-defence. We reply, this is a deception in the translation, done by the English bishops. "So shall he *astonish* many nations," is the true translation. "Baptizing with water," in seven passages, as a general reason, is also adduced. This is a deception also in the translation, as we have shown. "Immersing *in water*," is the literal translation in every instance.

But baptism, it is said, "is the ANSWER of a good conscience," and therefore we may sprinkle or pour; and may sprinkle children or not, just as we please. We answer that that translation is a deception also. No such latitudinarian license is given to us to make our own pleasure our rule. "*Test* of a good conscience," is the literal translation. Baptism tests the conscience whether it be good, and whether we will wholly obey Christ in that ordinance, or not. But infant sprinkling, it is said, is a token of the tendency of the piety of parents in its influence to convert the children. We answer, the influence of the piety of the church also tends to the conversion of the impenitent part of the congregation. Why not sprinkle the impenitent in the congregation also, as a token of the same tendency of piety in the church, to *their* conversion? But it is asked, how can so many be deceived? I answer, how can so many be deceived by other delusions? It is all the result of following a blind impulse, through the influence of others, and neglecting to guide ourselves exclusively by the word of God.

In the absence of every thing else, the delusion leaps back some thirty-five hundred years before its real existence, and lights on *circumcision*. I have read every Pædobaptist publication I could find or hear of for twenty-five years, and have patiently again and again followed them all through the quagmire and wilderness of this pretended argument; and long before I relinquished the delusion, I was convinced that *here was no real argument at all*. The Bible teaches that baptism does NOT come in the place of circumcision. Paul was circumcised and yet was baptized. The male part of the three thousand converts in Acts ii. had doubtless been circumcised, and yet they were all baptized. And so of all the other converted Jews. Circumcision administered while the law was in force, would have been sufficient for those so circumcised, if baptism came in its place, without baptism. Moreover circumcision was applied to all the males in the nation. If baptism comes in its place, it must also be applied to males only, and *to all in the nation!* When it can be shown that the law of circumcision authorised Calvin, the British Parliament, the church of England, and the Westminster Assembly, between 1556, and 1644, to establish the sprinkling of babes by law, and excused all Christians from doing it till that time, then and not till then, will we admit there is an argument for it from circumcision.

LETTER X.

NO AUTHORITY IN THE BIBLE FOR IT—ALL HISTORY AGAINST IT.

The law enforcing circumcision on all the males, whether pious or infidel, as a national arrangement to prevent intermarriages with other nations, and to keep the nation distinct from all others, was twenty-two hundred years anterior to the beginning of the practice of the *immersion* of babes, and thirty-four hundred and fifty years before the custom of *sprinkling* babes began. The Parliament and lords spiritual, that use such stratagems and commit such crimes as we have seen, in order to justify a national organization, under men, would, of course, light upon the national circumcision of the Jews, and make it subservient, if possible, to their purposes. But the astonishment is, that rational men, in a free country, should become so deluded and crazed with baby-sprinkling, as to suffer themselves to believe there is really any divine authority in the laws of circumcision, favoring a delusion so remote as infant sprinkling—an invention of men—a gross stratagem—and brought into existence under such circumstances, and for such purposes, as we have described.

When we consider, however, another delusion, and the greediness with which other delusions and fictions have been drank in, in different ages, the wonder ceases.

Free-masonary, during the first thirty years of its commencement in London, was an object of universal derision, and was all revealed several times. To shield itself against the shafts of ridicule, it began at length to pretend that it was very ancient—that it existed in Solomon's temple—that prophets and apostles were its patrons, and the like. To the astoishment of the *interested ones*, these pretensions *took* with the craft; and in less than eighty years, these perfectly groundless pretensions became universally credited by the craft, and confided in by the most intelligent of our citzens as if it were true, notwithstanding all the old masonic books dated themselves at its real orgin, in 1717. All this only shows how greedily a delusion is drank in, and often too, by the most intelligent of men, if only a bias is produced in its favor on their minds, and if successors are only kept in ignorance concerning the deception, or the origin of it.

It is not possible in the nature of things, that so ancient a thing as the national circumcision of males among the Jews, can justify the modern sprinkling of both male and female babes, in these churches; a practice so recent in its origin, and introduced in such a deceptive and wicked way. A man must be greatly deluded, seriously to think such a thing possible.

It is often inquired, by those under the delusion, "When Christ said, '*Suffer little children to come unto me*,' did he not baptize them?" I reply, Christ did not baptize at all, but his disciples. John iv. 2. As there is not a word said about his baptizing them, it must be a deluded state of mind that is anxious to find infant baptism and infant sprinkling where they are not to be found.

They were *not* babes, because they were old enough to "come to Him," but were "little children." "Suffer little *children* (not babes) to come unto me."

Similar remarks are pertinent to the passage, "Go teach all nations, baptizing them," &c. Such commentators as Doddridge, Baxter, Barrow, Freeman, and Calvin, tell us it should be rendered, "Go *disciple* all nations ; he that believeth and is baptized," &c. The persons to be baptized must be old enough, then, to be *disciples* and to *believe*. A delusion must be very strong, and in great trouble for support, in order to be so eager to find a proof where it is not to be found.

The deluded mind lights on Acts ii. 39. "For the promise is to you, and to your children," &c. What promise, I ask? According to grammatical construction, and according to the theme the Apostle has in the mind's eye, it is the promise of the Holy Ghost. To assert that "promise" here alludes to Gen. xvii. 7, is to assert a thing which can never be proven, and a thing which is totally foreign from the main subject; and nothing but delusion would think of making such an assertion. The delusion attempts also to sustain itself by the passage 1 Cor. vii. 14. "The unbelieving husband is sanctified by the wife, and the unbelieving wife by the husband, else were your children unclean, but now are they HOLY." This passage merely asserts that the piety of the wife naturally tends to the conversion of the husband; and the piety of the husband to the conversion of the wife ; and the piety of both parents is conducive to the conversion of the children. The fact that their children were "holy"—were *converted*, is the proof of this leading principle. The delusion has wasted much strength to give such a coloring to this passage as would justify the practice. Poor delusion!—in as much trouble to find a support, as ever free-masonry was. I truly pity those who have been fooled with it. It misdirected all my energies by fooling me for a great many years. It led me to build against the real kingdom of Christ, and in favor of the kingdoms of men, even usurpers, for a great many years, without knowing what I was doing ; and led me to deceive thousands of others with this deceptive stratagem, because I was deceived with it myself, and all this without seeing or surmising at the time, there was any deception in it. It cost me, when I discovered the deception, an immense amount of trouble. It is a cruel and troublesome business to be made the dupe of this delusion by parents. The honesty of the parents and of the minister, makes no more diminution in fact, than the honesty of the free-masons and Mormons, in propagating their delusions. The evil is, in fact, worse to the child, than if the parent and the minister meant to deceive ; because their *honesty* only causes the *delusion* in the child to be engrained the deeper.

The delusion tries also to find support in the baptism of the jailer. It is said, " He was baptized, and all his straightway." But it is also said, "They spake unto him the word of the Lord, and to *all* that were in his house." And it is said, " He rejoiced, believing in God with all his house." Such Pædobaptist commentators as Dr. Doddridge, John Calvin, and Matthew Henry, all agree in the opinion in view of this language, that these were all converted. As baptism was the the only custom of those times, and for fifteen hundred years after, there can be no possible ground for the support of baby sprinkling here.

But Cornelius, and his household, were baptized. These were Gentiles. The apostle asks " Can any man forbid water, that these should not pe baptized, who have received the Holy Ghost"—were converted—" as well as we." This looks like adults, not babes.

But the word household is also used in the case of Stephanus, 1 Cor. i. 16. It is supposed by many that Stephanus is the name of the above jailer: if so then we have said all that is necessary. In 1 Cor. xv. 1, this household are said to have "addicted themselves to the ministry of the saints." They of course, were not babes. Baby immersion never came into existence till the year 255, and after. Baby sprinkling not till 1556, and after. Of course there was no baby sprinkling here.

But the household of Lydia is triumphantly adduced. The account is given in Acts xvi. 14, 15, 40. She was at Phillippi, 200 miles from Thyatira, her home: was a pedlar—had a hired house, and hired servants—and calls it "my house," and the sacred historians call it the "house of Lydia," into which the apostles entered. All this is a conclusive proof that she had no husband, and no babes. A wife with babes is not very apt to be 200 miles from home on such a business. The deluded must prove,

1. That she was ever married.
2. That she had then a husband.
3. That she ever had any children.
4. That any of them then were babes.
5. That she had brought her babes along.
6. That her babes were baptized.
7. That they were baptized on her faith.

But when he has done all this, he has only proved their immersion; for this was the only baptism at that time, and for fifteen centuries after. In order to justify his delusion, he must prove further (1.) that the babes were sprinkled, (2.) that this false naming of the thing was done in the name of the Trinity, and (3.) that there was a divine warrant for this sprinkling, and this misnomer of it, before he can find the shadow of a justification for his delusion.

The old Abrahamic covenant is urged by some as a reason for infant sprinkling.

What was that covenant? It is in these words: "I will multiply thee exceedingly"—"thou shalt be a father of many nations,"—"I will make thee exceeding fruitful,"—and "I will make nations of thee, and kings shall come out of thee,"-"Thy name shall be Abraham, for a father of many nations have I made thee;"—"I will be a God unto thee, and to thy seed after thee,"—and I will give unto thee, and thy seed after thee, the land"—all the land of Canaan, for an everlasting possession. "And I will be their God." A national promise is all that can be made out of all this.

By seed, descendants are here meant, as in the promise of the land, and so in the other promises.

To be a God to them in all generations is to be just what God was in fact to them as a nation, to wit, their protecto and shield and benefactor. All the males had the foreskin circumcised, as a national 'mark.

If infant sprinkling, a modern delusion, comes in lieu of it, why not confine it to the males, as was the custom in circumcision; and then, when they are converted, still baptize them, as the apostles did?

I have no recollection of any other passages being used in order to justify the practice of infant sprinkling. Even the deluded themselves must see that at least uncertainty rests upon all their pretended proofs. They must be void of all reason as of all reasoning about it, not to admit as much as this. But to defend a practice so suspicious, and with no express warrant, and by passages of even *doubtful* construction, is perfectly inconsistent with the retention of a good conscience, and with logical accuracy. In an earthly government, how would men appear in enforcing a practice so vital in its deleterious bearing on the unity of the nation, and with no more appearance of a law to justify it. If the officers under a government should persist with the pertinacity we see in the case of infant sprinkling, and with no better authority, the government would dismiss them with disgrace. If this would be an offence against an earthly government, how much more rebellious is this pertinacious course against the government of heaven. If God requires the practice, let the deluded point us to the chapter and verse. Let them disprove all our historical statements, our biblical criticisms, and all the statements of Encyclopædias and other standard authors. Let them prove that the Presbyterian and Episcopal organizations have not, between the years 1556, and 1648, done these deeds; altered divine ordinances, enforced this substitute, committed these treasonable acts against heaven, perverted the scriptures as we have stated, assumed and usurped their self created powers, bred these divisions against the kingdom of Christ, repealed his statutes, and substituted others of their own formation, propagated these delusions and stratagems, and assumed to themselves to lord it over God's heritage. Let the deluded only awaken from their delusion, and begin candidly to examine, and there is no question what will be the result. To begin to examine, and be honest and free from delusion, and to persevere, will be productive of a sure result.

Many pædobaptist authors, who, for *some* reason, continued either the immersion or the sprinkling of babes, have left in their writings the full conviction of their minds, that there is *no authority in the Bible* for infant baptism. Bish-

G

op Burnet, Fuller, S. Palmer, Philip Limborch, Curcellæus, and Cellasius, Richard Baxter, the author of "Saints' Rest," Bishop Prideaux, Thomas Boston, author of " Fourfold State," Bishop Sanderson, Martin Luther, Erasmus, Œcolampodius, and Bishop Stillingfleet; all of them careful and prayerful readers of the Holy Scriptures, and Pædobaptists too, have recorded that, in their opinion, there is no authority for infant baptism in the Bible.

Standard authors, who were pædobaptists too, fully agree also in the fact, that there was no infant baptism in the first two centuries. Bishop Barlow says, "I do believe and know that there is neither precept nor example in scripture for pædobaptism, nor any just evidence for it, for about two hundred years after Christ."

This coincides with the statement we made in our seventh letter.

Dr. Chambers, in his Cyclopædia, says, "It appears that in primitive times none were baptized but adults."

The Episcopal Wall, who defended immersion as the divine ordinance, from the beginning, against Calvin's substitute, but who was exceedingly anxious to carry the fact of pædobaptism as near the apostles' time as possible, in his preface, p. 3, says, "There is no particular direction given what to do with reference to the children of those who received faith. Among all the persons that are recorded as baptized by the apostles, there is no express mention of any infants." This admission, from one so anxious to defend the practice, is of *much weight*. Martin Luther says, "It cannot be proved by the sacred scriptures that infant baptism was instituted by Christ, or begun by the first Christians after the apostles." The learned De La Roque, of Roan, in Normandy, says, "The primitive church did not baptize infants, and the learned Grotius proves it."

Grotius says, "You will not find in any of the councils, a more ancient mention of the baptism of infants, than the council of Carthage, in the year 418." That council met at Mela, a neighboring village; and hence is sometimes called the Melavitian council.

Salmasius says, "In the first two centuries no one was baptized, except being instructed in the faith and acquainted with the doctrine of Christ, he was able to profess himself a believer because of these words. ' he that believeth and is baptized,' &c."

Episcopius says, " Pædobaptism was not esteemed a neces

sary rite till it was determined so to be in the Melavitian council, held in the year 418."

Curcellæus says, "The baptism of infants in the first two ages after Christ, was altogether unknown; but in the third and fourth, was allowed by some few. In the fifth and sixth and following ages, it was generally received. In the former ages, no trace of it appears, and it was introduced without the command of Christ."

Suicerus says, "The eucharist was given to infants, after pædobaptism was introduced."

Erasmus, on Rom. v. 14, says, "Paul does not treat of infants. It was not yet the custom for infants to be baptized."

The learned Neander declares there was nothing of it in the times of the apostles, and for some time after.

Mosheim, though a Lutheran, still asserts, that all who were baptized during the first two centuries, were adults professing repentance, and were *immersed under water:* and indirectly asserts that infant baptism was introduced afterwards.

Limborch says, "There is no instance that can be produced from whence it may indisputably be inferred that any child was baptized by the apostles."*

The Magdeburgh Centuriators, say, "The apostles baptized none but the aged or adult, whether Jew or Gentile."†

Olshausen. "By the introduction of infant baptism, which was certainly *not apostolical*, the relative position of baptism, after the ebullition of spiritual gifts had passed away, was changed."‡ Also in vol. i. p. 158; "In infant baptism, which the church at *a later period introduced* for wise reasons, (a pædobaptist thinks it wise) the sacred rite returned back, &c."

Hughes, the Catholic, tells us that infant baptism is not in the Bible, and is only a tradition of the church.

Kaisend. "Infant baptism was not an original institution of Christianity."‖

Corrodi. "At the time of Christ and his disciples, only adults were baptized."§

Baumgarten Crusius. "Infant baptism can be supported neither by a distinct apostolical tradition, nor apostolical example."¶

Neander. "The practice of infant baptism was remote from the spirit of this (the apostolic) age. Not only the late appearance of any express mention of infant baptism, but the

---
* Body of Divinity, p. 789.   † Hist. of facts, p. 176.   ‡ Vol. ii. p. 454.
‖ Biblical Theology, vol. ii. p. 158.   § Dressler, p. 154.   ¶ Hist. Theo. p. 1208.

long continued opposition to it, (after it was introduced,) leads us to the conclusion that it was not of apostolical origin.*

Strabo says, "In the first times, baptism was wont to be given to those only who were come to that integrity of mind and body, that they could know and *understand* what profit was to be gotten by baptism."†

Greg. Nazianzen says, "None were baptized of old, but such as did confess their sins."‡

Beza says, "The baptism of children was unheard of in the primitive church."‖

Dr. Hammond says, "Anciently all men were instructed in the faith before baptism."§

Ludovicus Vivus says, "None of old were wont to be baptized but in grown age, and who desired and understood what it was."¶

Jacob Merningus states that he had a confession of faith of the Waldenses, written in the German language, in which is the following statement, "In the beginning of Christianity there was no baptizing of children, and our fathers practised no such thing."**

The Encyclodædia Americana says, "It is certain that infant baptism was not customary in the earliest periods of the Christian Church. In the middle ages, also, it was declared invalid by many disputing parties, as the Petrobrusians, the Catharists, the Picards," &c.††

Many more who declare the same, might be quoted, if necessary. It will be asked, Why then did such Pædobaptists practice it? Limborch, and many others tell us, It was thought better to do it than to rebel against the government of the Church; and expose one's self to the penalty of rebellion against the government over the Church, in which they lived. It was the arm of despotism enforcing it for the sake of uniformity, which crushed the people, and coerced subordination to this and other *ordinances of men.*

Mosheim mentions no appearance of any thing like infant baptism, till a sect of pedaizing Christians, called Ebonites, at Pepuze, in Phrygia, who were extremely heretical, baptized either youths, children, or babes; probably the former.‡‡

Robinson tells us there was no trace of infant baptism in Spain, earlier than 517.

---

* Apostolic Age, vol. i. p. 140. † De Reb. Eccles., as in Hist. of Facts, p. 177. ‡ Orat. III. in the same, p. 174. ‖ Exto. Idem. p. 182.
§ Lib. i. cap. iii. p. 23. in eodem. ¶ Extr. in Suppl. Athen. Vol i. p. 174.
** Mern. Hist. Part II. p. 738. †† Art. Anabapt. Philadel. Edit. 1830.
‡‡ Eccles. Hist. Cent. II. Chap. iii.—v.

The following modern German authors attest the same historical fact:

Rheinwald, p. 313, of his works, says, "The first traces of infant baptism, are found in the Western Church, and after the middle of the second century."

Matthies, De Baptism, p. 187, says, "In the two first centuries no documents are found which clearly show the existence of infant baptism at that time."

Prof. Haken, Theolog. p. 556, says, "Neither in the scriptures nor during the first 150 years, is an example of infant baptism to be found; and the opposers of it cannot be contradicted on Gospel ground."

Tertullian, of the second century, says of the Apostles. "Their business was first to preach, and afterwards to dip; and that those who are ready to enter on baptism should give themselves to frequent prayers and fastings."

Jerome says, "First they teach all nations, and when they are taught, dip them in water."

How perfectly evident it must be, then, that infant baptism is a deceiver when it pretends to be divine; and that it is just what we have before stated; and that the "scandalous subtitute of a substitute," as Wall calls it, so prevalent in our country, is profane; and that all who have a conscience in favor of it, are grossly deluded by their feelings.

LETTER XI.

MY OWN EXPERIENCE—HOW IT WAS IN GERMANY.

In my earlest years, the sprinkling of babes was an occurrence which was constantly presenting itself, and it was always called baptism. All the influence of ministers, of pious parents, and of other Christians, favored it. Of course, I imbibed the delusion at that early period. All those were denounced by them who rejected it. A prejudice against them was thus produced. One bred under such influence, and whose reading afterwards was entirely on one side, of course, would not begin to suspect it to be a delusion; and after imbibing the delusion in that way, it would naturally become stronger and stronger, and his whole subsequent reading, would naturally strengthen it the more and more firmly. Those ministers, parents, and Christians, had themselves been so deluded, and conformed in the delusion the same way.

The free-masons were just as ignorant of the fact that *they* had been deluded. Our ignorance that it was a delusion in each case, and our confidence thus secured by the influence of others, led us to become the unconscious tools in deluding others also. The same principles that account for the extension of the one delusion, account for the extension of the other. And the same honest but blind delusion, reproduced itself in other confiding minds, without even surmising that it was generating a delusion,—and in each case precisely alike. I was familiarly acquainted with both—having thoroughly examined the origin and movement of both—and know to a demonstration that it is even so in both cases. My excuse for having once favored the one is precisely my excuse for having favored the other,—viz., I was deluded, and I knew it not. There is as conclusive evidence that the one is a delusion as the other. Every mind that will candidly and patiently examine the subject, must see it is so. The same principles that account for the one, account for the other.

I shall ever recollect with gratitude that faithful minister,* who *crowded* the examination of baby sprinkling (as well as the nature of baptism) upon us, in the village where I was preaching. I sketched off all his remarks, in order to refute them before my own congregation. In my efforts to do it, I found I must study. Delays for the sake of investigation, in order to do it more thoroughly ensued. The more I examined the darker the subject became. Yet so strong was my delusion, that I was poring over the subject by turns, nearly a year. I ultimately resolved I would *follow truth*, let it lead me where it would; and it was not long before the bubble burst. Still, so strong were my prejudices and delusions, it was six months more before my mind became wholly disenthralled so far as to begin to be established on the original principles of the gospel, in relation to church order.

No one can know the injury done to a mind, by thus enthralling and enslaving it in infancy to this and concomitant delusions, within the wrong fold, under the wrong jurisdiction, the wrong bias and prejudices, the wrong training, the exclusive reading on one side, and the mind set against the right side by the influence of others, and all of it having its origin in the modern farce of baby sprinkling, whereby we are secured and fenced within the wrong fold, as church members in our helpless state; an operation so perfectly at war with our subsequent personal liberty, until he has both expe-

---

* Rev. William Arthur.

rienced it, and been reclaimed; and also unil he has carefully examined its bearing on the Kingdom and cause of Christ. It is all but the assassination of the prospective usefulness of a child, to infix this delusion upon his mind in childhood. and to train him up in this separate state from the real fold of Christ.

It is a consciousness of these facts, which leads me to use great plainness of speech. Who can avoid seeing that a *pretended* oath ot allegiance to Christ, but in reality a corrupted altered, and vitiated, oath, and corruptly administered to the unconscious; thereby treacherously binding them, in fact, to other lords in other folds, is a base deception, and a treasonable transaction against the King of Zion; and that the agents have nothing but the delusion of their own minds to plead as a palliation for such an offence. And who does not see that if the child confides in it, it will pervert his whole life, from the real kingdom of Christ, and lead him to propagate the same delusion in others, unless he is reclaimed. When will parents and ministers cease the propagation of this pernicious delusion!

In sketching the liberties that have been taken with the ordinance of baptism, the real oath of allegiance to Jesus Christ, as it was originally intended to be; (and such liberties with such oath of allegiance are always deemed High Treason in all civil governments) I here introduce the prevalent views in Germany, as late as 1712; which proves the Government there did not *change* the ordinance from immersion to sprinkling till after that period.

Philip Limborch filled the office of Professor of Divinity, in the Pædobaptist Seminary at Amsterdam, from 1664 to 1712. His views are, of course, the views of the Pædobaptist clergy in Germany, and of the national church of those times. As I have never heard of but one copy of this book in America, the quotation may be grateful to many. John Le Clerc, Vossius, Episcopius, and Stephen Curcellæus, all of them noted for their protound erudition, successively filled the same professorship, and confirm the same views, and give the same opinions.

"Baptism (he says) is that rite or ceremony whereby the faithful, (i. e. adults) by immersion into water, as by a sacred pledge, are assured of the favor of God, remission of sins, and eternal life,—and by which they engage themselves to an amendment of life, and an obedience to the divine commands. Christ (he says) appointed it, and it was confirmed by the practice of the Apostles."

"Baptism consists (he says) in washing, or rather immersing the whole body into water; as was customary in the primitive times."

On the question whether immersion be *so* necessary, that there be no baptism without it, inasmuch as it had become changed in England by the civil government; and as all in those times construed the principle of "submission to the powers that be," as a submission to the civil rulers over the church, let them be what they might, and alter ordinances and religion ever so much, be under the influence of such a principle of allegiance to false rulers says:

"Upon great and emergent occasions, some allowances ought to be made, especially in cold countries, and in case of infant baptism, since their tender bodies might receive damage, if the government require it, &c. This is the reason why sprinkling is at present so customary in the western climates, (i. e. England, &c.) and although it *deviates from the primitive institution* of dipping," &c.

In his remarks, also, on the questions, What we ought to think of the baptism of infants, and whether infant baptism is necessary, he says:

"We say, for our parts, it is not absolutely necessary. (1.) Because there is no express command for it. (2.) All the passages commanding baptism do immediately relate to adult persons. (3.) There is no instance that any child (babe) was baptized by the Apostles. (4.) The necessity of it was never asserted in any Council, before that of Carthage, in the year 418. It is true it was used in Africa before this; but it was only used as a rite that might lawfully be administered, without any notion of the necessity thereof." So that since there are no marks in antiquity, before the said council, of the *necessity* of infant baptism, "there is no reason why at present it should be held as necessary." These are the honest and published views of him to whom the education of the Pædobaptist clergy was committed, at that time, in Germany.

Concerning the families baptized, as mentioned in Acts xvi. 15, 33, and I Cor. i. 15, he says, "There might be children in them, yet the holy Scripture furnishes me with no solid argument whereby I can *demonstrate* it; and if they were infants, we are not informed that they were baptized with their parents."

Concerning the promise, Acts ii. 39, "to you and to your children," as affording evidence for infant baptism, he remarks, "It cannot be proved, that by children *infants* are meant, but rather their *posterity*."

Against the notion that baptism came in the room of circumcision, he says: (1.) "Infant baptism is no where expressly commanded, but circumcision was. (2.) If it were so,—that baptism comes in its place,—infants must be baptized on the *eighth* day; nay, (3.) as soon as born—because they might die. (4.) As the male children only were circumcised, therefore it would be unlawful for female children to be baptized." "Baptism," he again defines, " an intelligent profession of the name of Christ."

"I think," he adds, "every one ought to be left to his liberty to make use of this rite (baptism) after such manner as he thinks most conducive to those ends, (the profession of Christianity, and a holy life.) If any man *offers* children to be baptized, they ought to be baptized; since pædobaptism contains nothing in it contrary to the genius of Christianity and it has been practised for so many ages. No one should *oppose* it, therefore, if he cannot do it without giving scandal to the church in which he lives." i. e. its regulations and government.

We make but three remarks upon this quotation, from this learned professor and instructor of young men at Amsterdam, for the ministry, in Pædobaptist churches in those times.

1. He plainly defends the present views of the Baptist churches, as the principles taught in the Bible.

2. We notice the *slender basis* upon which he recommends infant baptism at all, viz. "If any man *offers* children to be baptized,"—"pædobaptism contains nothing in it contrary to the genius of Christianity," (i. e. the national church of Germany being his exemplar as to the nature of that genius,)—" it has been practised for *so many ages*,"—no one should oppose it if he cannot do it without giving scandal to the *church in which he lives.*" As good reasons as an *honest* man can give.

3. We see to what extent the principle that we may organize churches as we please—of such subjects as we please—and under such rulers as we please—under the civil government, if we happen there—by the stratagem of immersing or sprinkling babes or not as we please—under the laws and alterations of those governments as is for our convenience, has been carried—and how ruinous it has become to the originally organized kingdom of Christ, under his own jurisdiction.

Salmasius, Curcellæus, and Episcopius, all of them by turns, Professors in the same Theological Seminary, tell us, "In the first two centuries no one was baptized but adults,"— that "the baptism of infants in the first two centuries after

Christ, was altogether *unknown*,"—and that "no *tradition* can be produced for pædobaptism till a little before that council in 418."

We notice, also, that the civil government of Germany, had not, at the above time, enforced infant baptism so strenuously as had that of England. And the effect of this liberty of conscience, was, that Baptist views, and the honest truth were taught, as being the truths taught in the Bible; and that too, by the most thorough scholars of the age, and those the teachers in the Seminaries of the National Church.

We add, that the Dutch Testament, as translated by Luther, renders baptism, in every case, honestly, by a word that signifies immersion, and that alone.

We also add, that the Dutch Confession of Faith, or Creed, enforces baptism, i. e. immersion, in the fullest sense of the word.

But since the above period, the civil government of Germany too, have followed the evil example of the British Parliament, and have *changed* the ordinance of baptism, to sprinkling. Because at present, (1840) the devoted Oncken, for no other offence than preaching the Gospel, and immersing believers, is arrested under the civil law, and is imprisoned, and his labors are broken up, by the arm of civil power.

I have been informed by many emigrants from Germany, that during about 75 or 100 years past, sprinkling has become the national baptism of Germany.

It is the arm of civil power, and ecclesiastical power, then, that has committed these treasonable crimes against Heaven, in *altering* one of his ordinances, and in *enforcing* the application of a substitute to babes, for the uses and benefits of such treasonable Governments, thus usurping dominion, and at antipodes against the jurisdiction and the original Kingdom of Jesus Christ himself.

This course has well nigh prostrated the real kingdom of Christ, in many countries; and has fixed almost insurmountable barriers in the way of the preaching of the Gospel of the kingdom, and the conversion of the world. It has substituted, in lieu of that kingdom, national establishments, under civil rulers; and modern establishments, under ecclesiastical rulers, in abundance. The jurisdiction of Christ is thus prostrated and the outlines of his kingdom trampled in the dust. If all this is not high treason against Christ, it is difficult to tell what is!

LETTER XII.

NEW-ENGLAND.

A sketch of some of the circumstances conducing to the pushing of pædobaptism to the utmost verge in England, and New-England, is this:

Popery had used that snare for catching babes, in successfully building itself up, for about a thousand years; when Henry VIII., the bishops, and the Parliament, resolved on a revolt, and on a rival movement against the Pope. Accordingly, they passed laws indirectly *enforcing pædobaptism* upon all babes, in order to ensnare them within the Episcopal national Church; and under the penalty of treating all as outlaws—disabling them from being known in law, if married—treating their descendants as bastards—disallowing them the power of inheriting estates, and the right of burial after they were dead; unless the parents consented thus to ensnare them, by pædobaptism, to that church.

The Congregational rulers in the true spirit of rivalship, seeing this, enforced pædobaptism upon *their* members; i. e. required them to ensnare their babes to them, by that ceremony, and under the penalty of excommunication. It is hardly twenty-five years, now, since that tyrannic rule, with them, even began to lose its force.

The Presbyterian rulers, in the same spirit of rivalship, in the time of Calvin, and since, enforced the same thing on their members, under the same penalty. These folds, all contrived by human beings, and ruled by human beings, and compelling their members thus to ensnare their children into the church, commenced their career from the year 1534, to 1545. The *immersion* of babes was the form they enforced for a considerable time.

Sir John Floyer, a learned physician, in England, in an address to the deans and high officers of the Church of England, as partly quoted in Letter V., says, " I appeal to you as persons well versed in ancient history, and in the canons and ceremonies of the Church of England, and as *witnesses* of the matter of fact; that immersion continued in the church of England, till about the year 1600," and adds, " I have proved the practice of immersion, from the time the Britons and Saxons were baptized, till King James' days." Dr. Wall says,

The first liturgy in the world that *prescribes* aspersion is in 1643." It was the Westminster assembly that voted it, 25 to 24.

In getting rid of immersion every variety would be resorted to; as

1 Pouring a large vessel full of water upon the candidate, so as to wet him all over, and yet the administrator keep dry. This was Calvin's first way; and was the "substitute for baptism.

2 Pouring out of a less vessel—wetting less. The conscience that could interpose in the first way, could make it a still more convenient, and a less self denying transaction.

3 Pouring out of the hand as much water as the hand would contain. Calvin's book—the Book of "the learned godly man, John Calvin," as on the title page, in 1558, enjoins this way.

4 Pouring a mere trifle from the hand.

5 Merely dipping the hand into the water, and laying it upon the forehead—baptizing the hand," and wetting the face of the candidate, as one satirically calls it.

6 Wetting the fingers and laying them on the face.

7 Wetting them, and fillipping them upon the face.

8 Ultimately and finally, as in 1643, by Presbyterian authority, wetting the fingers, and sprinkling a few drops in the face. This last, Wall calls "the substitute of the substitute."

The seven first varieties gradually and successively came along between 1556, and 1643. About 1643, and 1645, the eighth variety came into use, by Presbyterian, and afterwards by Parliamentary authority. Wall tells us, "It was at that time (1645) just beginning.

I wish here to record, that I have (perhaps improperly,) called all these varieties of aspersion sprinkling, because it would cost too much pains to make all the distinctions in the successive progress of all the varieties.

The rulers in these three organizations from and after about 1644, compelled their members respectively to ensnare their children to them, from that time forward, usually by sprinkling.

The King of England had presumed to become the head of the church, and had empowered the several governors and general courts in the several New-England States to be, in a measure, the head of the several churches there. Hence the Cambridge Platform, and the Saybrook Platform, were perfectly invalid, till passed into a law in each case by the General Court, and sanctioned by the Governors.

Previous to this, the New-England churches are said to be "the truest sons of the Church of England, and to maintain its fundamental Articles;" i. e. its thirty-nine Articles. (Magnalia II., 155.) Of course the immersion of babes and others, was originally the law of the New-England Churches. They would not otherwise be "the truest sons of the church of England," or "maintain its fundamental articles;" because these enforced immersion from the first. From 1620, the first settlement, till 1648, this was their state. The reluctance of the Westminster assembly to adopt aspersion, and doing it by a bare majority, as well as the fact that they had no other Creed than that of the church of England, previous to 1643, and the fact that they, as a people, had a conscience against interfering with the laws of Christ, gives us reason to believe the Presbyterians and Congregationalists, in large proportions, previous to 1643, were accustomed to immersion in England.

The Governor, and General Court of Massachusetts, by virtue of power (if any they had) derived from the usurpation of the King of England, against Jesus Christ, convened a Synod of all the churches at Cambridge, Sept. 30, 1648; five years after the Westminster Assembly had presumptuously *altered* the ordinance of baptism. The Synod adopted substantially the confession of faith of the Westminster Assembly—of course took upon themselves to join in altering the ordinance of baptism to sprinkling, and adopted a platform for the government and regulation of the churches accordingly, called the Cambridge Platform.

Prominent features of all those regulations, were based upon the assumption, that the General Courts or Governments in those States, had the right, as the civil governments did in Europe, to regulate, control, and rule in all matters of religion: that the part of the people was to submit "to the powers that be;" and that submission to the magistrate, in general terms, is abundantly enforced in the Bible. It was a belief in this latter principle, in its unlimited sense, that led the people, everywhere, to acquiesce in all these changes; and that emboldened their rulers to make changes, according to their pleasure.

The rulers in New-England, however, graciously acceded to the clergy the privilege of first acting in matters of conscience; by a mutual understanding, however, that when the the clergy had acted, the rulers, if the clergy pleased them, passed it into a law. The clergy were pleased with this high honor of being their tools; and the governments, in this way, easily accomplished their ends of ruling the church, and of enforcing uniformity, and by very plausible measures.

How true it is, that in proportion as human beings rule Christians, the real kingdom of Christ becomes prostrated, and the elements of it fail to be gathered under Christ.

The Legislatures were called "General Courts," the Governors were appointed of the crown of England. The rulers, as a whole, were called magistrates. The policy was to enforce uniformity in religion, and to have baby-sprinkling, which had five years before been adopted in Westminster, become the stratagem for securing the end; and to force the parents, by ecclesiastical power, to apply it to all their babes, and so make them church-members, and cause all to grow up in uniformity.

Under these circumstances, the General Courts of Connecticut and Massachusetts, in 1644, called the above Synod, to be holden Sept. 30; and according to the policy of the times, this Synod adopted the Westminster Confession of Faith; a prominent feature of which was, that all church-members should be required to have their children sprinkled into church-membership.

They reported progress to the General Court, and the latter passed it into a law: whereby baby sprinkling became the law of the land, in those States.

Roger Williams, and the Baptists, for pleading that no such authorities over the church were lawful, and that Jesus Christ alone was Head of the Church, were most shamefully persecuted for such opinions, by the same authorities.

The concentration of these movements in England, and in New-England, is quite striking.

The rights of conscience were not then understood. To think too highly of uniformity in the inventions of men, in religion: and too lightly of the real kingdom of Christ, is nothing strange for those times. To distinguish between the jurisdiction of magistrates, and the jurisdiction of Christ, was what very few were disposed to do. A total reformation from popery, would have been to reject all power of magistrates over the church—all the inventions of men—the traditions of *mother church*, and the stratagems upon babes. It is evident, therefore, there was but a very partial reformation from popery. "Midway," to use Lowth's language in the case, is as far as they had gone. The Westminster assembly had established sprinkling as baptism, by a majority of one, and made a Creed in 1643. The Parliament were imprisoning men for immersing persons into the real kingdom, and under the exclusive jurisdiction of Christ; had established sprinkling by law, in 1644;* and had passed the *gag-law* of May 2, 1648, which rendered all persons liable to imprisonment who presumed to speak against it, or say that such persons when grown up and converted, ought to be immersed. And all the Baptists in the realm, soon after, were required by law, to " depart out of the realm," While these things were going on there, these movements in New-England, began Sept. 30, 1648. They all stand connected, not only as to time, but also in design.

In 1657, the General Court of Connecticut requested the magistrates of Massachusetts, to convene another Synod; which they did, and accordingly it met June 4, 1657. The reasons assigned by Mather are, " That the ecclesiastical state of their posterity, was an object of great interest. Parents had become grand parents, and the sprinkled babes had become parents, and yet were not communicants. Some of these were willing to take their own baptismal (rantismal) vows, made by parents, at their sprinkling, upon themselves, although they were not converted. To make no difference between those and pagans, (an opprobrious epithet given to those who were not sprinkled) would soon abandon the country to heathenism. And yet if all were to become communicants, the church would soon consist of impenitent persons. The object of the General Courts was, to have the clergy attend to these matters; and particularly to attend to two poins: 1. Who are the subjects of baptism, (rantism.) 2. Ought the churches to be consociated so as to control each other, and all to be controlled by rulers over them?" On the first point " Who are to be baptized? they decided in substance, first, those who are members of the visible church; second, the members of the church are confederate believers, and their infant seed: also minors, where one or both parents are in covenant: third, all such children are members of the same church with their parents; and when grown up, are under the watch, discipline, and government of that church: fourth, not membership, merely, but conversion is necessary, in order to be communicants: yet, fifth, members thus grown up, though unconverted, if sound in the faith, and of good moral character, and *owning the covenant*, (the church government,) thereby subjecting themselves to the government of the church, their children must be sprinkled; sixth, such pa-

---

* Dr. Gill, and John Floyer.

rents dying, their children must be sprinkled: seventh, if such parents remove, their children should be sprinkled wherever they may go." Uniformity in these matters, was the object of the magistrates and clergy. These things were approved by the General Court. "Soon a law was passed enforcing upon every plantation, the duty of having the stated ministry." (Magnalia 11., 286.) But it must be a minister of this establishment; because the Baptists were persecuted to the utmost extent, by law, as they taught the exclusive jurisdiction of Christ over the church, and the original oath of allegiance to Him.

Another convention, in 1662, was convened, and passed this rule: "For any church to arrogate to themselves an exemption from giving account, or from being liable to censure by any other, either Christian magistrate above them, or neighbor church about them, is a *most to be abhorred maxim!*" In another convention, in 1679, it was decided " It would very much promote reformation among us, if all due means were used for the bringing of more than there are, and as many as may be, to submit unto the church watch." (Idem. p. 589.) Also " that union between the civil government and the clergy be carefully observed." In May 12, 1680, a similar convention, held in Boston, exchanged away the Westminster Confession of Faith, or Creed, for the Savoy Confession or Creed. Meantime, persecutions against the Baptists were carried to the utmost extent. (See Isaac Backus' History.) The General Court of Connecticut, at their May session, in 1708, passed the following act: "This assembly, from their own observation, and from the complaints of many others, being made sensible of the defects of the discipline of the churches, arising from the want of a more explicit asserting of the rules given for that end—from which would arise a more permanent establishment among ourselves—a good and regular issue, in cases subject to ecclesiastical discipline, &c., hath seen fit to ORDAIN and REQUIRE, and it is ordained and required, that the ministers in the several counties in this government, shall meet together at their respective connty towns, with messengers, on the last Monday in June next; there to consider and agree upon those methods and rules for the management of ecclesiastical discipline, which, by them, shall be judged conformable to the word of God: and shall appoint two or more of their number, to be their delegates, who shall all meet at Saybrook, at the next Commencement; where they shall compare the results of the ministers of the counties, and out and from them, to draw a *Form of Ecclesi-*

astical Discipline; which by two or more persons, delegated by them, shall be offered to this Court, at their session in October next, to be considered and *confirmed* by them. The expenses of said Convention to be defrayed out of the public Treasury. Albert E. Kimberly, Secratary."——Here the legislature and the clergy assumes to make laws and regulations for Church discipline, as if the jurisdiction was theirs, and as if their *substitute* for what Christ enforced in the 18th of Matthew, and established under his own jurisdiction, and to be observed within his kingdom, might be enforced by civil law, under their jurisdiction; and as if a Confession of Faith or Creed, enforcing sprinkling for baptism; and baby sprinkling into their jurisdiction, might be established by law. This Convention tinkered and adopted the Savoy Confession of Faith, enforcing baby sprinkling, and made themselves rules of Church discipline. The General Court, in Oct. 1708, acting under the principle that they were the head of the church, passed the following act. " The reverend ministers, delegates &c., met at Saybrook, Sept. 9, 1708, having presented to this assembly, a Confession of Faith—Heads of agreement, and regulations in the administration of Church discipline, as unanimously agreed and assented to by the Elders and churches in this government; this assembly doth declare their great approbation of such an happy agreement; and *do ordain*, that all the churches within this government are or shall be thus united in doctrine, worship, and discipline, be and for the future shall be owned and acknowledged *established by law*; provided always that nothing herein shall be construed to hinder and prevent any Society or church that is or shall be *allowed* by the laws of this Government, who soberly differ or dissent from the united Churches, hereby established, from exercising worship and discipline, *in their own way*, according to their own conscience. E. Kimberly, Secratary."——(See Trumbull's Hist. of Conn. also laws of Conn.) In these efforts on the part of the civil government, to stir up the deluded clergy to contrive their baby sprinkling creeds, and forms of churches and of church government, we have another specimen of rulers over the churches first fixing on a purpose, and then using baby sprinkling as the main stratagem in accomplishing that end. Uniformity in religion, according to the devices of men under the government was the object; baby sprinkling the means for securing uniformity, and the arm of civil power, the efficient force in securing the end. The "kingdom of Christ is not of this world,"—comprises converts alone; and membership is constituted by the oath of allegiance to Him as King, and is where the King has the exclusive jurisdiction and dominion, and where his his laws alone prevail. A government like the General Courts of New England, and the clergy under them, with baby members in greater numbers than Christians; with human laws, creeds, and rules of discipline, and the exclusion of Christian baptism into Christ, is a totally different government from the kingdom of Christ; a totally different jurisdiction, and is a great obstruction to the prevalence of the real kingdom.

As this baby sprinkling delusion builds up *imperiums in imperio*, within our own national government, it endangers our own national Government. Nearly two millions of our citizens, by it, are already subjected, and in their helpless state, to the dominion and jurisdiction of the Pope, a foreign despot. Probably two millions more are subjected, by it, to other ecclesiastical dominations, such as Bishops, Hierarchies, Aristocracies, Conventions, Conferences, Sessions, Presbyteries, Synods, General Assemblies, General Conferences, &c. &c. To suffer helpless babes to be thus cheated, enslaved, and deprived of their personal liberty, as is palpably the fact, under such *imperiums in imperio*, is perfectly inconsistent with the sound principles of *equal rights*, and of protection in a free government. That New-England, the land of boasted liberty, should have established it by law, as was evidently done, by the establishment of such Creeds, would be truly astonishing, were it not palliated by the ignorance of the times, and the example of Europe.

How cruel and treasonable against heaven, is the principle of persecuting and imprisoning men for baptizing converts into the jurisdiction of Christ, and contrary to the laws of the land; and how treasonable such laws are, as against the King of Zion.

Germany has since followed in the wake, and established the "substitute," as the national baptism, and enforced it upon babes; and prohibits, under the penalty of imprisoment, such an act as Christian baptism into the exclusive jurisdiction and kingdom of Jesus Christ.

It is unnecessary to sketch further the history of the New England churches. We see in this sketch, all the authority there is for baby sprinkling,—whence it originated—the fact that it is a stratagem—the authority by which it was commenced and propagated, from the first—the fact most conclusively demonstrated that it is a sheer delusion and deception, and of course, that it is treasonable and criminal, as against Christ, as it is the subsidary help resorted to by his rivals to compete for power and for numbers against him, in building up their rival folds.

We see also the reasons why it did not prevail much among the honest Dutch, for a long time, to wit, because the government let it alone for some time; and the reasons why it has been made to prevail so extensively in England, and in the United States; to wit, because civil and ecclesiastical authorities have *enforced* it under penalties, as a matter of policy in building up their rival kingdoms, and because the people have become *crazed* from infancy, with the delusion, which has been thus generated within them in their infancy, and grown with their growth.

The question, therefore, is palpably this: Whether the laws jurisdiction, and authority of Christ, are to prevail, or the laws jurisdiction, and authority of civil and ecclesiastical usurpers; whether treason or obedience to the rightful Sovereign, and whether the corrupted vitiated, and deceptive oaths of allegiance to the usurpers, and the falsehoods accompanying, whereby the people and babes are treacherously subjected to them, are to prevail, or the original oath of allegiance to Jesus Christ.

Here is all the authority there is in the universe, for the practice of baby sprinkling,—a true sketch of its origin, and the enforcements producing and extending it.

LETTER XIII.

ON THE RUINOUS TENDENCY AND EFFECTS OF TAKING SUCH LIBERTIES WITH THE KINGDOM OF CHRIST.

I cannot but stop here in order to advert for a moment to the ruinous tendency of these interferences with the kingdom of Christ, and with the oath of allegiance: also of usurpations of the government—such obstructions to his jurisdiction, and such prevention of the oath of allegiance to the King—such misapplication of it and the substitute to the unconscious, so as to secure them under usurpers—such alterations of it in the purpose and end to which it is applied, as well as in form—such amalgamation of babes, sinners, and converts, in churches—such contrivance and continuance of new folds, under men holding new offices, the inventions of men, in lieu of the command of God.

I. It has produced endless divisions. Each and every

change must either sweep all Christendom, and lead all Christians, and the King in Zion Himself, to adopt it, or it must from the nature of things, breed a division; the extent of which, and the evils resulting from which, in time and in eternity it is not possible to describe or to conceive. The divisions which have grown out of the misapplication of real baptism to the unconscious, out of the change of the ordinance, and the extension of the substitute; and out of the misapplication of the substitute to the unconscious, are exceedingly great. Popery, with all its horrors, has grown out of it. All the church and state organizations in the world, have grown out of it, interposing, as they do, so many obstacles to the prevalence of the real kingdom. The check of the reformation from popery, in 1534, and the consequent building up of the divisions comprising the Episcopalian, the Congregational, the Presbyterian, the Lutheran, and subsequently the Methodist organizations, have all grown out of these liberties taken with the ordinance of baptism. The consequent troubles, jars, and difficulties in the world, the obstructions thrown in the way of Christian union, and of united effort for the conversion of the world, and in the way of the millenium, have indirectly ruined millions! All these evils, originating, as they have, in these liberties taken, have now continued and been extending during some fifteen hundred years; and annually have occasioned either directly or indirectly, the ruin of millions of souls. Unless this career is checked, the millenium cannot come and prevail. It is impossible in the nature of things.

II. We see a ruinous and wide yawning principle of *substitution*. A substitution of something else in lieu of the real ordinance of initiation, has extensively prevailed, and been accompanied everywhere, with the general impression that strict obedience to Christ is not necessary. This accompanying impression has done immense mischief a thousand ways. The pleasure of each, has become a *substitute* for the will of Christ. The wish and law made by the candidate, has become a substitute for the law of Christ. Baptism has ceased to be the *test* of a good conscience; and *feelings* are the substitute. The yawning principle has been extended until we have an amalgamation of all the variety of characters for a church, in lieu of Gospel Churches; usurpers for rulers, in lieu of Christ; the constitution of men, for new folds, in lieu of his constitution; the laws of these human rulers as substitutes for his laws; capricious human beings for legislators, as a substitute for Him as Legislator; divisions in abundance as a substitute for His united Kingdom; and, in general terms, the devices of men to an unbounded extent, in lieu of the commands and ordinances of Christ, and " the commandments of men," as a substitute for the doctrine of Christ.

III. Strong delusions, and prejudices on the minds of those who are grown up under the influence of this state of things. These substitutes, as in popery, are taught to children where they grow up, as the real doctrine of Christ. Passages of holy writ, are perverted, wrested, and misapplied from their real intention, to favor those delusions. The ministers themselves, become filled with " strong delusions," as in popery, and propagate and strengthen them in others. The youthful mind from infancy up, as in popery, becomes strongly prejudiced in favor of these delusions, and against all those who oppose them. In this way, their minds become extremely dark towards the truth, on these points, while they are brilliant and well informed on all other subjects. In this way, each one becomes strongly biassed in favor of the peculiarities of his own sect, right or wrong, and against the real kingdom of Christ.

IV. Another result is a most selfish state of rivalship, in all, against each other, and against the real kingdom of Christ. To the liberties originally taken with baptism, and to the misapplication of it, as the origin, can be traced all these divisions, and of course all this bigotry, selfishness, and sectarianism. The delusions accompanying the defence of the peculiarities of the sects, in each case stir up all the selfish feelings of the natural heart, in their defence. This selfish state of feeling, and their delusions present almost insurmountable barriers in the way of wedging in a single ray of truth that is adapted to remove the films from the mental eye. This deluded state of their minds, exhibits almost insurmountable obstacles in the way of the prevalence of the real kingdom of Christ. Each can see it to be so in others, but his deluded mind prevents him from observing it in himself.

V. Another result is, the dark and confused views generally prevalent concerning the kingdom of Christ. Some define it as comprising all the converts in the world; others as comprising them and their children; others, all the Jewish nation; others, all who have ever been baptized or sprinkled; others, as comprising their own sect merely, (as the papists, and the high-Church-men)—others as comprising this many headed monster of Sectarianism, including all these folds of men; others, as comprising some one particular national organization, as the Church of England; others, as comprising all the national, together with all those other organizations; just as if that Kingdom never existed in due form, till all these sore evils sprung up. The darkness upon the mind is so great, in relation to the kingdom of Christ, and the prejudices are so strong, that scarce any will tear asunder the veil, and candidly search in the Bible for the original organization of the real kingdom of Christ. Many honest and intelligent minds seem to be perfectly benighted on this subject.

VI. Another result is, confused notions concerning the design of baptism. Some make it a token of a national organization—some the test of salvation. The papists tell their deluded dupes, that their children have *no souls* till they are *sprinkled*. Many teach they cannot be saved without it. It is usually shaped by the teachers in all the sects, so far as design is concerned, so as to favor their selfish sectarian purposes. Though the real design is made very plain in the Bible, yet in consequence of this state of things, the mass of mind has become exceedingly beclouded.

VII. Another result is, that the heritage of God is almost wholly placed in the hands of other rulers, and in a state of rivalship against the real kingdom. The idea may be conceived, by supposing the real kingdom to be a Ship, starting in the days of John the Baptist, which we will call the "Ship Zion," under the command of the Great Captain; and by supposing a number of rival ships, built afterwards, and controlled by human beings as commanders, sailing along by the side of Ship Zion, and all of them robbing the latter of its crew, as fast as possible, by stratagems, and by fixing the mimicry of the Great Captain's badge upon babes, so as to forestall them, and to secure them in their own rival ships; thus hindering his rightful soldiers, when converted, from going into His Ship; and securing them in this, and by diffusing their delusions, darkness, and prejudices over the minds they secure, and by inducing them, in this way, to believe that the more soldiers are drawn into their ships, and hindered from going into His ship, the greater service is rendered to Him.

The ship of the Pope was some two hundred years in building, and set sail in the year 606. The church and state establishments began to be built about those times, and set sail from time to time, as soon as built. The Episcopal Church of England, was built and set sail in 1534. The Presbyterian ship was built by Calvin, and set sail on the 20 Nov. 1541. The Congregational ship grew out of the division between those who adopted Calvin's Presbyterianism, and those who rejected it, and set sail soon after the Methodist ship was built, between the year 1739, and 1784; and was completed by Wesley, who had never been a Bishop himself, usurping the prerogatives of a bishop, and presuming himself to ordain one as a Bishop, during this year, thus treading down the principle of succession, and openly usurping a new succession.

We now see all these ships sailing along by the side of Ship Zion, robbing her of men and of means—slandering her and her crew—pretending great friendship to the Commander, that the more are secured within their ships, the more service is done to Him; and yet all are constantly attempting to crush His ship, and to rob Him of all his men. This is a perfectly treasonable state of things, against the Great Commander, however deluded and blinded the agents may be. It is a fair view of the origin of sectarianism. If just such persons had divided Moses' army, and travelled along by his side, competing for numbers against him, would the people still contiune to be Moses' army who submitted to such rulers? or other rival commanders? they would certainly be under another jurisdiction. If Washington's army had been so divided, under other competitors for rule, the same question might be asked. None of these can claim to be the original kingdom as organized by Christ himself, unless they prove that it never existed till the time such denomination began its career.

Another effect is that all deplore the evils of such division, but yet, not one in a thousand perceives, or is able to discover, where the difficulty is; and therefore, none seem to know how to remedy it. All have been biassed in favor of their own sect, and therefore, place the fault at their neighbor's door. Another effect is, a vast amount of wickedness, and crooked management, and dishonest contrivance on the part of professors. and especially the rulers and ministers, against each other, and against the real kingdom of Christ: being so perfectly deluded, "they know not what they do." Another *tremendous* effect is, a rapid approximation *towards Popery*, in many of the sects, without being aware of it. The strong delusions over the mass of the people, and the selfish adherence to party, prepares them to be easily misled and duped by their rulers. We see this approximation towards popery, in the inducements held out to the people to commit their babes in that stratagem. which has always been the ground and pillar of popery. We see it in the usurpation of such astonishing power over the people, by several rulers; in their crooked management; in the rival governments against Christ's; In the use of delusion in advancing their ambittous projects; in the stratagems and pious frauds practised; in the enforcement of the traditions of mother church, in each case; in their vast stretch of power; in the subjection of helpless babes to their control; in human beings assuming the entire reins of government; in the blindness of the people to their danger, through delusion; in the rapid strides by which the real kingdom of God is broken down, and in the strong delusion of the rulers over the people. The rulers over many of the organizations, assume a station but very little short of popery, even now. In these ways, the most alarming stumbling blocks are put in the way of extending the real kingdom of Christ. Christ says, ' Whosoever shall offend,' &c. i. e. put a stumbling block in the way of his people, &c. Another effect resulting from the stratagem with babes, is the amalgamation of the world and Christians together, and the consequent degradation of churches, as to spirituality, down towards the wicked world. By the principle of baby membership, large majorities of many churches in New England, soon were found to consist of impenitent persons. The impenitent portions became the majority, and in a vast many cases have seceded, and organized as Unitarians. So that the Congregationalists now stand aghast at their own dogmas in relation to baby membership. They have been obliged to practice close communion against their own members, and are growing ashamed, in many instances, of their own principle of baby membership. In all the national churches, there seems to remain but very little of piety. The form of godliness Is substituted for the power, where all the nation are members; and the effect is that souls are neglected, and perish in their sins. The national establishments present strong barriers in the way of missionaries ever preaching the gospel of the real kingdom among them. All this had its starting point in the liberties taken with baptism, the initiating ordinance under Christ, and the misapplication of it to babes. Almost the whole of Christendom, has, in this way, wandered away from the real kingdom of Christ. In the national organizations, the kingdom of Christ is nearly crushed by the arm of civil power.

Another serious effect is, that among this whole family of wanderers from the Fold of Christ, no possible basis of Christian union among themselves, can, from the nature of the case, possibly be discovered. As all things in which they differ from the real kingdom of Christ, are the *inventions of men*, it is impossible there ever should be any union in agreeing precisely *how many* of these inventions all will adopt. The

Congregationalists will want baby sprinkling, and civil government merely; the Presbyterians will want their Bishops, gradations of clergy, and successions, and aristocratic government; the Episcopalians their forms and ceremonies; the Methodists, their inventions, caprices, management, and government; the national churches theirs; the Lutherans theirs; and all the several grades of Scotch and Dutch organizations, theirs. During twenty years connexion with that vast family of wanderers from the real kingdom of Christ, I studied faithfully and perseveringly, to discover some basis of Christian union; and investigated all the propositions that were made for union. It is impossible, in the nature of things, that this vast mass of wanderers from the original Fold, should ever be united, as long as they remain in their present illegitimate folds, the devices of men. They must drop all the inventions of men, and return to Christ within his kingdom, and agree to take his revealed will as their exclusive guide, or there can never be union. Another effect is, that when people are baptized, on account of this thick darkness, they have very muddy views about baptism, and they hardly know whether they are baptized into subjection to Christ, or into subjection to human rulers. Also a vast amount of guilt is incurred by all this mass of wanderers, in *all they add to, and in all they take from*, the original kingdom, and the things of the Bible, so expressly prohibited in Rev. xxii. 18, 19; and under the most tremendous penalty.*
Another effect is, a perfect agreement among all the wanderers in one point, i. e. in censuring severely those who adhere to all the principles of the original kingdom, and for not wandering away with them, and for refusing to fellowship their inventions and wanderings. The wanderers agree in denouncing those who adhere to Christ, as bigots, and close communionists.

A large part of the Christian world, in these ways, is thrown into a treasonable state against their King and Redeemer, without being aware of it. Treason against the King of Zion is daily practised; and yet they know not what they do. This blindness to the offence, is the effect of their strong delusion fixed upon them in early years. The thick mist and fog that has been spread over the real kingdom of Christ prevents them from developing this " mystery of iniquity."

Another effect is, that multitudes under the influence of these " strong delusions," defend all these *substitutes* stoutly

---

* The same prohibitory law is reiterated in Deut. iv. 2, and chap. 12, 37; also in Prov. xxx. 6, and in a great many other passages.

as the real ordinances of Christ. Divine truth is misapplied in their support. Books containing the facts, are withdrawn from those who grow up in the delusion. A spirit of denunciation prevails, against those who defend the real truth. The arm of power, civil and ecclesiastical, as well as this strong delusion, made stronger by sectarian selfishness, and by use, exerts a mighty influence in defence of this whole wayward course against Christ.

And in a general view we perceive to how many different and wicked purposes baptism and the substitutes have been applied since such treasonable liberties have been taken with the kingdom of Christ.

Baptism was originally intended to initiate converts exclusively under Christ. Yet in the year 256, it was loaned to the purpose of shielding babes against heathen depredations—afterwards to that of a passport to heaven to the sick, in consequence of a wrong interpretation of John iii. 5;—afterwards of a passport to sick babes to heaven—afterwards, when the clergy had assumed the reins of government, about 418, to the purpose of building up treasonable folds under their jurisdiction, and to securing babes by stratagem, under their treasonable rivalship—afterwards, to gathering up nations, whether saint or sinner, under the Pope, to gratify his ambitious and treasonable designs against heaven—afterwards, to gathering babes by stratagem, for the same treasonable purposes—afterwards, to the treasonable purposes of building up national jurisdictions and governments, as against the jurisdiction and kingdom of Christ, and the securing of all, both good and bad, and babes, in a state of uniformity, to accord with the selfish and worldly purposes of the governments—afterwards to the worldly and selfish purposes of the national church of England, enforced by law upon all, both good and bad, and babes also—afterwards to building up the purposes of the Presbyterian aristocracies, and to the securing of all their babes for sectarian rivalship—afterwards to similar purposes with the Congregationalists—afterwards it was exchanged for a substitute in form,—afterwards for the "substitute of a substitute," in form—afterwards the substitutes have been applied to all the varieties of selfish, sectarian, and treasonable purposes, with all its attendants of misnomers and untruths accompanying—afterwards to the purposes of the Methodist rulers over a sect—and latterly, ministers of the Gospel have set themselves up to *deny* its original form and purpose, and have resorted to stratagems and deceptions, to alterations of Lexicons, and to new definitions, in order fritter it away in form and principle; and finally, Bucher has defined it, a mere token of the necessity of purification, like a Jewish type or shadow.

Before we close, we will simply add, that there are twelve points, each and any of which demonstrate an organization not to be the original kingdom of Christ:—1. If the organization originated since the ascension of Christ, and since the days of the Apostles. 2. If it recognize any human rulers, so as to interfere at all with the exclusive dominion of Christ. 3. If it have any constitution contrived by human beings. 4. If it have any law-making, or law-repealing features. 5. If any but professed Christians are admitted as members. 6. If members are *admitted in any other way, than by the real oath of allegiance* which Christ established. 7. If the churches are so joined together, as to control each other, whereby Christ fails at all to have the exclusive dominion. 8. If men are permitted to obtrude any of their laws or inventions. 9. If any popish, or other tradition of men is recognized. 10. If any stratagem to catch babes is recognized. 11. If the initiating ordinance as administered stands connected with any interference at all against the exclusive jurisdiction of Christ. 12. If church discipline, by usage, be performed in any other way, except according to the express command of Christ in the 18th of Matthew, as by delegated power expressly emanating from Him.

It is preposterous to call that state of things the Kingdom of Christ, where other lords have formed the constitutions; where other members are admitted, than those He approves; where other rulers hold the reins of government over the people; and where the sect is palpably of very recent origin, or where it misleads Christians away from the exclusive jurisdiction of Christ.

LETTER XIV.

THE KINGDOM OF CHRIST.

By "Fold of Christ," and "Kingdom of Christ," we understand the same thing. "The law and the prophets, were until John; since that time the *Kingdom of heaven* suffereth violence," Matt. xi. 12. Of course it exists since then. "Since that time the *Kingdom of God* is preached." Luke xvi. 16. John was sent of God to say, "Repent, for the kingdom of God (*engike*) has come," or has come near. This fully expresses its existence from that time.

Christ repeatedly used the same expression, if it had been properly translated, and he taught his disciples and Apostles when they went forth, to use that expression. The Bishops have perversely covered up its force, by rendering it "*is at hand.*" A verb in the perfect tense is thus grossly perverted, and made future, to get rid of the argument against a national organization, in John's baptism. Christ teaches, John iii. 5, "Except a man be born of water and of the Spirit,"—that is, be baptized as well as converted, " he cannot enter the kingdom of God." In chap. v. 3, he says in substance, Man must be converted, in order to *see* that kingdom; and in verse 5, says, "He must be converted and be baptized in order to ENTER it." All this shows its existence. He is doubtless speaking of this same kingdom, and in the midst of baptisms, as is evident from chap. iv. 1. Christ himself was baptized, and thus formally introduced into it, by God's Messenger, and said, " Thus it behooveth us to ratify every ordinance.'* He introduced into it more disciples than John. He uniformly teaches, "Except a man be converted, and become as a little child—Except your righteousness exceed that of the Scribes and Pharisees, ye cannot enter it;"—thus intimating the necessity of piety, in order to membership. The number within it was so great, that he was seen of above *five hundred* brethren at one time; (*brethren*, being a name of church-members) 1 Cor. xv. 6. The sacrament of the supper, as well as the ordinance of baptism, both of them peculiar to this kingdom, were administered within it before Christ's death. If Christ deemed the strict observance of the initiating ordinance so necessary, before he should officiate within it, it would be a reproach upon his consistency to suppose his disciples and apostles were not of the baptized also.

When John baptized, teaching his disciples "they must believe on him that was to come, then they were baptized into the name of the Lord Jesus;" that is, into him who soon was found to be the Lord Jesus. But for the perverse purpose of the Bishops, this, as it was the truth in fact, would have been the real representation of Acts xix. 4—5. The fact was even so. "*This*," in italics, verse 4, is supplied by the bishops. "Him" or "John," would doubtless have been the supply, if they had not had a purpose of their own to advance; and then the meaning would have been plain. John baptized in-

---

* Campbell's Translation.

to Christ, substantially telling the people to believe on Him; "He is mightier than I,—He must increase,—His shoes I am not worthy to unloose,—Behold the Lamb of God." Christ himself, acting within it, says, "Verily, verily, I say unto thee,"—the very language of authority. The first converts were "added to them;" not constituted anew:" and other converts "were added daily," i. e. such as should be saved—converts. Jesus, thrice or more, calls it "my kingdom," before his death—declares that he was "born a King," and to Pilate's question, replied, "Thou has said," and "thou shalt see the Son of man," &c. Circumcision as Jews was not making them members; for Christ, and Paul, and the 3000, and all the Hebrews, (Heb. x. 22.) were added to this new kingdom by baptism, just as other converts. Circumcision therefore, did not introduce them into this new kingdom. Conversion and baptism, as Christ taught, was indispensably necessary with Jews and Gentiles, in order to become members of this new kingdom.

Besides we have no account of his organizing a kingdom after his resurrection or ascension, and if it was not organized at the time we have named, we have no account of its ever being organized."

And of the "Fold," he says, "I am the door of the sheep, If any man enter by me he shall be saved."—"I am the good shepherd," (referring to Isaiah xl. 11,) who "giveth his life for the sheep."—"I, the good shepherd, know my sheep, and am known of mine."—"Other sheep (that is, prospective from the Gentiles,) have I; them also I must bring or gather, and they shall hear my voice, and there shall be *One Fold, and One Shepherd*," or King. And of the sheep the description is, —"hear my voice,"—"follow me,"—"I give unto them eternal life,"—"shall never perish,"—and the like. Converts were the only persons within that Fold or Kingdom.

All the institutions in the 18th of Matthew, concerning Church discipline, contemplate the Church as already in existence. The direction to forgive offences to a brother, contemplates the same church state before the death of Christ. But for the perversions of the bishops, no one would have doubted the existence of that kingdom, from the baptism of John, and forward. The fact would have been so plain, the way-faring man, though a fool, need not have erred.

In all the revivals as mentioned in the Acts, the converts were added to them. But not a word is said of adding any others, but converts. Those churches comprising this kingdom, are addressed in this language: "Called to be saints,"—

"have put on Christ,"—"beloved of God,"—"sanctified,"—"help together with your prayers,"—"are called into the grace of Christ,"—"are faithful,"—"chosen in him before the foundation of the world, that they should be holy,"—"are partakers of his grace,"—"in whom God hath begun a good work,"—"saints and faithful brethren,"—"have love to all the saints,"—"have the work of faith, and labor of love, and patience and hope,"—"have been buried by baptism,"—"their bodies washed in pure water,"—"are saved by the washing of regeneration," (that is, the washing pertaining to the second birth,)—"are born of water and of the Spirit,,'—"baptized into Christ, and have put on Christ,"—"have faith which groweth exceedingly, and charity which aboundeth,"—"elect according to the foreknowledge of God,"—"have obtained the like precious faith with us,"—"rejoice with joy unspeakable, and full of glory,"—"are sanctified by God the Father, and preserved in Christ, and called,"—"cannot bear them which are evil,"—and are uniformly taught to put away from them "those who disobey the gospel of God."

While these descriptions are so frequent, there is not one word said about babes being members. Hundreds of passages describe the churches as saints, and not one passage that even remotely alludes to babes as members! This view is further evident,

1. Because the Bible then recognized but two kingdoms: the one comprising Christians, as soon as gathered under Christ by baptism, which all converted did, in those times; and the other the kingdom of darkness. The intermediate kingdoms, comprising sinners, saints, and babes, and under human rulers and usurpers, were not then in existence.

2. John and Christ baptized none into that kingdom but the *penitent.* "Repent, and be baptized," was the uniform direction. When the impenitent Sadducees came to John for baptism, he said, "Bring forth fruits meet for repentance." "Say not within yourselves, 'We have Abraham to our Father.'" Not a single instance can be named of one being baptized by either of them, but adults, and professed believers. Christ himself made disciples, i. e. constituted them scholars, before he baptized them, (John iv. 1.)

3. The commission of Christ did not authorize the baptism of any but believers. "He that believeth and is baptized;" "Go disciple all nations, baptizing them," &c. These must have been *old* enough *to believe* and be discipled, whom they were instructed to baptize.

4. The Apostles, after the ascension of Christ, baptized no

others. In all the accounts given, none are mentioned as having been baptized but believers, who voluntarily subjected themselves to Christ in baptism.

5. All the churches are uniformly addressed in the scriptures, as we have seen, as a company of saints.

6. Baptism, the initiating ordinance, is spoken of as the washing that pertains to the second birth. There is a washing pertaining to the first birth, and there is a washing pertaining to the second birth. In Titus iii. 5, it is thus mentioned. In Heb. x. 22, it is spoken of in connection with the profession of religion, and of course, it was applied only to Christians. In Col. iii. 3, the members are represented as *dead to sin*; such language does not apply to babes.

7. Baptism, the initiating ordinance, is a token of resurrection to newness of life.—Col. ii. 12; Rom. vi. 4; 1 Cor. xv. 29. All this brings us to the same conclusion.

8. It is a token of an intelligent engagement to serve God—baptized into Christ—is putting on Christ: an act of adults only. Col. iii. 27; and baptism into Father, Son, and Holy Ghost, as in the commission, plainly teaches the same. It is a willing and intelligent subjection of the baptized under Christ.

9. Ecclesiastical History is perfectly plain and clear on this subject. Even Mosheim, the Lutheran, testifies of the first two centuries, that none were baptized into the kingdom of Christ but believers.

Clemens, of that century, tells us that the proper subjects of baptism are such as have passed through an examination, and received instruction. Ignatius affirms that baptism ought to be accompanied with faith, love, and patience. Justin Martyr, a disciple of John, tells us, that those who are to be baptized, must "first be instructed in the faith," and that no man is to be admitted, but such as "believe the truth of the doctrine, and live as Christ has taught."

Richard Baxter informs us, that Tertullian, Origen, and Cyprian, of the second and third centuries, all affirm that in the primitive times, none were baptized but such as personally *promised* to obey Christ. The Waldenses, who were so bitterly persecuted by the Catholics, for rejecting infant baptism, Beza assures us, "were the very seed of primitive and purer Christian church—they having been upheld by the wonderful providence of God;" and affirms, that no "persecutions could ever prevail on them to bend or yield to any other course." When some imprudent persons, near the end of the second century, began to hurry the catachumens in the schools to baptism, before they gave clear and full evidence of conversion, Tertullian raises his voice against it, and cautions against receiving them till they give full evidence of conversion. The most decided opposition to infant baptism, was raised every where, after it was invented and came into being.

England, and Ireland, were both subject to the Welsh government until about the year of Christ 450. The Welsh, at that time, were driven into that part of the country now called Wales, and other governments were established in England and Ireland. The gospel was first planted in the then Welsh kingdom, in the year 63, i. e. thirty years after the death of Christ, and by the apostle Paul, as Theodoret, and Jerome affirm, who was aided, as some assert, by Joseph of Arimathea. The gospel met with wonderful success; and when the inhabitants by wars were afterwards driven to the west, into the country now called Wales, they still continued the same church order and faithfulness in the service of Christ. Two native Welshmen, in the second century, named Faganus, and Damicanus, on visiting Rome, were converted, and ordained at Rome, and had preached there for some time with great success.

In the year 180, they were sent back to assist in spreading the Gospel in the country, then Wales, now England. That church proceeding then from the organization of Paul in Rome, and in Wales, now England, has been perpetuated, and still continues in regular organization in Wales, and has been prosperous there, amidst all the darkness that has spread over other parts of the world. It has been demonstrated from the records of that church, in all ages, and from the first, and from the writings of her sons in their connexion, eminent for piety, preserved amongst them, written during every succeeding age, from the first establishment of Christianity in the Welsh and Latin languages, that this same church so planted, from the first has always adhered to the same fundamental principles as are now maintained by the Baptists of our country. That is, infant baptism has always been rejected; believers, and they alone, are admitted. Immersion, in the name of the Trinity, has always been the initiating ordinance. Subjection to the exclusive authority of Christ, the rejection of human rulers, the equality of the members, the churches independent of each other, as to government, and every church considered as a school of Christ, where his doctrines and spirit are taught, and church discipline performed by the church under his authority, are the prominent features.

We have here, then, a regular succession of the kingdom of

Christ, as he organized it, in the succession of the Waldenses, in all the various branches from the apostles, and also in the regular succession from the original church of Rome, as organized by the apostles, through this Welsh church; and also through the same, the regular succession of it, as it was organized in the year 63, by the apostles in England, then Wales. The gates of hell have never prevailed against it.

We notice in view of all this, 1. That Jesus Christ is King and sole Monarch over his people. John prepared a people for the Lord. The very language "my kingdom;" "my sheep;" "one shepherd;" "to this end was I born;" and the like, proves it. Baptizing into Christ, implies the same. He is set far above all principalities and powers; "God hath put all things under his feet;" "given him to be head over all things to the church, which is his body." The Government was to be upon his shoulders. "I have set my King upon my holy hill Zion;" is the language of Jehovah. He is Prince of Peace; and of his rivals it is said, "He shall break them in pieces." No officer has any power in the church except that which is expressly delegated from him, and be used solely for his purposes. "He that would be great was to be least of all, and servant of all," and "he that would be least, (i. e. had most humility) was to be greatest;" solely because he would be free from arrogancy and usurpation, and yield to Christ his place. Such officers as Bishops, beyond the station of an humble overseer of a single church, are the effect of selfish ambition. The offices as now in vogue, of Bishops, Deans, and Prebends; of Popes, and Rectors, of national governments over national churches, of M. E. Bishops, Presiding Elders, and subordinate rulers; of General Assemblies, Synods, Presbyteries, Sessions, and Ruling Elders, of Annual Conferences, and General Conferences, and the joining of all the churches of a sect, in a state or nation together; so that such rulers can control them, and gratify their ardent love of rule, are entirely the inventions of men, and the effect of an ardent desire "to be greatest." The two sons of Zebedee were sharply rebuked for a much less love of rule.

All these things are a direct and treasonable invasion of the prerogatives of Christ. If "offending" (literally, *obstructing*,) one weak Christian were so abominable, that "it were better a mill-stone were hung about the neck of the criminal, and he cast into the depths of the sea," then what punishment may not those expect, who build up and perpetuate such large and treasonable invasions of the prerogatives of the King in Zion; and present such large obstructions to the prevalence of his kingdom? All those who aid, abet, or in any way assist, directly or indirectly, will be held as criminals, as well as the principals in this vast amount of crime, and these machineries for the continuance of crime against the rightful Head of the church.

This whole movement on the part of rulers, is high treason against Christ, in the fullest sense of the expression, and antichrist is stamped upon this whole usurpation of jurisdiction and of dominion over his people. The whole adaptation of the immersion and sprinkling of babes, is, or has been, to build up this treason. False pretences are held out to beguile the parents to subject their babes, by that delusion, in building it up; and therefore, those who beguile the parents are guilty of *swindling* also; that is, obtaining babes by false pretences, bating all the allowance in the eyes of omniscience, on account of the delusion and ignorance of the offender. Until such offices came into existence such stratagems were not needed, and such wanderings from the fold of Christ, and such divisions did not exist; and of course, none being deluded, there were none prepared to delude others. I warn all who read, against all this treason in all its branches, and in all the variegated machinery; the *love of rule is at the bottom of the whole*; this mass of treason is not the kingdom of Christ. The United States, since their revolt, and establishment of another government, might just as well be called a British colony. The King, rejected as such—usurpers enthroned—a new and separate government established—and his subjects cajoled and subjected under usurpers, and beguiled to subject their helpless babes; and yet the hypocritical pretence be held out by such rulers—the insult added to injury—that all this is the kingdom of Christ! It is an insult to heaven. When did Jesus Christ resign his throne to such proud aspiring rulers? They stand forth before the world convicted by the word of God, of usurpation and treason against the Saviour. For those who dethrone the King and take such liberties with the oath of allegiance to him, to pretend to the people they have beguiled, that they are still within the organized kingdom of Christ, is an insult to common sense. Many of the most lovely Christians are deluded, blinded, and seduced away from the real kingdom of Christ by these rulers. Were it not for the selfishness of these rulers, the people would readily return to the fold of Christ. In the real Kingdom of Christ, his exclusive jurisdiction prevails—His will is law—and there is one fold, and one Shepherd. Additions of all descriptions, and especially such additions of new rulers, and new folds, and such treasonable machinery as the above, is prohibited by the King, under the severest penalty, even "all the plagues that are written in in his Book." Rev. xxii. 18.

2. In the kingdom of Christ, none were received but converts. This we have proved. Babes are made church members only in rival folds, for the purpose of subserving the ambitious purposes of the rulers.

3. Each church, according to scripture, and according to all history, and especially Mosheim, stood disconnected with all others; was a simple school to learn the doctrines and spirit of Christianity; all the members were on an equality; all the watching over each other, was according to the 18th of Mtthew, and done under the jurisdiction of Jesus Christ, and by power expressly delegated from him; the officers, being two, viz., an overseer, teacher, or usher under Christ, to teach these things; and a deacon, or deacons to serve the church. In this simple and natural organization, all was peace and harmony.

4. All the members were subjected to Christ by baptism. This is a humiliating ordinance to every feeling of the natural heart, croping to pride, to the love of the world, and not affording gratification to a single feeling of the natural heart. Like the anxious seat, it tests the good conscience of the convert. It strikes at the root of his strong and proud propensity to try to be a Christian in secret. As the soldiers in a mutiny, though they repent, are still viewed as mutineers, until by some public act they return to the army; so the alien from Christ, even the converted in heart, is viewed as still of the class of aliens, and the reproach of having been in the rebellion cannot be wiped away only by a public return to the Saviour. And all this self denial of washing in pure water, is appointed by the Saviour, to constrain the convert publicly, and in this humiliating way, to subject himself to the jurisdiction of Christ; thus testing his conscience, his sincerity, his willingness to bear the cross, and his willingness to do whatsoever the Saviour has commanded, and his willingness to take sides with Christ.

The phrases, "Baptizing them into the name of the Father, Son, and Holy Ghost," after they are discipled, "As many as have been baptized into Christ, have put on Christ;" (implying, that as many as have put on Christ, have also been baptized into Christ,)—"Buried with him in baptism,"—"Having your bodies washed in pure water," (connected as it is with the "profession of faith." Heb. x. 22, 23.)—"baptized *in* water," in ten instances, if properly translated: and *immerse*, and *immersion*, in the almost one hundred instances, if it had been translated, in lieu of the transfer of the Greek, all teach what is the mind of Christ too plain to be mistaken.

This and other views of the kingdom of Christ, are necessary, because baptism was intended to introduce the candidate into the real Kingdom, and exclusive jurisdiction of Christ.

LETTER XV.

SECTARIANISM—ITS ORIGIN AND PROGRESS.

This view is necessary, in order that the honest friend of Christ may know when he is not baptized into the exclusive jurisdiction of Christ, according to the original intent of the ordinance: and the minister, when he is not being ordained; not baptizing, and not acting under the jurisdiction of Christ.

According to the constitution and kingdom of Christ, as we have seen, no church is to exercise any dominion over any other church. The principle of the exclusive dominion of Christ over all, so vital to his kingdom, expressly forbids one church to rule another. A church may say she has no fellowship for another, if justice requires it; but this is all she can do. Hence, each of the churches in the New Testament is spoken of as being independent of the dominion of others. In all that is said by Christ, and in all that is said by the apostles in the Acts, and in the Epistles, not a word is said about one church controlling or governing another,—or about churches being joined together under any large jurisdiction. Mosheim (Cent. II. chap. ii. § 1, 2, 3,) tells us, in substance, that during the first, and greater part of the second centuries, the churches were entirely independent of the dominion of each other. Each church took care of its own affairs, except that Christians would always befriend each other. One teacher, or bishop, he says, presided over each assembly, or church; to which office he was elected by the people: and each church was a little state, governed by its own laws, (or rather by the laws of Christ,) that the people were all upon an equality; and that their privileges and prosperity were far greater then than afterwards..

He tells us, that "near the last part of the second century, they formed themselves into large ecclesiastical associations, like confederate states, having stated meetings to deliberate about the interests of the whole." This step, it is evident, must have been based upon the false axiom, that the people instead of being subjects under Christ, according to his laws, may become the fountain of power, and make and alter laws themselves.

This false maxim is at the root of all the troubles in the church, in all ages. This movement, he says, "originated among the Greeks, whose states were thus confederate; but soon became universal among all the churches. By the Greeks, these associations, or delegated conventions were called Synods, by the Latins, councils. These soon changed the face of the church, and gave it a new form. These ecclesiastical bodies soon assumed *legislative* powers—"enacted canons, or laws—abridged the privileges of the people, and augmented constantly the power of the bishops, or clergy: of course they abridged the jurisdiction of Christ. Although at first these Synods or councils acted as representatives from the churches, as if deriving their warrant from the people, yet soon they asserted their right to *prescribe* authorative rules and laws to the churches, and to dictate.

"Ambition for ascendancy, and emulation for power, constantly increased, until it eventuated in Popery." Congregationalism resembles these councils and synods, in their first state. Like the moderate drinkers, they are "*on the road*," making rapid progress in their pursuit, after they begin to travel towards the summit. The Presbyterians, Episcopalians, and Methodists, are already where the rulers "assume legislative powers, enact laws, abridge the privileges of the people—are constantly augmenting the power of the bishops, or clergy, and assert their right to prescribe authoritative rules to the churches."

The churches in these several kingdoms are already bound together in large national compacts, contrary to the constitution of Christ, and the state of the first churches, and inconsistent with his entire jurisdiction. All the Methodist churches in the nation are bound together under one large human jurisdiction, to gratify the ambition of the rulers. All the Presbyterian churches in the United States are bound together under another large human jurisdiction, and for the same purpose. All the Episcopal churches are joined together by their constitutions in similar large compacts, within the diocese of each of their Bishops, and are under those

J

bishops as rulers. According to Mosheim, all this, in each of these organizations, is but one step short of absolute popery. It is entirely different from the gospel of Jesus Christ, and inconsistent with his exclusive jurisdiction.

The people who would be Christians according to gospel order, must always keep the place of humble subjects under Christ. Let them once assume the axiom that they are the fountain of power, in religion, and they immediately invade the prerogative of Christ, as he alone is, and must be, the *fountain* of power, in fact.

Having once assumed this false axiom, associated together, and agreed on the convention of a council, who are to act as rulers, and as representatives from the people, soon such council will make laws, and soon will assert their rights to "*prescribe authoritative rules and laws* to the churches." This is but one step short, wherever it is found, of popery. There never can be safety only by recognizing Christ as the fountain of all power—the sole Ruler and King in Zion, having the sole jurisdiction.

Sectarianism, from *seco* to cut, is the cutting up of the people of God into separate folds, under human rulers. The elements of the kingdom of Christ, viz., **Christians**, trusty and well-meaning, and that **ought to be gathered under Him**, within his fold, are constantly, through the intrigues of rival rulers, and the delusions they disseminate, and by the barriers placed in the way of their escape, (whether they were secured when babes, or later in life,) misled, deprived of personal liberty, and kept away from the real kingdom and exclusive jurisdiction of Christ. The **blame and odium of sectarianism, is therefore on the rulers and not on the people so much.** The intrigues of sharpers are not more shrewd than those of these rulers in cheating Christ out of his sheep and lambs, and in cheating all other folds. This iniquity has become so prevalent, that Christians have lost almost all their influence in the conversion of sinners.

The love of rule in these rulers, is the foundation. Delusions, intrigues, and **crooked management** are the means.

The first beginning of a secession from the original fold of Christ was near the end of the second century, and originating with the joining of churches together, and in the ambition of the clergy prompting them to assume the reins of government, thus to establish a rival jurisdiction against that of Christ. This usurpation of the government progressed so far that in 418, we find a council at **Mela**, making laws at a tremendous rate; enforcing the death of church members, in certain cases; excommunicating persons for calling on the clergy to do secular business; enforcing the administration of the supper to babes, and also enforcing the baptism of babes, to gratify their love of power, and of monopoly. This love of rule during the next two centuries, prompted many more to carry their usurpation of power, even to a far more extravagant length, so that the jurisdiction and kingdom of Christ, as far as their influence extended, was entirely prevented. In this way his kingdom was obstructed. Infant baptism became gradually established far and wide, as far as this despotism prevailed.

Popery, absolute, became established in the year 606, and was a perfect despotism. The will of the Pope becoming law in all matters whatsoever. The mockery of baptism upon babes, was universally enforced by him, for the sake of establishing and confirming his monopoly. This was the entire annihilation of the kingdom and jurisdiction of Christ, as far as it prevailed. It was only those who secreted themselves in mountains, and vallies, and in remote places, that now constituted the real kingdom of Christ, or remained under his jurisdiction. In the successive efforts of the Pope to subdue them, he commonly sent messengers, proposing to them to consent to the adoption of infant baptism, and a few other preliminaries towards popery, and threatening them, in case of refusal, with a war of extermination. By these means infant baptism was extended, and the abrogation of the jurisdiction and real kingdom of Christ, kept pace with the prevalence of these things.

In the days of Constantine, the project was also devised of governing the church, under the pretence of protection, by the arm of civil power. Soon this custom extended all over Europe. As the civil governments assumed the jurisdictio`, and extended infant baptism to secure all in the nation in a state of uniformity under the government, and oppressed and persecuted those who adhered to Christian baptism, according to the laws of Christ ; i. e. the baptism of converts into subjection to him ; in that proportion, the kingdom of Christ became frittered away.

The whole aim of national governments over churches, has been to establish a monopoly under their own jurisdiction, and to exclude all other jurisdictions, even that of Christ. They have persecuted to the utmost extent, those who recognized, defended, or promoted his jurisdiction or kingdom at all. In proportion, therefore, as these have prevailed, his kingdom has become extinct. And as infant baptism, the main subsidary of these governments has prevailed, the same result has followed. The reason is, that infant baptism has always been used to build up a rival government and jurisdiction against his. It has also degraded the church to a worldly state, and has screened and excluded those thus secured by stratagem against the "preaching of the gospel of the kingdom." Thus by means of the clergy, from the second to the fifth centuries assuming the reins of government; by popery —and the national governments, and by infant baptism as the means, the kingdom of Christ became excluded, whole nations became nominal members, uniformity in the devices of men became estabished in lieu of that kingdom, and all the evils of the dark ages, during nearly a thousand years followed.

Yet the Kingdom of Christ was not entirely extinct, after all. A regular succession of Baptist churches in the western part of Wales, beginning in England, A. D. 63, recognizing no jurisdiction but that of Christ, and no baptism into his kingdom, but that of believers, has continued down to this time. All the Christians also that were not engulphed in Popery, in national churches, and under the jurisdiction of usurpers, continued in the regular form of the kingdom of Christ, always repudiating infant baptism as fully as they did, popery itself, as well as all rulers over the church, except Christ himself. In England, large portions of people were of this description, many of them being persecuted and slain as martyrs to the truth long before the Reformation. In Queen Mary's reign, also, 800 of them suffered martyrdom in five years. Those in Europe, who escaped the control of popery and of despots in succession, often bore the names, more or less of them, of Petrobrusians, Henrisians, Albigenses, Waldenses, Waterlandians, Mennonites, Wickliffites, Hussites, &c. The Papists called the people that held believers' baptism, and the exclusive jurisdiction of Christ, "the *oldest heresy in the world.*" Mosheim says, "The true origin of the Baptists is lost in the remotest depths of antiquity." When Luther arose against the church of Rome, the Baptists he says, arose from all quarters of Europe, to second his efforts. But finding his views did not go so far as to promote the exclusive jurisdiction of Christ over the church, or to building churches of converts only, they receded, and Calvin, and the Lutherans opposed and persecuted them bitterly, because of their difference in these points. (See Mosh. c. xvi. chap. iii. sec. 3. Part II.) In vol. iv. p. 426, he speaks of the Baptists "starting up all of a sudden in several countries at the same point of time, on some emergencies." Their peculiar views, as he says, p. 427—9, same volume, are, "That the Kingdom of Christ was an assembly of true and real saints, exempt from all those institutions which human prudence suggests:" thus honestly teaching the exclusive jurisdiction of Christ. In all those periods, according to President Edwards, there were multitudes who adhered to the principles of the exclusive jurisdiction of Christ; and according to the testimony of the papists and others, they generally adhered to the immersion of believers only, in the name of the Trinity, and denied that pander of popery, and of the national governments, that delusion, infant baptism.

We now approach new obstacles in the way of the real kingdom of Christ, and establishing new divisions.

After the reformation had progressed some fifteen years, it was checked, in England, as Lowth expresses it, in 1534, by the establishment of a national church, then under the King, Parliament, and Bishops. This new jurisdiction still prevented the people from returning to the original jurisdiction of Christ, and obstructed the extension of his kingdom there. That I may not seem invidious, I will here give the description of it, as it exists, very nearly in the words of another author.

The King, whether an atheist or a believer, stands at the head of the Church of England: next to him ranks the Archbishop of Canterbury, who is called the primate of all England. Next to him is the Archbishop of York, called the primate of England. Under these are twenty-four Bishops; all of whom, except the Bishop of Sodor and Man, are peers of the realm, and hold seats in the House of Lords.

The interference of the Bishops in the political concerns of the nation, has been a stain upon their character. Under the late spirit of reform, a loud demand has been made to exclude them from their seat in Parliament.

The revenues of the bishops are princely. It was stated in 1830, in the House of Commons, that the income of the Bishop of London, would soon amount to £100,000; i. e. about $450,000 a year!! and that of the Bishop of Winchester, to 50,000 pounds sterling per annum; equal to 225,000 dollars!! These bishops pretend a divine right to appoint successors in office as long as the world shall stand; and that no baptism is legal, but by their license.

Some of their clergy, as a writer remarks, are oftener seen at Epsom, Doncaster, and New Market, and at the sporting parties of Norfolk and Yorkshire, than in the pulpit. Those who wear the clerical costume in England, do not hesitate to appear at balls, routs, and in Opera stalls. And they have no scruples in appearing in a box at the Adelphi, or the Olympic.

This laxity of manners grows out of the *right of presentation to the Churches;* whereby individuals have the power of placing just such a clergyman over the people as they please. The people have no choice in the election of their ministers. The right of presentation is in the King, and in the Bishops; in the Lord Chancellor; in the Cathedral and Collegiate establishments, and in the aristocracy, and in the gentry. For example: The King's patronage is the Bishoprics, the deaneries, thirty prebends, twenty-three canonries, and a thousand and forty-eight livings. The Lord Chancellor presents to all livings under the value of twenty-five pounds in the King's Book, which are seven hundred and eighty, besides twenty-one prebend stalls. The Bishops have in their hands, sixteen hundred places of church preferment, at their disposal. The two Universities have six hundred livings at their disposal. The colleges of Eaton and Winchester, have fifty-seven. One thousand are in the gift of Cathedrals and collegiate establishments. The remainder are in the gift of that community called the Aristocracy and Gentry. In 1814, there were 6311 church livings held by non-residents; that is, ministers who did not live in the parishes. Of these 1523 employed curates, leaving 4788 churches entirely neglected, notwithstanding the salaries were extorted.

Men void of piety, of course, are put into office, and secure the livings. Piety suffers, religion is degraded, infidelity increases, and souls perish in consequence of such an establishment. There are many clergymen who preach the gospel in a degree of purity, it is true, but the larger portion seem perfectly reckless.

On certain occasions, the Parliament originates, and the King ordains a Fast. No one ventures to refuse to abstain from food, or to turn the measure into ridicule; but all must attend worship as a form. See Goodrich's Universal Traveller, p. 224, 225.

A seceding clergyman, says of that church, that a man, who by reason of his immoralities, was adjudged in law, incompetent and unworthy to direct the education of his own children, still held the patronage of seven livings, and the right to select clergymen to guide the immortal souls of seven parishes. He selected one clergyman to a living, of late, who, during the first week after induction, never retired to his chamber at night sober. The livings are purchased by parents and friends, of such patrons, at large prices, for incumbents, irrespective of their piety or talents. Livings are advertised, and sold to the highest bidder like merchandise. One advertisement reads, "Single duty—a living of —— in a good *sporting country*," &c. Such sales of livings, by patrons, he says, are as common as the shining of the sun. The book is headed "Present State of the established Church," 1840.

Here is a specimen of national churches, the effect of such jurisdictions, and of national rantism, as a stratagem with babes. Thousands of helpless souls are engulphed within such establishments annually, by the profane practice of baby sprinkling, wherein the clergyman falsely tells the parent that the child is made a member of Christ; a child of God; and an inheritor of the kingdom of God, and "is born again." Such falsehoods are more palpable, than those uttered in the ceremonies of free-masonry itself.

It is a rival jurisdiction, excluding the jurisdiction and kingdom of Christ by law, and those who have undertaken to promote it, have been imprisoned, fined and whipt. It is a most powerful obstacle in the way of the prevalence of the real kingdom, and jurisdiction of Christ.

Those who through love of forms, or from any other motives are anxious to build up this establishment in the United States; this obstruction to the real kingdom of Christ, are not to be envied, either for their respect for the kingdom and laws of Christ; their patriotism; their regard for immortal souls, or their regard for the feelings of Christ, which so ardently desire the prevalence of his own kingdom, and the union of all his people within it. Here is the interference of a government against the real kingdom of Christ.

In seven years after the origin of this, another sect was contrived.

The circumstances relating to the origin of Presbyterianism are these. John Calvin was first put to study, by his father, in order that he might become a Roman Catholic priest. Afterward he was put to the study of the law, and practised as a lawyer of those times of oppression, for a period. He afterwards became a Catholic priest, and was ordained a presbyter in the Catholic church. In 1534, he joined the reformation. In 1535, wrote his Institution of the Christian Religion and went to Geneva, persecuted the Baptists bitterly, and by informing against Servetus, a Baptist, and a Socinian, occasioned his death as a heretic. The great disturbance excited by these movements caused him to leave. After a few years, his friends solicited his return. He refused, unless they would adopt some system of church government whereby he could hold the people in subjection. During these negotiations, he, with his love of rule, his Catholic, and lawyer like traits previously acquired, contrived the constitution of church government for a Presbyterian church. The outlines of it, are, that four or five rulers over the church are appointed for life, (called ruling Elders) who, together with the minister, constitute the session. This session, so appointed for life, has the entire and exclusive jurisdiction over the church, and has a new form of church discipline, by citation, by appeals, and by a many-headed jurisdiction.

The Presbytery consists of all the ministers, and one of these rulers from each session. The Synod is a convention from all the Presbyteries. The General Assembly is a representation from all the Presbyteries. The people, therefore, are subject to the whole, and have no representation. The session governs the church, the Presbytery governs the sessions, the Synod governs the Presbyteries, and the General Assembly governs the whole, in its whole practical operation, by legislative, judicial, and executive powers.

A portion of the people of Geneva subjected their necks to such a jurisdiction, Nov. 20, 1541, as the price of Calvin's return. Their constitution, and form of government was made by Calvin, and was never in existence till the above period. Their creed was, for a long time, that of the church of England, for they had no other; when a convention made the Westminster Confession of Faith.* It was transferred in 1789.

The fundamental principles of Presbyterianism, as in practical operation, recognize not Jesus Christ as head of the church, but the General Assembly. This government, as well as the national governments, is perfectly at war with the exclusive jurisdiction of Christ.

The difference between Calvin and the Baptists, at its origin, was, they were for the exclusive jurisdiction of Christ, *he* was determined to have a new constitution, whereby he could rule. They were for each church standing independent and alone, as at the first. He was determined to join them together, so as to rule the greater number. *They* were for " baptizing into Christ" those, and those only whom Christ had required, and the apostolic example justified, *he* was determined to make babes church members, so as to monopo-

---

* See Life of Calvin, prefixed to his Ins. Chr. Relig. Glasgow, 1749, and Mather's Magnalia.

lize the more. They were for uniformity according to the apostolic usage, he was determined to enforce a uniformity according to his pleasure. The same contrast continues even until now.

The people cannot serve two masters, i. e. the General Assembly, with the other conjoined aristocracies, and Jesus Christ. "No man *can* serve two masters." It is impossible in the nature of things. It is a great pity those excellent Christians should be cramped by such a government, and when they have so warm a disposition, should actually be prevented by it from promoting the real kingdom and jurisdiction of Christ. These are not the kingdom of Christ, not because they are not Christians, hearty and devoted; but because other lords have the dominion over them, and totally prevent them from subjecting themselves to his jurisdiction, and from becoming members where he alone is King.

Here is another obstruction interposed at that time, in the way of the reformation, to check it mid-way, and to leave such a government over all it could control, as hindered the re-establishment of the real kingdom of Christ, and has thus far hindered it in just so far as that government has prevailed. The litigious character of the courts under this government, and the unchristian spirit they engender is notorious.

The Congregationalists never had a systematic organization, till after the organization of Presbyterianism. They consisted, at first, of that portion of pædobaptists, in those periods of partial reformation from popery, who refused to subject their necks to Calvin's Presbyterian aristocracies. They stand in the posture of the Synods and councils of the second and third centuries, in their departure from the original kingdom of Christ; only since they have adopted the "substitute of the substitute," in lieu of Christian baptism, and continue to apply it as a stratagem to babes; and are treading hard upon the heels of Presbyterianism, and fast passing into it. By their early alliance with the civil governments of New England, and their persecutions of those who rejected infant baptism, and defended the exclusive jurisdiction of Christ, and their continued opposition against the real oath of allegiance to him: they have demonstrated (whether they see it or not) that their organization has been a great obstruction in the way of the real kingdom of Christ. How lamentable it is that those who have so good hearts and intentions, should by being unfortunately entrapped by baby-sprinkling, be blinded all their lives, and be made blindly to hinder that, which in heart, they would most cordially desire to promote. Their leaders, by blindly misleading them, without even seeing it themselves, are doing a great injury to them, and a great injury to the real kingdom of Christ, however unconscious of it they may be. As a son of New-England, I fearlessly make these remarks, with a readiness to meet them in the scenes of the judgment.

And still another advance towards the right ways of the Lord, in a revival of religion, and yet the establishment of an illegitimate government, which checked it midway, and thus hindered the people from returning to the exclusive jurisdiction and kingdom of Jesus Christ.

John Wesley, in 1735, commenced an honest effort for the revival of religion in his own heart, and in 1739, commenced public efforts for the salvation of others, and was very extensively blessed. Bred in the church of England, and inured to such a construction of the passage, " Submit to the powers that be," as led him to feel bound to ecclesiastical domination, he had, by delusion, or the influence of parents, or use, become strongly prepossessed in favor of its forms, ceremonies, jurisdiction, government, and pretensions of powers, a regular succession of Bishops, strait from heaven, through a period of 1500 years before it existed.

" We believe (said he) it would not be lawful for us to baptize, if we had not a commission from the bishops; whom we apprehend to be in succession from the Apostles."—" We believe in the three-fold order of ministers, &c. (Jour. L. 514.) " By baptism (said he) we are made the children of God, and are made members of Christ its Head," p. 399, 400. " By water, we are regenerated, or born again."—" Our church ascribes no greater virtue to baptism than Christ."—" Herein (in baptism) a principle of grace is infused, which will not be taken away, unless we quench the Holy Spirit."—" In the ordinary way, there is no other means (than baptism) of entering into the church, or into heaven." (Jour. p. 401.) That which originated then, in 1534, out of popery, was, under the jurisdiction of the King, Parliament, and Bishops, so corrupt, and yet pretending a divine succession, entirely back to the Apostles—makes baptism a means of conversion and salvation—and yet allows no power to administer it only to such as emanates from those bishops. This is admitting that baptism and salvation *is in their gift!* And yet the Parliament had dashed baptism away, and established a " contemptible substitute:" as one of their ministers calls it.

[Query. Was it the doctrine that this "*substitute*" had converting and saving grace in it? We do not reproach

Wesley in all this. We simply take another peep at mother church, and at the arrogant pretensions she taught her sons and at the opportunities Wesley enjoyed. Another query: Was not Free-masory intended, in part, to take off and hold up to ridicule some of these pretensions? If so, it certainly had one good design.]

But to the Government: Wesley, for a long time, had no thoughts of leaving mother church, till at length he found it necessary. Believing that no ordination was valid without a bishop's hands, of course, his clergy being void of this gift, were unable to administer ordinances; and being obliged in his absence, to call upon other ministers, to administer sacraments, he felt his lameness. Before he left mother church, he made some overtures towards becoming ordained a bishop in the Episcopal church: but failed. In 1764, he procured one Erasmus, a Bishop of the Greek church to come to England, and he sought Episcopal ordination from him;* but failed again. Twenty years more passed. At length, in 1784, he practically usurped the Episcopal office, by proceeding to ordain Thomas Coke as a Bishop; gave him a certificate that he was a bishop; and sent him to America to ordain Francis Asbury; and then to tell him and the people that he was a bishop also.† But solemnly, this is quite as good Episcopal ordination as popery could bestow after all. It reminds us of the masonic ordination of High Priest. Now let us see to what extent this farce (for such it was in fact: Wesley having no more power to begin such a movement, than any other man,) has been carried. It has built up one of the most arbitrary hierarchies in the world.

About 1825, or 1827, a number of clergymen seceded from the Methodist Episcopal church, on account of its government, and published the following statement.

"1. The Methodist Episcopal government is an *Hierarchy*, administered solely by itinerant preachers. Every local minister, and lay member, no matter how well qualified by age, experience, piety, and knowledge, is *excluded* from all participation in the government, except *so* far as he is permitted to act as the *officer* or *servant* of the travelling preacher. The servant thus is often a man grown grey in the church, and the master an inexperienced youth.

"2. In the Methodist Episcopal church, there is no constitution to prevent the travelling preachers from introducing the most pernicious changes in doctrine, discipline, and gov-

---

* Toplady's Lett.   † Toplady's Lett.: Meth. Dis. Ed. 1806.; Port. of Meth.

ernment. What are called the "Restrictive Articles," authorize them, when they shall be so disposed, to "alter any," and "all" the restrictions, and *change* the articles of religion, the general rules, the discipline, and the entire government, and independently of the people.

"3. In the Methodist Episcopal church, a spurious and universal Episcopacy exists, with power to control the destinies of the travelling preachers; and to overawe and lead into submission those of them who may be desirous of a reform.

"4. The Presiding Elder's office is filled (1827) by about ninety preachers, each of whom receive support, for riding round a district, to do what could be as well done without him. It is called a "growing aristocracy."

"5. In the Methodist Episcopal church, Committees of trial are appointed by the preacher in charge; and the person accused has no privilege of challenge, or to object to any member of the committee, [the preacher appoints] and is bound to abide by their decision, though his greatest enemy be one of the jurors. In 1824, it was moved that the person about to be tried should have some share in choosing the committee of trial, but it was defeated, on the ground that it *would lessen* the power of the **travelling** preachers. If the person tried, appeal to the Quarterly Conference, the *tools* of the preacher are there also, to vote a second time for his condemnation. This is adapted to enable a travelling preacher to EXPEL ANY MAN from the church, against whom he is PREJUDICED.

"6. There is a rule, p. 91, of the Discipline, liable to interfere against the *freedom of speech*, and of *the Press*. It gives the preacher the power of *silencing* every inquiry into the nature of the government, or into their own acts of mal-administration.

"The principle upon which the Methodist Episcopal government is based, is this: That all power, in every department of the government, emanates from the travelling ministry; and no part from either the local ministry, or the *people*. Nothing can be done without the presence and direction of the travelling preachers. Without them, no rule can be made for the government of the church; for they are the sole legislators. Without them the government cannot be administered, for they are the only executive officers. Without them, no office can be filled; for they, directly or indirectly, hold the appointment of all officers, in their own hands. A trustee cannot be appointed, unless a travelling preacher nominate him; nor can a steward be elected, without his naming him for office. A class leader can neither be appointed nor removed, unless the preacher in charge *do it.* No one can be received into the church, except the preacher admit him. Nor can a man be expelled for immorality, or for any other cause, unless the preacher direct the trial, pronounce the sentence, and carry it into execution.

"What makes this the more exceptionable is, that these preachers are in no manner whatever accountable to the church for their moral, religious, or official conduct. They try, acquit, or condemn each other, as they themselves judge proper. And *their* trials are conducted with the utmost *secrecy*; as no person but a travelling preacher is permitted to be present.

"They claim also a divine right to exercise authority in all matters of church government and discipline, independently of the local preachers, and the people. One of the present Editors of the "Christian Advocate and Journal," (1827) has published—'Those ministers whom God selects to be the Shepherds of his flock, and the guardians of his people, possess the right of governing themselves, in religious matters; and all those committed to their care. After having demonstrated the divinity of their mission, in the awakening and conversion of souls, have they not a right to govern those who have been thus given them, as the fruit of their ministry? Let those who call this right in question, if they are able, produce a better. As long as these officers move in this way, so long the people are bound to submit to their authority, in all matters of church government and discipline. Those restless spirits who rebel against the order God hath established, rebel against God; and shall receive their own punishment. This is not pleading for submission to man. It is the authority of God. This is the order he hath established for the peace and prosperity of his church.'"

All this is a quotation from the statement of a large number of Methodist ministers, who seceded, as published in their "Brief History of Reform," published in Baltimore, by Lucas and Deaver, 1829.

This is entirely a new sort of jurisdiction, and a phenomenon. Jesus Christ has the right to the exclusive jurisdiction over all his people. These ministers, in just so far as they simply preach the gospel, and labor for souls with a disinterested spirit, are doing good. But in just so far as they are employed in treacherously beguiling people under such a jurisdiction, by baby sprinkling and the class paper, and train-

K

ing them to oppose every thing that does not come under this hierarchy, they are doing injury. Is such a spurious hierarchy thinking to govern the world? Christian Baptism is the subjection of converts to the exclusive jurisdiction of Jesus Christ. Whence did this hierachy derive its power to control the people of God, in this sectarian, selfish, shape—thus counteracting the exclusive jurisdiction, dominion, and the real and exclusive kingdom of Christ.

As further specimens of such wicked usurpation, and domination over Christians, coercing them into a sectarian shape, the Presbyterian aristocracies of Ireland, have repealed the law of Christ, as to the form of baptism, and established the "substiute of the substitute," and the people are degraded to a state of absolute subjection to them in all things pertaining to religion. The Presbyterian aristocracies of the Kirk of Scotland, exercise a domination not less tyrannic; and have also established the "substitute of the substitute" for baptism, for their convenience, in the same way, and all this since 15 8. The national Government of Germany, since 1712, have wiped out baptism in form from the national escutcheon, and although the Rubric still enforces immersion, as of old, still their civil law now enforces the "substitute of the substitute."

As a specimen of lording it in the United States, the Old School Presbyterians disfranchised five Synods, comprehending some 500 churches, and some 400 ministers, because of some different views, on some little points, as to the philosophy of the human soul. They have also recently established close communion by law, against the New School Presbyterians, unless they come up to their views as to the materiality and philosophy of the soul, the mechanical and passive imaginary process in regeneration, and such a way of explaining the doctrines of grace, as accords with this philosophy of the dark ages, and in general terms accede to their domination.

And as Christian baptism is "baptism into Christ,"—into the sacred Three,—into the exclusive jurisdiction of Christ, according to the usages of the first churches, all these governments, by treacherously beguiling the people, and securing babes by stratagem, under their own domination, entirely defeat the nature and effect of Christian baptism, the oath of allegiance to Him, within his own kingdom, and under his own exclusive jurisdiction.

The people, then, are not so much to blame for this heinous state of sectarianism, especially where they have not the power to help themselves. It is these tyrannic, heaven-daring, treasonable dominations, established over them, springing up, as we have sketched it, building themselves up by wrongs, stratagems, and frauds, against Christ, assuming the tyrannic, popish principle, of the right of appointing successors in their usurped offices, *ad infinitum*. On a partial reformation, as it was called, from popery, there sprang up in lieu of it swarms of hungry popes, and swarms of popedoms, as we have shown, have been established.

Now each of these popedoms, under these usurping rulers, is high treason in the fullest sense of the word, against Christ. If such governments were to spring up in the United States, such *imperiums in imperio*, ensnaring our citizens under them, or if it were to occur in any other nation, the cry of *treason* would resound throughout the nation, and there would be no rest till the rebel leaders were subdued. Reader, this treason is against Jesus Christ, and against his kingdom, and is therefore a thousand times more heinous, than treason in a national government. Are you engaged in it? Repent of this thy wickedness, and forsake it.

It is an imperious duty, resting upon every Christian, to come out and be separate, to repent, and in practice to wash his hands and soul of this foul stain. Christian, can you expect to be saved, if, after being shown this world of iniquity, you do not forsake it, absolutely, and wholly, publicly, and firmly.

The reason why Christian baptism is so necessary, is, because it puts the convert under the exclusive jurisdiction of Christ, within his kingdom, and because it builds up the kingdom of Christ, as it was intended of God it should do. There is no Christian baptism, however correct it may be in form, unless it in principle and effect, puts the convert under the exclusive jurisdiction of Christ.

The reason why the popes over all the masses of abused Christians, are so much opposed to Christian baptism, is because those so baptized, are gone into the kingdom of Christ, and they feel that they have lost them, and a sort of vague condemnation of themselves, comes across them. The reason why they falsely and foully slander those who build under the jurisdiction of Christ, with being equally sectarian, is with the same selfish feelings, that prompts to other slander.

The reason why Christians ought without delay to come out from under this mystery of iniquity—this treason against Christ—this domination over Christians—this profane invasion of the prerogatives of Christ, the participation in the guilt, and the continuance of these delusions and stratagems which sustain it,—are, in the rights and equities of Christ—the injury they have already done Him—the desirableness of Christian union—the blessed state of the primitive churches, when the Kingdom of Christ alone prevailed—in the importance of the millenium—in benevolence to the right organization of churches, as the gospel is planted in heathen lands—and in the fact, that unless we are willing to forsake all sin as fast as we see it, we have no reason to believe we are Christians, or to expect salvation, or to think for a moment we are receiving the approbation of Christ.

We see in this glance, 1. The vanity of jurisdictions, as the ambition of the clergy prompted them to usurp the reins of government, in different countries, between the third and seventh centuries. 2. The usurped jurisdiction of the Pope in all ages. 3. The usurpation of national jurisdictions, in all ages. 4. The usurpation over the national church of England. 5. The usurped jurisdiction of Calvin's Presbyterian aristocracies. These, like the frogs of Egypt, have spread into France, England, Scotland, Ireland, Germany, and America; and now, like free-masonry, pretend to be of divine origin. 6. The several usurped jurisdictions established in the Congregational Sect. 7. The Methodist hierarchy. 8. The modified forms of national governments. 9. The Episcopal jurisdictions, under various other modifications.

We see, also, why their energies have been directed, in all ages, either to the converting of baptism (immersion) to their own sectarian purposes, by applying it to adults and babes, and using it in subjecting the people to themselves, or else in frittering away its form, to wit, because of their rivalship against the kingdom of Christ, and because Christian baptism as such, had an exclusive tendency to build up the kingdom of Christ; a kingdom which those rulers have uniformly opposed. Again, we see why Sir Isaac Newton made the remark, that the Baptists were the only Christians who had not symbolized with Antichrist; and he inclined to consider them one of the two witnesses; to wit, because they had always contended for the exclusive jurisdiction of Christ, for the oath of allegiance to him, and for implicit obedience to all his commands. And finally, we see that the usurped jurisdiction of men over Christians, has been the fruitful source of all the sectarianism that at present exists, and to the same cause we trace the origin of all our troubles. The idea of uniformity is but a small remuneration for such broad, and deep, and lasting injuries, to the kingdom of Christ and to the world.

LETTER XVI.

SECTARIANISM—ITS FEATURES.

Sectarianism is the cutting up of the heritage of God, into separate folds, by those who think highly of themselves, and have a great love of rule, and who, from time to time, seize the reins of government, clothe the office they assume with a dignified name, make arrangements to give permanency to it, usurp the dominion, provide for a succession, gather up the people, and then make arrangements to secure their descendants, whereby an entire secession from the original jurisdiction and kingdom of Christ ensues.

In looking at the mass of sectarianism, mentioned in our last, a number of points strike the attention.

1. The love of rule, was the first beginning of it. How faithfully did the Saviour reprove this spirit. The rulers of the Gentiles are called benefactors, "but it shall not be so with you." Ye are my disciples, then, *and only then*, when ye do whatsoever I have commanded you. "The disciple is not greater than his Lord."

2. Such sect ceases *abinitro* to be the kingdom of Christ. If others rule, Christ does not. If it becomes a new government, it ceases to be the original. If other rulers reign, they hinder Christ from reigning. If in all respects, it agrees with the original, it remains and coincides with it. But the moment it differs in so material points as become a separation, to have new rulers, and regulations, it, of course, ceases to be the original government. As well might the United States be still considered as belonging to the Government of Great Britain, notwithstanding the separation. When the ambitious clergy, from the third to the seventh centuries, in different places, assumed the reins of governmens, and became rulers, the sections they misled, ceased to be the kingdom of Christ; because wherever his kingdom is, he is King and sole Ruler. Wherever he is dethroned, his kingdom so far ceases. So when popery became established—when the civil governments began to rule the church—when the King, Parliament, and Bishops, of England, began to rule in England over a pretended church—when Calvin, and his aristocracies

began to rule portions of the Christian community—when other rulers in succession, and when Wesley's bishops, and hierarchies began to reign, in each and every case, from the nature of things, those communities ceased to be of the kingdom of Christ. When others rule, Christ does not. The kingdom of Christ was quite another government, organized on different principles, for another purpose and had another Ruler.

3. Each and all of these, in just so far as they differ from the kingdom of Christ, are so far wrong—are unprincipled, are wicked. They differ in the separtion, and in all those points which make a separation necessary—in establishing a new government, and in all those movements and that course of action, which gives permanency to this separation.

4. In looking at this mass of sectarianism in a general view, we cannot but see the whole of it is treason. It is high treaso against heaven. The particular illustration of this we reserve for another place.

5. We notice that the office of the ministry, is. and must be illegitimate, in all these separate folds. With those who first separated from the kingdom of Christ; if they had a regular office, of course, they could not carry it out of the regular jurisdiction, where it was bestowed, and still exercise it. A Justice of the Peace cannot exercise that office within another government. This is true of all offices. As soon as they went under another government, they had no legitimate office.

6. Those churches are not legitimate churches. Christ authorized the organization of churches under his own jurisdiction, bur never authorized a secession from his kingdom, or any kind of movement, except such as fell strictly within the scope of his own jurisdiction, according to his laws. " Then (and only then) are ye my disciples, if ye do whatsoever I command you." No provision is made for the organization of churches under other commanders.

6. We notice the principles upon which the rulers claim the transfer of the office of the ministry. One is, that this whole mass of sectarianism is the kingdom of Christ. But nothing can be more absurd. Those changes, secessions, assumptions of new offices, new governments. new rulers, new sects, jars, contentions, usurped power, addition of men's constitutions, laws, regulations, and contrivances, and especially such great stretches of power, make it absurd to pretend it is still the kingdom of Christ. Nothing is the kiegdom of Christ

but that which remains under his jurisdiction, and accords with his regulations.

A second pretence is, that the office of the ministry may be carried any where out of the kingdom, as well as in, and connected to a treasonable agency in building up treason, rebellion, secession, and rivalship, against the King, and still be a legitimate office! This needs only to be looked at, in order that its absurdity may be seen. No office conferred in one jurisdiction, may be carried into another jurisdiction, or into a rebellion, or be turned against the government who conferred it, and yet retain even the pretence of legitimacy. The opposite of this might be crowded upon people in the dark ages; but will not do for these.

The other pretence is, that officers have the right to appoint successors *ad infinitum*, out of, as well as within, the kingdom or jurisdiction. So a Captain in Great Britain, may claim the right of appointing all succeeding Captains, not only in Great Britain, but may come to revolted America, and claim and exercise this appointing power. A President—a Governor—a Justice of the Peace—a Postmaster—may all claim the right to appoint all successors, and each may monopolize the appointing power in relation to successors. This may go in the dark ages of popery, in the church and state establishments, and under the tyrannic government of the Bishops in Great Britain. But it cannot go in an enlightened community. Every civilian, statesman, lawyer, and enlightened Christian, knows that each government, or rather the fountain of power within that government, has the sole right of appointing all the officers; and that it is tyranny for an officer to claim the prerogative of appointing successors, and above all things, after he has left the original jurisdiction for him to hold out such a pretence, is absurd. "Those things which thou hast heard of me before many witnesses, the same commit thou to others," &c., is a passage which many superficial readers think favors this absurd principle. But this passage relates, not to the office of the ministry, but to the faithful defence of divine truth. It is "things which have been heard," which are to be committed to others,—truths. The instructions are to one already a minister, to be faithful in preaching. Jesus Christ has the appointing power in his kingdom. To the church is committed the responsibility of guarding itself against false pretensions, of examining candidates, of deciding on the evidence that Christ has called the person to the ministry, and praying over the case, and thus commending him to the work. *Cheiropoico*, is the word which often expresses this action of the church. It expresses the vote of the hand, or the decision. *Diatithemi*, to appoint, sometimes is the expression of the action. Paul never monopolized this appointing power, and of course never conveyed it. The Head of the church says, "Separate me Barnabas and Saul, for the work whereunto *I* have called them." When and where did Jesus Christ surrender his right to call to the ministry, and relieve the church and ministry conjointly, of acting in such cases, in deciding as far as they can, whether Christ has called the person to the work or not. But we must be members of Christ's body, the church, in order to have anything to do with it. And no one, though converted, is a member till he has subjected himself by baptism, to the jurisdiction of Christ, within his kingdom. Under another jurisdiction, he is not a member here. For persons who were never converted, who live in luxury and wealth, like the bishops of England, who have never become members of Christ's body, the Church, to claim the monopoly of appointing all his ministers, of giving permission to baptize, or rantize, by which they pretend persons are converted and saved, is as absurd as any other part of popery, that has ever existed.

Christ appoints his own ministers, by his Spirit, and by bestowing evident qualifications. The supervision and scrutiny of the case rests upon the church and ministry conjointly. All they do, however, is to decide that in their opinion, Christ has called the candidate, to pourtray his duty before him, and to pray over his prospective labors. The imposition of hands, an unmeaning ceremony, except as a token of friendship. The appointing power is exclusively with Christ, the evidence to the church is the spirit and ability, so far as they can judge. Theirs is the delegated prudential part to examine the case, to join in the responsibility, to decide approve and pray. In this way, the man becomes appointed exclusively by Christ. All the church and ministry do, is to act the part of his agents.

Now for human beings to monopolize this appointing power, is to carry it out of the kingdom of Christ, into their revolted folds, is high treason, is the crime of injured Majesty, is robbing God, is dethroning the King. Foreigners cannot exercise the appointing power, when it is the exclusive prerogative of the crown and his council. Christ is this King, and the Church are his council, not to advise him, but to act under him, in counselling others. To assume, therefore, that a minister may monopolize the appointing power, may revolt, as in the fourth or fifth centuries, and establish a new jurisdiction, may in succession go into popery, that treasonable state of war against Christ and his kingdom, may, in 1534, monopolize the exclusive appointing power, in the kingdom of Great Britain, may, in the person of Calvin, revolt from popery, and assume the right of appointing Presbyteries, Synods, General Assemblies, Ruling Elders, &c., and may in the person of Wesley, a mere priest, or deacon of the church of England, appoint bishops, who shall from him, monopolize the appointing power, in a new sect,—is to assume a prerogative that is popish, revolting, treasonable, robbing God, and dethroning the real King, so far as it goes, or at least to invade his prerogative. This principle of men being clothed with the appointing power, wheresoever they may go, into whatsoever jurisdiction, and so may carry the monopoly of the rights of the King into popery; into Episcopacy; into Presbyterianism; and finally, into Wesleyan Episcopacy—is revolting to every principle of justice, and to every righteous claim of the King in Zion.

No one is even a member of his kingdom, only by being baptized into subjection to him. And here are revolters, who claim to have stolen the exclusive livery and prerogatives of the King, and carried it into all these revolts, shaped it into the office of a pope, of an Episcopal Bishop, with his princely salary, and his vices, and monopoly of appointing power: the several offices of the Presbyterian aristocracies, and the office of Wesley's bishops! Popery itself has never been more absurd.

It is palpable that there is no legitimate ministry at all, away from the jurisdiction of Christ. Wherever other rulers have ascended the throne, it ceases to be the kingdom of Christ. Those even, who had an office in the kingdom of Christ, at the beginning of this revolt, could not exercise it. It becomes illegitimate, even when first carried into such revolt. A revolted succession of fifteen hundred years, does not cause it to become legitimate, by the lapse of time, It is all perfectly spurious, however pious and honest the men may be, solely because it is all out of the jurisdiction and out of the kingdom of Christ. No person was ever a member in the kingdom of Christ, until he had been baptized into the exclusive jurisdiction of Christ. Piety shows right feelings, but baptism puts him under his jurisdiction. Much less is one an officer in that kingdom, who is not a member. The pomp and parade of self-complacent dignity, was as visible in the officers of free-masonry, as it is in the pompous ceremonies of other pretenders. When did God authorize the revolts of the fourth and fifth centuries; of popery; of the Episcopal, the national, the Presbyterian governments, and the governments of the Wesleyan Bishops, as substitutes for the original kingdom, under Christ?

8. In looking at this mass of sectarianism, we see the Lord has a vast amount of property there. Probably the majority of real Christians are there, and large numbers, of good, well-meaning, and well-qualified men for the ministry, are serving there in this illegitimate way, who have never become even members of his jurisdiction. They have grown up under revolted jurisdictions, and never been shown the wrong, and never suspected any, but have always been tampered with, in a way that has filled them with prejudice.

All this is a wrong to Jesus Christ. He has need of them all: that they should labor, work, and pray, and preach, under his jurisdiction, and not within revolted folds, and under competing jurisdictions.

9. In looking at this sectarianism, we see the fallacy of the commonly received opinion, that one denomination is just as good as another, and those who gain the most proselytes are the most to be commended. The true principle lies far back of all this. The claims of Jesus Christ are entirely different from the claims of revolters, and usurpers, and illegitimate folds. The original Fold, where the lawful King, and his laws and regulations prevail, and where allegiance to him, however self-denying, prevails, is entirely different from the revolted folds of men, where men have contrived the constitutions, rule the people, make many of the laws, and blindly encourage a revolt from the rightful King.

10. We also see that religion, in this mass of sectarianism, is wrought into merchandize, and made to be a trade for a living, in many cases, as an end, when the end ought to be to advance the kingdom of Christ, and through that the best interests of the world, and the glory of God. From the first, where men have assumed the reins of government, they have made merchandise of the people. Sprinkled babes, if they grow up as they would wish, become fit subjects of merchandise. The princely salaries in the church of England, the merchandise of the livings, that are bought and sold, and the sinecure offices of the ministry, are all in point. The hands of the people are tied, and they have not even the privilege of promoting the real kingdom of Christ. In Germany, the government extort the salaries by direct tax, and appoint all the ministers, who fill their places for pay, rarely see their

parishoners, live in wealth, and thus the cause of Christ languishes. The same remark is true, to greater or less extent, in all the seceding fold.

11. We see how difficult it must be for Christians in these folds, daily to pray, "Thy kingdom come." Refusing to become members of it, in a state of alienation from the jurisdiction of Christ, never having put themselves under his own jurisdiction, within his kingdom, but having always remained under revolted jurisdictions,—and yet required daily to pray "*Thy Kingdom come!*" How can they do it with sincerity, while their practice contradicts their prayers? How can they pray for a kingdom, at the same time the Lord requires them to become members of it, and yet they refuse to do it?

12. We see what it is that has built up infant baptism, and baby sprinkling. It is interested feelings in these revolted folds, who use it for sectarian purposes, to secure numbers.

13. We see how Christian baptism has become so much frittered away. It was originally the pledge of the convert, whereby he volvutarily subjected himself to the jurisdiction of Christ, within his kingdom. It remained such, till these revolts began. When the aspiring clergy, in the fourth and fifth centuries, assumed the reins of government, then they procured the babes to be baptized, from selfish motives. The principle of subjecting believers to Christ, was left, and the principle of subjecting babes to usurpers became the substitute. The principle of subjecting them to popery, soon became the substitute. The principle of subjecting them to national governments, soon was also a substitute. The principle of building up the national church of England, after 1534, was a substitute. The principle of building up Presbyterianism, and Congregationalism, by securing babes, soon became a snbstitute. The sprinkling of babes, it was soon found would subserve the interests of these revolted folds just as well, and so became a substitute. Wetting, pouring, sprinkling, or immersion, just as suits the candidate, whereby they become subjected to Wesley's hierarchy, became a substitute. And finally, baptism is nothing but the token of the need of divine purification.

In the early governments, in popery, in the Episcopal, Presbyterian, and Congregational governments, infant baptism, or the substitute, has always been enforced upon the parents, and the penalty was excommunication, until the last fifteen or twenty years. The immersion of converts into subjection to the exclusive jurisdiction of Christ, is what he requires, and what these all war against. Those who obey Christ are dubbed as Baptists, and held up to odium, and persecuted, and opposed. Who does not see through all this, and discover what is right?

13. We see, in looking at this mass of sectarianism, the true idea of close communion. While all Christians continued to be baptized into Christ, as soon as converted, according to the command of Christ, and enjoy the privileges as soon as they become members, there was no close communion. Our denomination, during 250 years, held precisely the same principles as now; and yet there was no close communion. After sections begin to secede, and organize in another way, and to wander wider and wider, then close communion exists. We have not wandered or altered, but still obey the regulations of Christ. It is the wanderers, then, who have made it, by fixing their own folds, presenting their own terms, demanding of us to follow, and because we would not wander too, have charged the fault of the separation upon us. Had they never wandered from the original Fold, of Christ, there never would nave been any close communion, but the kingdom of Christ would have been prosperous and happy. We simply ask them, therefore, to return to the original fold of Christ. The path is simple. Be baptized into the jurisdiction of Christ, and there is no close communion. Remain under the jurisdiction of men, and it will remain. Because Christ has made no provision for incorporating such a revolt, into his kingdom, only by the return we have named.

But here the objection comes up, "If all this is so wrong, why then does God bless those so much, who have thus wandered?" We answer, God is infinitely merciful, and blesses all people, as far as he possibly can, consistently with their circumstances. He blesses them *so much*, because they have not consciously, *any more* of these wrongs. The inference is, that if they *had less*, he would bless all still more. And if all were entirely rid of these divisions, and alienations from Him, and all were one in his Fold, as they were during the first and second centuries, blessings would be poured out in such abundance, that there would hardly be room enough to contain them. The Kingdom of God would come with power, and the earth would soon be filled with the knowledge of the Lord; missionary operations would cease to be embarrassed; our divisions among ourselves would cease; our united influence would be exerted upon the world; and they would hear the voice of God and live.

LETTER XVII.

FRAUD UPON CHRIST.

When our dear pædobaptist friends were sprinkled as babes, it was done under the wrong jurisdiction. So modern a jurisdiction, of course, cannot be the right. This sprinkling was a snare, which confined them in the wrong, and kept them from the right jurisdiction. No jurisdiction can possibly be right, but that of Christ exclusively. A jurisdiction of men, clothed with imaginary offices, which have been invented within a very few centuries, must be a spurious jurisdiction, and the offices be spurious. The jurisdiction of the rulers in the Episcopal, Presbyterian, Congregational, and Methodist organizations, are palpably such. Their rantism, and subsequent training, caused them to grow up under the wrong jurisdiction; one that sprang into existence in all those cases, within three hundred years, and without any divine warrant for such divisions, for such new offices, or such new and rival folds. *Adding* them to Christianity, is as much forbidden, as adding any thing else. And yet these frauds have perhaps grown up without beginning to suspect any wrong.

Ministers, when first invested, were hindered from Christian baptism; i. e. from subjecting themselves to the exclusive jurisdiction of Christ. They devoted their lives to the wrong jurisdiction, became ordained—i. e. *appointed*, to officiate under the wrong jurisdiction, and have been sprinkling babes into the wrong jurisdiction, thus ensnaring them also, and confining them wrongfully under the same. Now as the jurisdiction is spurious, all these operations are spurious.—Sprinkled when babes—a false confidence secured—the influence of the parents, and the sect devoted to continuing them there—converted to Christ, and then neglecting to take the oath of allegiance to him, within his kingdom—but in the delusion and blindness of the mind, becoming more and more strongly attached to that spurious jurisdiction, he devotes his whole life to it; and thus, in all probability, does more hurt than good. With one's hands to the plough, and his head

L

turned back, he can cultivate the field, as well as such a minister, with his hand turned away from the real kingdom of Christ, and devoted with the spirit of a bigot, to a spurious fold, that he can benefit that kingdom. Instead of this, he works against the real kingdom of Christ, during all his life, and consecrates all his energies to building up an opposition fold, and a rival jurisdiction.

Reader, baby sprinkling has done all this. If rival governments were to spring up in the United States, against the General Government, and you were to devote your whole lives to building them up, and become ordained under them, the case would be precisely parallel. And if you were to get babes and others committed, then it would be the same in effect, as your baby sprinkling.

Suppose you are a minister there. Whenever you have sprinkled, you have wronged the truth. 1. In saying, "I baptize," without doing it. 2. In using the name of the Trinity, as authority for it at all, and especially when it is not done. 3. In pretending the babe, or person sprinkled, is thereby put into the jurisdiction of Christ. 4. In pretending the child, in such case, is, in fact, devoted to Christ. In Calvin's time, and long after, the language was "Giving them to the Church." This was telling the truth. 5. If, in prayer, you told the Lord, the dedication had been made to him, you uttered a falsehood in prayer, and yet, probably knew it not. 6. In pretending to the congregation that the Lord even authorized such a mockery, as never existed till 1556, except in the case of popery, after 1311. 7. By your life and influence, in sanctioning all this mass of iniquity, in all the popish national, and hierarchial dominions, who have carried on this fraud for so many centuries. It is all treachery and fraud upon Christ, however honest you might have been in heart.

The effect of the class paper is also to put people into the wrong fold. It is simply building up a wrong jurisdiction, and confining you away from the jurisdiction of Christ. Ministers, then, who are employed either in managing either adults, or helpless babes into these wrong jurisdictions, are doing immense injury to Christ, are promoting a treasonable state against him, and are, in fact, cheating all the parties concerned.

All must admit that Christ alone, on principles of common justice, and common equity, is entitled to all Christians, as his own property. "Ye are not your own—ye are bought with a price." "My sheep,"—is his endearing appellation. They are "redeemed unto himself,' "redeemed by his blood," and "redeemed unto God." But the rulers in these modern folds of men, act on the principle that they have a better right to Christians than Christ himself—to use them for their selfish sectarian ends. Hence the most fraudulent measures are often resorted to, in order to defraud Jesus Christ out of them. "We have labored and prayed for you," is the language often used, "and therefore you owe yourselves to us;" i. e. to our sect, and to our selfish purposes. Just as if the Lord had no righteous claims to them—as if a few such efforts had bound the converts to give away themselves, not to Christ, but to a selfish sect, to usurping rulers, and to a rival jurisdiction.

The whole policy of baby sprinkling, was intended by the original contrivers, to cheat Jesus Christ out of the babes, by stealth, and is therefore, an imposition upon the parents, the child, and upon Christ, and is a perfect cheat on Christ, in its effect. The honest parents are duped thus to betray their children into the hands of human rulers, under the pretence of giving them to Christ. The command, that there be no divisions, prohibits the existence of these other folds, and these usurpations—and of course, prohibits the building them up by such stratagems, and such a mockery of Christ's ordinance, and the building them up at all. The partaker is as bad as the thief.

If all Christians and all converts are Christ's property, then all such movements are frauds upon him. To steal our neighbor's sheep, and secure his lambs prematurely, by stealth and stratagem, is not worse, in principle, than it is to seduce the sheep of Christ, and secure babes by stealth, so as to possess them at all events, when they are converted. To steal from Jesus Christ, in order to build up usurped jurisdictions, is worse than common theft, because of the dignity of the Person defrauded—the great value of the property stolen, and the application of it to build up an opposition against him. People have become perfect maniacs in these matters. They steal in open day-light—steal from Christ—steal as if they were doing God service—and are so crazy with sectarianism, many of them verily believe the more they steal the more they do God service. They lay the most subtle plans, to steal from and rob the dear Saviour of his rights, and do it under a pretence of having authority from him. They steal for the glory of God, and, in the name of Christ. All this grows out of the establishment of these competing folds of men against the kingdom of Christ, and the delusions therewith connected. Consequently, every thing which tends to build them up, even baby sprinkling, is wickedness, is immoral in its whole tendency, and stands connected with a general course of frauds, which, if committed under a civil government, would expose the offender to State's prison. To let down the fence, and seduce sheep and lambs away from a neighbor is certainly no better in principle, than it is to seduce sheep and lambs from Christ. The very existence and continuance of these other folds, than Christ's, and the building them up, is a succession of such frauds and thefts, however honest, deluded, and deceived the agents may be; it is high treason against heaven.

Paul "verily thought he ought to do many things contrary to the name of Jesus of Nazereth." But when he came to himself, he found that he needed "mercy" for those same transactions. These men, who, in modern times, are doing so much against the kingdom of Christ, and yet "verily believing they are doing God service," will find sooner or later, that they must have great mercy from God, and that they must "weep bitterly," as did Peter, for thus denying the ONLY LORD, and for building up other lords, the usurpers of his power, who are thus lording it over his people against his will, or they will weep eternally.

In the civil governments, every man is *obliged* to KNOW the law. And if he breaks the law through ignorance, it is no excuse, if he has the means of knowing it. Men would be indicted daily for defrauding a civil government, as they daily defraud Christ. What if a rival government in our midst, and at the expense of our government, were daily building up, and the agents were daily to practice such stratagems, to enlist our babes under them, and to seduce our citizens—to use class-papers, and baby sprinkling, as we daily see it, and were so perfectly deluded as to see no evil in it! How long would it be before the leaders, *en masse*, would be sent to State's prison, as a warning to the rest. The honest intentions of the thieves, or their delusions, would never be admitted as an excuse.

This is not a highly painted description of the sectarian thefts continually and openly practised under the cloak of religion, in our country.

Baptism, into Father, Son, and Holy Ghost, implies exclusive subjection to the Triune God, in that ordinance. "Baptized into Christ," implies subjection to Christ. The baptized were "added to the Lord. Acts ii. 41. "Baptized into Moses," (the literal translation,) implies subjection to Moses; "baptism into death," (Rom. vi. 4,) i. e. into the great principle of our death to sin, implies subjection to that fundamental Christian principle; baptism into the death of Christ, implies subjection to the great fundamental principle of salvation, by his atonement; baptism into the kingdom of Christ, implies subjection to the rules and regulations of that kingdom, under the great Ruler, and rightful King. The prominent idea in Christian baptism, in the kingdom, is subjection to the proper authority, viz. Christ. It is true, the *willingness* to die to sin, the burial in baptism, and the resurrection, have an important resemblance to the *voluntary death*, the burial, and the resurrection of Christ; and as Christ, after his resurrection was in heaven, in glory, so we, after our baptism, are in the church, where we must " walk in newness of life." The resemblance, however, is collateral and incidental in its bearing, although of vast importance; and the argument thence derived to enforce " newness of life," is also of inconceivable importance.

The prominent and chief idea of Christian baptism, then, is subjection to Christ. The baptism of believers into the kingdom of Christ, accumulates to him, " gathers with him," and under his jurisdiction, where there is " one fold, and one Shepherd. But gathering, by another initiating ordinance, under other rulers, who have usurped the dominion, " scatters abroad from Christ.

Subjection to the usurpers of his power, therefore, is a mockery. Such a use of the real ordinance, or of the substitute, or of the sacred words used in baptism, or of the ministerial office, in relation to either adults or babes, as in fact gathers not with Christ, but scatters and subjects them to usurpers is a mockery, is profane, and is abomination in the sight of God. The kingdom of Christ, therefore, should be rightly understood, and these folds of men should be rightly understood, as baptism, or the substitute, is, in fact, the initiating ordinance under the rulers, in all the several jurisdictions, wherever it is done. Babes are considered by all governments, as subjected under the rulers, wherever they are sprinkled. Parents and candidates should therefore know to whom they subject themselves and their children, not merely in intention, but in *fact*. If it is, in fact, a subjection to usurpers, and of course, a lothing to Christ, it should be known, and the parents should awake from their delusion. What is, in fact *done*, not what the deluded *mean*, is the true test of the transaction. That, which, in fact, " scatters away from Christ," should not be through delusion, viewed as " gathering to him."

All these things must be understood, or we shall never have

adequate ideas of what is, *in fact*, done in baptism, or in the substitute, or in the modern delusion of baby sprinkling

The usurpers of dominion, are the Pope—all the variety of hierarchies, the church and state establishments, the Bishops and governments established by law over the church of England, Wesley's bishops and subalterns, with their several Conventions, and Conferences; the Aristocracies, and Hierarchies, in the Presbyterian church, consisting of Sessions, Presbyteries, Synods, and General Assemblies; including the Ruling Elders, the mere tools of the hierarchies,—and those *particular* ministers in all the several folds and Conventions, who seem perfectly intoxicated with the love of pre-eminence and the love of rule, and all the rulers elsewhere, who assume the reins of government over the people of Christ. All these dominions and offices (the office of the ministry, simply excepted) have come into existence long since the times of the apostles, and all of them, except popery, within three hundred and six years. Their position on the map of history, and the times when they came into existence, demonstrate them to be the innovations and devices of men. Constitutions, the devices of men, within that period, are the only authority they have; and this is no authority at all. The fact that others had filled such offices before them, is their only pretext. The love of party, in the people, and the love of rule in the rulers, are the bonds which cement them together; and the cheat, the profane hoax, of baby sprinkling, is the main dependance for enlarging these dominions of men. Babes thus imposed upon, should spurn it with indignation, and revolt from the dominion to which, by the delusion of their parents, they were subjected in their helpless state, as soon as they are old enough to understand it.

We have, then, a vast amount of real popery now in the country. It stalks abroad in these dominions, with an unblushing face. The usurpers of such exorbitant powers, are imperceptibly extending their dominions by stratagem, far and wide, and are thus hindering the prevalence of the real dominion of Christ. Every sprinkled child, according to these constitutions, is considered as subjected to the powers that be, wherever it is done.

Now baptism, and the substitute, should always be honestly and intelligibly performed, without any falsehood, or prevarication, or deception. If the minister is to sprinkle; the candidate should insist on his saying, "*I sprinkle.*" If he is to pour, should insist on his saying, "*I pour.*" If he is to baptize, then, and only then, let him say, "*I baptize.*" Let him use just such words as convey the exact truth. How can the candidate serve God in a transaction which is performed with falsehood in the language, and in the act, however deluded and honest the minister may be. It is deception of the grossest kind, to lie or prevaricate in so solemn a transaction, or for the candidate to suffer it to be done. The candidate is a partaker in the sin, if he suffers it to be so done and said, as is contrary to truth.

And further,—the minister should be required to tell what the real fact is that is done in the transaction. If the child or candidate is to be subjected to the Presbyterian governors and rulers, then insist on the minister telling the plain truth, and saying, "I baptize, sprinkle, or pour, thee, (as the case may be,) into the Sessions, Presbyteries, Synods, and General Assemblies, of the Presbyterian government." To pretend to subject the candidate to Father, Son, and Holy Ghost, when in fact he is subjected to other and human rulers, is deception. The candidate as he values his soul, should not allow it. If he does, he is partaker in the guilt. Let the honest truth be told without any deception.

If the candidate is to be subjected to an Episcopal hierarchy, he should insist upon the minister's telling the truth. To pretend, in such a case, to subject the candidate to Jesus Christ, is just as deceptive as it would be to pretend, in enlisting soldiers that it is under American colours, when in fact they are, by stealth, subjected to French or British colours. Such deceptions, however honest the minister may be, is too barefaced. "I baptize, I sprinkle, I pour thee, and into subjection to the Pope, to the Episcopal Bishop, or to Wesley's Bishops," (as the case may be,) must be the substance of the language of truth, if the candidate chooses to go under such human rulers. This custom of deceiving people, as to the nature of the transaction, and as to the rulers to whom the child or person is subjected, should no longer be continued.

The sprinkling of babes and others, never subjects them to to Jesus Christ. Because Jesus Christ never allowed it. The name of the Trinity, therefore, should not be mocked with it. Its prototype, the immersion of babes, was introduced during the growth of popery, under a state of things similar to that now in our country, and was always intended to subject the child *ostensibly* to Jesus Christ, but really to other lords, and under other governments. The parent should not allow the deception, but should demand of the minister to have the honest truth fairly told. Let the minister then say, "I sprinkle thee into subjection to the

Presbyterian rulers, or to the Methodist bishop, or to the Episcopalian bishop," just as the truth in the case may be, and cease the mockery of the sacred Trinity.

All these governments hold the child as subjected to them, wherever he is christened. Let the plain truth then be told. It is lying and deception, therefore, to pretend that it subjects them to Christ. Let the plain truth be told, and the bubble will soon burst, and the delusion soon end with the intelligent.

The sprinkling of babes is never any thing else but a subjection of them to illegitimate rulers.

The whole business of deceiving and being deceived, in the way of treacherous enlistments, by baptism, or by its substitute, and under human rulers, is fast accellerating the establishment of popery among us; and in every step of it, is defrauding and cheating Jesus Christ. For if under the pretence of his colors, the soldiers and the babes are in fact enlisted, and committed by delusion and deception under other rulers, and within the modern folds of men, then Jesus Christ, the only rightful ruler, and his kingdom, are cheated by it. Insult should not be added to injury, by pretending to do it under his colors, and in his name.

This whole movement on one side is building up popery, increasing the power of the usurpers, is at antipodes against the kingdom of Christ, and against the safety of our country, and the best interest of the world. When will parents see that this baby sprinkling movement only *fools* them, is unprincipled, is profane, is anti-christian, is a solemn mockery, and is, in fact, treacherously building up the cause of the enemy, under the pretence of building up the cause of Christ. Parents deceive their children, and yet ignorantly, and with honest motives. Children grow up with the deception, and become ministers, and deceive others, though they may mean no such thing. Thus all pass along, deceiving and being deceived, destroying all peace and harmony among Christians, and in the Christian world; robbing Jesus Christ, of mocking his ordinance, uttering falsehoods in the mock service, and building up false rulers, who are stretching further and further to a state of absolute popery and monarchy over Christians.

Even the immersion of a Christian, if it subject him to the wrong rulers, and in the wrong government, is a baptism, *ostensibly* under the colors of Christ, but, *in fact*, deceptively, under a totally different ruler, and different government, and for this reason, is not Christian baptism. Jesus Christ must have all the dominion, where we are, or we are not baptized into his kingdom.

When will people awake, and enlist under the banner of Christ, instead of enlisting under that of usurpers, and rebels, and self-created rulers. The building up of these monarchs and rulers by the stratagem and deceptions of baby sprinkling, counteracts the dominion of Christ, and the spread of his kingdom, as he originally contemplated, hinders Christians, after conversion, from being exclusively under him. Whosoever is not with Christ is against him. What a pity so many good ministers, and so many babes, by being fooled, should be prepared favor during all their lives, the above popish state of things, to at antipodes against Christ, and in favor of his rivals.

This baby sprinkling, we cannot but see is a gross fraud. It obstructs the prevalence of Christ's kingdom; it cheats him out of the true intent and effect of his own initiating ordinance, by using the mockery of it, and the words of it, and for another purpose; it cheats him, by teaching that the will of men and of parents may make the law,—thus trampling his authority, and his right to make the law, in the dust; it cheats him, by preventing him from ever having those who confide in it, in a state of oneness under himself, in his own kingdom; it cheats him out of their usefulness to him, and their right example; it cheats him out of the privilege of ruling his own people for their own best interest under himself, and for the best interests of a perishing world; it cheats him, by the obstructions it throws in his way; it cheats him out of the privilege of gathering them all in his own way, and of seeing them all happy as one, and enjoying free communion as he would have it. The ministers who were cheated with this delusion in infancy, became the blind and unconscious tools in cheating others. They are cheated into the belief that it is divine, when it is only a palpable *modern hoax;* and being so cheated, they cheat others during all their lives with it, and all this without knowing it to be a cheat. By confiding in this baby sprinkling, they become instrumental in all this world of iniquity, and know it not. They do a great injury to the kingdom of Christ and to the world, and breed and perpetuate divisions, and know it not. They mean to build up the kingdom of Christ, but in reality build up the fold of usurpers, when they say, "I baptize," tell a falsehood, and do not know it: and in this way cheat others by the falsehood, and know it not. When they add, "In the name of Father, Son, and Holy Ghost," if they mean by authority of the great God, they tell another falsehood, and know it not; and thus cheat the congregation by this falsehood, and know it not. If, in the use of these latter words, they mean to say they subject the babe to Father, Son, and Holy Ghost, in that, too, they tell a falsehood, and know it not; for in fact they only subject the child to human rulers in an earthly kingdom, the device of men. They cheat the people, and know it not, when they teach that the child is by that fiction subjected to Christ or baptized. If after this they pray to God, and say to him that it has been done according to his instruction, they tell a falsehood to God, and know it not; and thus cheat the people, aud know it not, by a solemn falsehood uttered in prayer. When they publicly defend this delusion as divine, they defend a false pretender, and know it not, and in this way cheat the people, and know it not. When they encourage the parents to it, they of course cheat the parents, and know it not; and the parents, too, cheat their babes; for while they really mean to give up their children to God, they only in fact bind out their children as slaves to other lords, and thus cheat their children out of the privilege of being devoted to the right Lord, and in the right kingdom; and the child is cheated as he grows up, into a belief that he is in a right kingdom, when in fact he is only in a fold whose constitution was contrived by men, and is ruled by men; and being so cheated, he is also cheated out of the idea of ever joining the right kingdom in the Lord's way after conversion. And so the Lord, the kingdom, and the world, are cheated out of his usefulness; and not only this, but he becomes, in his turn, a cheat to cheat others, and all this without knowing it. And if he becomes a minister, he becomes prepared to cheat thousands of others in the same way, without knowing it is a cheat. Such cheated parents, cheat their children into the belief that they are baptized, when they are not, and all this without knowing that what they say or do is a cheat, and also that it would be wrong to renounce it, when in fact nothing would be more pleasing to Jesus Christ.

All babes who are cheated with this fiction, become prepared to cheat others with it during all their lives. The Christian world are cheated by this delusion out of the gratification that Christian union, under Christ would afford them, by the divisions it produces, and in the jars, the jealousies, and misdirected expenses and efforts it occasions. It cheats a perishing world out of such an infinite and invaluable privilege as a state of union in the Christian world. It cheats benevolent individuals, who have contributed their substance and their efforts to benevolent institutions, out of the privilege of realizing the objects which their expanded and benevolent hearts desire. It cheats the Christian world, by the blinding and darkening influence of such a delusion, out of the privilege of discovering any possible way in which Christians can be united together. It does all this by building up the modern folds of men under managers, whose hearts are full of the love of rule, and are perfectly blinded by delusion, and under systems and constitutions which are the contrivance of men, and of modern origin. It counteracts and obstructs the prevalence of the real kingdom of Christ, under his own organization, where he shall have all the power and all the dominion. Of all the delusions, therefore, which have ever prevailed, the misapplication of the initiating ordinance of Christ and of its substitute to babes, in its tendency to build up popery, and the other rival folds of men, to gratify those who have the love of rule, and who are willing to gratify it at the expense of dividing the kingdom of Christ, and continuing these divisions, and of robbing him of his dominion, and in its tendency to promote and extend delusion, disobedience to God, rebellion in Israel, and its tendency to destroy the usefulness of those who are duped by it after their conversion, and in leading them to build up other lords, and under other constitutions, than the Saviour and his constitution, has doubtless occasioned more real injury to the kingdom of Christ, and thrown greater obstacles in the way of Christian union, and of the conversion of the world, than any device or stratagem of the grand adversary, that was ever contrived.

As those constitutions formed by the Pope, by Henry VIII, by Calvin, and by Wesley, conveyed, in fact, no power, (for the makers had none to convey,) as God is the only source of power in these matters, and not the people, or any rulers, and as those, therefore, who step into power, under them are usurpers, the ordinations derived from such usurpers can not possibly be valid; because a usurper, having no power but what he usurps, conveys none but a usurped power, and this is none at all. It is all done under the wrong constitution, in the wrong fold, and under the wrong rulers. Nothing is done right, except that which is done within the kingdom and government, and constitution, and jurisdiction of Jesus Christ. If the beginning is usurpation, the succession is nothing but usurpation. The very existence of these other folds is rebellion. The builders of them and the rulers have ten thousand times more cause to weep bitterly than Peter had. He never went so far in denying his Lord, as to assume the reins of government, and build up opposing folds, and frame constitutions, usurp the dominion over his people, ordain subalterns, and provide for a succession, and provide to forestall numbers by securing babes by stratagem. Peter's was a sudden emergency, and he immediately repented. But these modern rulers seem to show no disposition to repent.

From the principles laid down, it is evident that every bishop, officer, and ruler, holding on to the reins of government, should immediately cease his usurpation, and repent of his rebellion against the rightful and only Lord over Christians, and cease to perpetuate this treason, as he would meet it at the bar of God. Every subaltern minister, however honest in deriving an office from such usurpation, and under such rebellion, should see and candidly turn away from his mistake, and set an example that is adapted to remove such rebellion, and such a treasonable state of things. The original usurpers had no power but that which was obtained by robbing God; of course they did not have it in fact; consequently they conferred none. Every transaction, so far as the power is derived from such usurpation, is void from the first.

Christians who find themselves subject to usurpers, should immediately withdraw, and subject themselves to him who alone has all the power, and who has bought them with his blood. Ministers under usurpers, if they go on, and attempt to gain proselytes, should be aware that in every step they are defrauding Christ, by attempts to get away his rightful subjects, and to subject them to the usurpers under whom they act. Such ministers are promoting rebellion, and it is an imposition upon those with whom they tamper, and it is perpetuating rebellion against Jesus Christ and against his dominion.

Those who were sprinkled in infancy, were only sprinkled into subjection to these usurpers of dominion. It was false in principle, and a profane use of the words connected with baptism, and the sprinkling was nothing but a stratagem, the device of men. As soon as converted therefore, they should immediately subject themselves to Christ, just as if nothing had been done. If any confide in it as a substitute for circumcision, they should remember that Paul, the three thousand, and the five thousand, were probably all really circumcised, and while the law was in force, too, and yet, as soon as converted, they were all subjected to Christ in baptism. Wherefore, go thou, and do likewise.

For honest Christians to get on board the wrong ship, in these times, is no uncommon occurrence. They should immediately rectify the mistake. It is a disgrace, and dishoner, when apprized of it to remain. But it is an honor to rectify, and get on board the ship of Jesus Christ, where he alone is commander. Under the wrong commander, all is wrong. One error as to church organization, always needs human rulers to take care of it, and these by a stretch of power soon mislead the church and decoy it away from the rightful Captain. No organization can possibly be right, except it be where Christ himself has all the power, and where Christians are subjected exclusively to him. Let each organization be tested by the leading principles we have given, and let each minister test himself, and decide under what government he is building, and whether he derives his authority from Christ, or from usurpers, and whether he is accustomed to baptize into Christ, or rantize into subjection to usurpers.

LETTER XVIII.

PRETENDED SUCCESSION IN OFFICE.

No being in the universe but Jesus Christ, has any right to the dominion and jurisdiction over his kingdom as emanating from the sacred Trinity, the true source of all power.

The covenant of redemption eternally subsisting between the three persons in the Trinity, has acceded this right to reign exclusively and permanently to Jesus Christ. He is placed upon the holy hill, Zion, and he is to reign till all enemies are subdued at his feet. All power in heaven and on earth is given to him from the true fountain. (Matt. xxviii. 18.) The chain of title is unbroken and direct. In matters of religion, the people are not the fountain of power, but God. The tail is not to be the head, nor the head the tail. In civil and political matters the people are the source of power, but in religion God is the only source of power, and he has given it to Christ. Where did the chain of title to power, among these modern rulers over these modern folds, built by men and enlarged by these stratagems begin? In the kingdom of the Pope, the usurpation began with the first founder of popery. In the church of England, it began with Henry VIII. his Parliament, and the wicked bishops. In the Presbyterian kingdom it began in 1641, with Calvin. But Calvin was only a subordinate officer under the Pope—had never gone into the kingdom and jurisdiction of Christ—had never learned nor acquiesced in the principles of that kingdom under Christ: of course never having a membership

M

there, he never had an office from the kingdom of Christ. His office was illegitimate, and yet his is all the office out of which Presbyterianism has grown. As popery was in the revolt, it had no legitimate offices at all, and of course, none to confer. Calvin had none but of them; of course it was none. As the Presbyterians have never returned to the original Fold of Christ, by being baptized into him, they can have no legitimate offices, of course.

A revolt from popery took along all the offices which the Church of England ever had. Wesley's chain of title to an office began in the church of England. But what was his office? merely that of a Priest or deacon.

The chain of title to office then, in his bishops, began with him. Any other person in the world, and just as much out of the jurisdiction of Christ, has just as good a right to start and head a succession of bishops. But as Wesley had no such power to convey, of course his succession of bishops have none. When did God authorize Wesley in 1784, to begin a line of bishops, and to clothe them with such powers? If he had no such authority, and no such powers, his bishops have none, and those who hold offices under them have none. The chain of title to power in the Methodist jurisdiction, began at Wesley, in 1784.

So in the kingdom of free-masonry, the chain of title to power began with Elias Ashmole, in 1717. In the kingdom of Mormonism, at Joe Smith, in 1830.

Suppose Beelzebub had an office in heaven; could he exercise that office in the kingdom of darkness? Were the terms upon which he received that office such, that he might exercise it in heaven a while, then rebel, and revolt, then be thrust down to hell, and still exercise that office in hell? Suppose the founders of popery held offices in the kingdom of Christ, were they empowered to exercise those offices; first in the kingdom of Christ for a while, then to rebel, then to build up a rival and opposing kingdom, and still to exercise those same offices in this rebellious and new formed kingdom? When an officer of an army becomes the head of a mutiny, and revolts, and fights the army whence his power was derived, does he hold his office any longer, as of the original army? Certainly not. As soon as an officer of any description begins to act in a revolted, or another competing kingdom or government, his office from the first, in the nature of things, ceases and becomes void. To pretend to exercise it in another government, or kingdom, or army, or country, or jurisdiction, than that where it was conferred, is perfectly absurd in the nature of things. To turn vulture upon the government which conferred it, and still to exercise it as of that government, is the most absurd thing in nature. It could not be so.

If the first founders of popery had offices under the kingdom of Christ, yet as soon as they began to build up popery —an opposing government—their offices ceased. They usurped and assumed all the power they exercised in the new jurisdiction after that. So also when Henry the VIII. and his bishops revolted from popery, they all lost the offices they held even from the Pope, and from that time forward assumed and usurped all the power they exercised.

Wesley's was no better than such as these revolters from popery had to confer. But as soon as he revolted from them, he lost even the office he received from them; because it was not, in the nature of things, conferred to be exercised in another revolted and opposition fold or kingdom. How does Wesley look, then, in presuming to confer the office of bishop; in establishing a new fold, with nothing but an inferior and spurious office himself? And how do successors look, in holding on to such powers, when their chain of title goes back only to him? And how do minions look, in extending the powers and jurisdictions of such Rulers, and by such stratagems, as we see. When at the reformation those who were thoroughly reformed, and those who were in the kingdom of Christ, were minded to act exactly according to the Bible, and to build exclusively under Christ's jurisdiction, and by gospel baptism into subjection to him, so many of them as were seduced into the observance of the stratagem of baby immersion, in order thus to build up *another* kingdom, part clay, part brass, and part silver,—as soon as they decided to do it, their office, if they held any, ceased at that time, from the nature of things. Because they never received it to build up such other folds. And as soon as Calvin and associates decided to build up an aristocratic or Presbyterian fold, and commenced subjecting the people under four aristocracies, in present Presbyterian form, they lost their office, from the nature of things, which they received in any other fold, if such offices existed. Because it is impossible for an office to be legitimate, out of the jurisdiction which conferred it.

Beelzebub might just as well carry his office from heaven into the kingdom of darkness, and exercise it there, in the nature of the case, as Calvin and associates carry an office received to build up popery with, into a newly contrived and totally different fold, and so much at variance from the purpose for which they were in that jurisdiction originally appointed or ordained. A Justice of the Peace appointed in one county, can not exercise that office in another county. A civil officer in one State, cannot exercise his office in another, or for another purpose, or within another jurisdiction.

The founders of popery, then, lost all the office they possessed as soon as they began to build in another jurisdiction than that of Christ. The bishops and clergy, in the time of Henry the VIII., lost all the offices they held from popery, as soon as they began to build in another, a revolted jurisdiction. And Wesley lost all the office he held, even of the Episcopalians, as soon as he began to build in another, a revolted fold. The Congregationalists lost their offices, if they had any, as soon as they began to build in another kingdom of medley mixture, different from the real kingdom of Christ. And Calvin and associates, lost their office, as derived from popery, whence it came, as soon as they began to build up another, an aristocratic fold, under Calvin. The whole of this *governmental* operation, then, from the first to the last, is *usurpation*, and based on nothing.

What is the chain of title through popery worth, if it could be traced? What was the office the first founders of popery possessed, while under Christ? Not the office of a pope, but merely the office of a *minister*,—a servant. Changing that into the office of pope, or a bishop, in the modern sense, is absurd,—is an usurpation, even if an office could be carried from one jurisdiction to another. The office of pope often was interrupted, and for a great many years at a time, and once was filled by a woman. What is such a popish succession then worth? A chain of succession through the kingdom of darkness up to Beelzebub, would be just as good, and worth just as much. A chain with so many broken links, as exists in the succession in popery, is no chain at all. It begins with antichrist at the head, and continues with antichrist wherever it is found. The chain of succession up to Beelzebub, may be described in the same way, and is just as good.

As no one ever had permission from Christ to establish a popish government, an Episcopal government, a Congregational separate jurisdiction or fold, a Presbyterian aristocratic government, or a Wesleyan government; a chain of succession through popery is good for nothing, if it could be shown. It stops at a usurper, even at the head of popery Where in the Bible is there the least evidence that a succession in office from one man to another, is indispensible. As well might our Presidents, and all our civil officers claim a *jure divino* right to appoint successors in office, as these rulers over Christians claim such a right to appoint successors in office.

Ordination is *appointment*, as the Greek word in the New Testament denotes. This *appointment*, as the original Greek implies, was often made in the apostolic churches, by raising their hands. If a succession from one officer to another is indispensible, none of us have it. It is certain, as we have demonstrated, that it is not found in any of these revolted folds.

It is not necessary. If it was it would have been preserved. If it is preserved, it is only with that succession which begins with John, continues on under Christ and the apostles, continues with the primitive churches, all of which held, as we have demonstrated historically, the same sentiments and principles as those churches which have more recently been *dubbed* as Baptists. The succession continued with those who were driven by popery into the dens and mountains, by persecution, because they adhered to the same principles.

It continues also with the Waldenses, Petrobrusians, and Henricians, who still adhered to the same principles, with the first Christians under the reformation, and with those who in such vast numbers suffered under the cruel bishop Bonner, and associate Episcopal bishops. By a regular succession they can easily be traced down to this time.

But what do we so trace? Not a succession of rulers and usurpers, forming separate jurisdictions, ambitiously assuming the reins of government. But we trace a humble penitent, persecuted, obedient people, acceding all the power, and jurisdiction to Jesus Christ, appointing or ordaining his ministers, according to his word. And such an appointment or ordination, even without tracing any regular line, if performed according to his law, and under his jurisdiction, is valid. When the question about an office, and its validity, is raised, the question is not such as regards a line of succession. This is only a notion of papists, and tyrants, and lawless usurpers. The only question is, Was he appointed under the right jurisdiction, and to act in the right jurisdiction, and in behalf of the legitimate government. If he was appointed in the wrong jurisdiction, to act under an illegitimate government, and for their purposes, it is all void, and just as if nothing had been done.

How then do the Papists, the Episcopal bishops, Calvin and his aristocracies, and Wesley, and his bishops, appear:

as well as the civil governments in usurping such powers over the abused people of Christ,—in insulting heaven by pretending a divine descent, under such circumstances—in building up such rival folds—in dividing the people of God—in treacherously misleading the people of God—in building up such treason, and in using such stratagems for the accomplishment of these nefarious purposes?

These have all built up revolted folds, seized the reins of government, opposed baptism into the jurisdiction of the true King, and managed the people into their own fold, under themselves, and by stratagems, when it is, in fact, treason to build up such folds—when they never were authorized to gather up the people under themselves, when the law is, that all be gathered under Christ—and when from the true fountain of power, Jesus Christ stands forth as the only King in Zion, and nothing is done aright unless it is done under his jurisdiction.

A person who has never been made a member of the kingdom of Christ, and only been made a member in an illegitimate fold, acting under an illegitimate jurisdiction, never been by baptism put into the kingdom of Christ, but always stood at antipodes against it, if he is ordained in such illegitimate jurisdiction, still it is all illegitimate. It is not a succession of immersines, that authorizes one to immerse into the kingdom of Christ. Offices and baptism do not derive their validity from succession, but from jurisdiction. Such a person even immersing within the wrong jurisdiction does not subject the baptized to the jurisdiction of Christ,—an effect always contemplated by Christ. A person who has always remained an alien, with an office from another government, might as well administer the oath of allegiance without even being a member himself, as for one to think he is baptizing into Christ when he has never been introduced into the fold of Christ himself.

There is then no succession of bishops, and no legitimate succession of any kind out of the kingdom of Christ. But on the contrary, from the first revolt from the kingdom of Christ it is nothing but a succession of a revolted state, from the jurisdiction and kingdom of Christ.

Christ has a succession as we have traced. Every minister in gospel order is made such by Him, and recognized by his church, who are under his jurisdiction.

Those who are under the jurisdiction of other rulers, are all wrong from first to last, and will continue so until they return to the jurisdiction of Jesus Christ.

LETTER XIX.

WICKEDNESS OF RULERS.

I was illustrating the prominent principle, that in the kingdom of Christ, he alone has all the power, and showing where this principle clashes with the Christian kingdoms of men. I say *Christian* kingdoms, because so many excellent Christians are by *some* means gathered into them; *kingdoms of men*, because men continued the constitutions, and men govern the people who are gathered. In the kingdom of Christ as it is defined in the scriptures, he alone forms the constitution, and he alone governs the people. Of course kingdoms of the former description, are not the kingdoms of Christ. He, in scripture, recognises that only as his kingdom, where he has all the dominion. In just so far as men rule, he cannot; and it therefore ceases to be his kingdom, when they usurp the dominion, or govern at all according to their constitutions. I have not a word to say about the comparative excellency of Christian character, among the Christians in either of the kingdoms. Very probably there are as devoted and pious Christians in the Christian kingdoms of men, as there are where Christ has the entire dominion, and controls all the external and internal regulations. And we charge no special dark design upon the human rulers. So far as it is possible for men intoxicated with the love of power, and with constant strife for the pre-eminence, and exercising usurped dominion over the rightful subjects of another, and that other the Lord Jesus Christ, to be so far deluded as to be hones in heart, so far we admit they may have honesty of heart, and refer the whole judgment of their hearts, to the Judge of all the earth. Their course is exceedingly unjust *in fact*, however unconscious of it they may be. They interfere with his right to spread his own kingdom exclusively, by his agents, without being obstructed by *them* and their agents, in spreading their dominions. They interfere with his just rights, and with his title to all the people, to all the power, and to all the dominion, and with his right to have all the Christians and ministers employed in building up his kingdom, according to his pattern, exclusively.

The course of these rulers is treason and rebellion, in fact, of the darkest dye. Delusions from infancy up, and familiarity with this treasonable state of things, and these delusions and the defence of them, that is often made in true Roman Catholic deluded style, by minisiers, by parents, and by others, who are as perfectly crazy with them, as the papists were with their delusions, may possibly diminish some part of the guilt in the eye of omniscience. We leave all that to the rightful Judge, and deal only with facts. It is usurpations, rebellions, treasons, frauds, and wrongs, in fact, against Christ as King, and sole King over his people. It is interference, in fact, by these rulers, the maker of these constitutions, and the successors in the usurped dominions, against the unity of his people, under him, and against his right to have all the Christians one under him, and against his right to their united influence with him, and exclusively with him, for the conversion of the world It is fraud, in fact, upon him, upon his kingdom, and upon a perishing world. It is treason, rebellion, and usurpation, in fact, of which we treat. We present Jesus Christ as the only being in the universe, who has the right to exercise any dominion in the kingdom, any control and power, (except that which is expressly required by him to be done in benevolent discipline in his behalf.) We present the rights of his down trodden standard, and oppressed kingdom, as above defined. We present the great advantages of Christian union under him, and the claims of a perishing world to the influence, and useful tendency of such union to their conversion. In view of these we most affectionately remonstrate with these rulers over the Christian kingdoms. We know you are blinded by delusions which have grown with your growth, and strengthened with your strength. You have all that love of power, all that love of party, all that habitual delusion from infancy, all those habits of thinking in a particular deluded channel, which throw difficulties in the way of your reformation, which are natural to those who grow up under such a state of things. And like the sinners who are banded together, ye have the influence of each other to prevent any misgiving in any. And moreover, ye are strengthening the same delusions, and selfish love of party, and delusive habits in your subjects. But after all, he that has the means of knowing the law, and knows it not, or for any reason fails to learn it, is held in civil governments, and doubtless in the divine, equally criminal for transgression, as if he knew it. Ye are guilty of usurpation or treason, and of perpetuating rebellion in fact. And every candid dispassionate person sees it. God sees it, and angels see it. And *ye* will see it in the great day.

We say, and every one knows, that the popish powers, that the church and state establishments, that Henry the eighth, his Parliament, and those bishops, that Calvin, that the Congregational powers, and that Wesley,—never had any permission from the Lord of all power, to form such constitutions, to suit themselves severally, under which to gather up sections of his people, or put themselves into power over them, or to rule them according to those constitutions, or to authorize successors to do it, or to authorize the people of Christ to remain since their time, subject to such governments. The want of permission from the true source of all power, amounts, in fact, in all governments, as a permanent principle of invariable application, to an express prohibition. It is also expressly forbidden in such passages as Rev, xxii. 18, 19; Deut. iv. 2, and 12—37; and Prov. xxx. 6.

If it is right for you to go on with such a state of things, and holding up such dominions of men, then it is wrong in Christians during fifteen hundred years to neglect such a state of things. But if it was right in the Apostles, and primitive and successive Christians, to neglect such a state of things, then it is certainly treason for you and your predecessors to *begin* and *continue* these things from those times, without an express warrant from the true King, and Lord of all power. For the *beginners* of this business to frame such constitutions, and to put themselves thus into power, and to gather up sections of Christ's people, was usurpation and treason, *ab initio*, against the rightful king. Of course it is no less usurpation, and treason, in successors to continue it. And to use such stratagems as we have named, to take such advantages of the delusions of the people, from infancy up, and to ordain subalterns in such a rebellion, who should extend the delusions, decoy the people, and aid you in extending these usurpations, and in building up these kingdoms of men, however honest you and they may be in heart, on account of your delusions, —is, in fact, a treasonable and rebellious course. You fill up the measure of your fathers in the use of these means, by continuing and enlarging these usurpations. Ye are the chilof them that commenced the rebellion, formed the schemes, and foisted themselves into usurped power. Ye are guilty with them in fact, whether ye see it or not, of the blood of all souls that will perish in consequence of this deranged state of Zion.

These *imperiums in imperio* are in competition against

the rightful and exclusive dominion of the Great King in Zion, against the unity of his people, and against the best interests of the world. And ye are now in fact at the head of the whole of this disturbance, whether ye see it or not. If ye hold on, this whole world of iniquity will fall upon you. Ye have not even the excuse that the beginners of this business had, as ye have more light, less seeming necessity from the external state of things, and from such ignorance in the people as then existed. But ye have, in your love for power, and your greediness for the pre-eminence, stretched and spread yourselves far beyond everything which they originally contemplated. And ye shield yourselves under their piety and good name for a cloak Ye bishops, ye rulers of every description, ye petty monarchs, behind the curtains, with your subordinate clergy, and agents, entirely under your control; ye move the whole machinery by chords which vibrate exactly according to your pleasure. Ye control the stratagems. Ye inherit your dominion from those who usurped it. And yourselves continue to exercise a usurped dominion. Ye should repent, and restore it to the only rightful Lord and Saviour without delay. If ye hold on, ye are responsible for all this treason against heaven, for all these stratagems and pious frauds, for all that is done by your subalterns, who are moved in the machinery by your own wills, and for all this world of iniquity. The subalterns are the catspaw in your hand. Ye are unseen by the people while ye move the wires, and build up this rebellion in Israel, and all this by usurped powers.

The people are kind hearted, are deluded by what they see and hear in early life, and feel perfectly unable to unravel this "mystery of iniquity," and feel as if they were deprived of the power to help themselves. They seem to be enslaved to usurpers. The exercise of usurped power over the people of Christ, under the forms of religion, and under a sanctimonius garb, is the very gist and essence of popery. It will be a fearful thing for you who presume to exercise dominion over the people of God, to fall into the hands of the living God. Those clergyman who can consent to act as tools in these dominions of men, and on the principle of passive obedience, and non-resistance under these lords spiritual, exercising such usurped powers against Christ, cannot be supposed to have much manliness of soul if they continue in it, unless we suppose them to be awfully deluded.

An office derived from usurpation is no office at all. Because those who are usurpers have no offices to confer, emanating from any correct principles that relate to original rights. A catalogue of regular successors for a thousand years of such usurpers and rebels against Christ, presents no more authority, *jure divino*, for the continuance of any usurpation than if it proceeded from those who usurped dominion in heaven, and in consequence of this usurpation, were thrust down to the pit. A catalogue of one such succession, is just as good as the catalogue of another. It is the original right emanating from Christ, to act on behalf of Christ and in his kingdom, and here alone from whence any valid commission is derived. And as soon as such power is transferred to a revolted kingdom, under other lords, it becomes null and void. The power of the angels to act in heaven, is not to be exercised in a revolted government. It is preposterous to suppose a succession of popes—those *false Christ's*—and as perfect rebels as the rebel angels, continue a valid office, or that such succession continues it at all, any more than such a succession through the infernal pit would do it. Whoever of us act under the exclusive dominion and jurisdiction of Christ, retain and derive our offices exclusively from that fact, and from the fact that we do not act under other lords, or derive our offices from usurpers.

In the sectarian folds of men, ambition for the pre-eminence extensively prevails and succeeds. But Christ declares it shall not be so in his kingdom. There, whosoever wills to be great, shall, on account of that fact, be least of all and servant of all. Suppose these usurpations of the rightful power of Christ, had began at those times, in heaven, under those self-created authorities, and with such constitutions and stratagems, and the usurpers of the dominion in the newly created folds, had ordained them ministers to act in their behalf, to proselyte against the kingdom of Christ. How would subalterns appear in heaven, deriving their power from such a source and ordained to act in such a business, and in such a revolt, how long would they be endured in heaven? But whatsoever would be wicked there, is wicked here. Whatsoever the Lord would loathe there, he loathes here. Whatsoever there would cause them to be thrust down to hell, will, if done here, cause you to be thrust down to hell, unless you repent. And whatsoever state of things *there* cannot be called the kingdom of Christ, has no more claim to be called the kingdom of Christ here. Whatsoever things there, would be usurpation and rebellion, are equally usurpation and rebellion here.

Suppose the modest Moses after conducting the children

of Israel ten years, had had a pope, a British King, Parliament, and bishops, a Calvin, and a Wesley, in succession, forming just such constitutions as they did, in order to gather up sections of the people, and babes by stratagem, and to take advantage of the delusions of the people, so as to put themselves into power. Suppose they had gathered up more or less of the people, contrived the stratagems, and ordained their subalterns to act in their behalf, in using the stratagems, in proselyting against Moses, and in order to make greater encroachments upon the army of Moses. How contemptibly should we look upon those subalterns, ordained to such a business and continuing it. These facts would be clear to all. 1. These subalterns, so ordained, could not be said to be gathering to Moses, while they were gathering under rival competitors, or to derive their commission from Moses. 2. Those who joined under these other captains, even though they were honest, and though it was by the same initiating ordinance in form, still could not be said to belong to Moses' army, as long as they were under these other captains. 3. Every body could have seen where the blame was in the production of these divisions, viz. chiefly in those who contrived the constitutions, usurped the power and dominion, as bishops, and rulers, under all the various names, and their successors in the usurpation, partly in the tame, passive subalterns, ordained by them to act as tools under such a government, and to extend such rebellion and witchcraft, and to act just as the wires are drawn by the usurpers, partly, though least of all, in the deluded and misguided people, for not awaking from their delusion. As delusion needs great plainness of speech in order to make things plain, I will present still another case. Suppose Jesus Christ had remained on earth in person, and had personally governed his own kingdom till this time. By kingdom of Christ, all along I mean precisely that organization, including king laws, and subjects, that is described in the New Testament. To use it in any other sense is to pervert the truth. Suppose these same men had provided those constitutions at terms, foisted themselves into power, taken the reins of government, provided them subalterns and agents to attend to the stratagems, and to act under their authority in all respects just as we see things move now in seducing people under themselves. Suppose not a word had been said to the people till now in relation to this rebellion, and all things had moved on just as they have; and the people had not even surmised there was any rebellion in building up such mixed kingdoms of Christian babes and others, under human lords, and in thus competing against the kingdom of Christ. Suppose that by this time their delusions and love of party had become so strong, that all concerned in the rebellion had become so much intoxicated with ths love of power, and the love of party, that each and all would be offended if a single doubt were expressed. Suppose the Saviour should then call them all before him, and by a miraculous flash hold up to them all the divine law in the case, all his rights, and the evils of those divisions and usurpations just as they will see them in the great reckoning day, and show who are the guilty ones. In view of all these things, the rights and claims of Christ, of his kingdom, and of a perishing world, and the injuries eight hundred millions of souls so many times over had suffered, by the embarrassments thrown in the way of laboring for their welfare would not these self-called lords, bishops, and rulers, of every description, melt away like wax before his presence, and hide their heads in confusion and despair. Would they not call upon the rocks and mountains to fall upon them, and hide them from him whose power they had usurped. Their guilt, in view of their usurpations, the rebellions they had promoted, and the evils they had produced, would not be a desirable load to bear. And the subalterns under such usurpers of the rights of the Saviour, would not present an enviable appearance.

LETTER XX.

TREASON.

Allegiance is the tie that binds the subject to the rightful sovereign. The King in Zion claims it from every convert. It is a debt of gratitude, and a rule of equity, which can never be forfeited, altered, cancelled, or annihilated, by the subject. The Lord holds all Christians as his own property. and as obliged to be joined with him in his kingdom. As they are "not their own." they are not *capable*, by reason of this allegiance, of contracting themselves away to other lords, in other folds, any more than a wife is capable of contracting herself away to another husband. As the contract would be void should she do it, so it is equally void when they do it. His claims are inalienable, universal, permanent, of universal application, and such as will never be abrogated on his part.

N

All their wanderings, therefore, and seeming contracts to other lords, in other folds, are only so many treasonable abuses of his love; but void in their nature, *ab initio*, because they had no right or power to contract themselves away.

Taking the oath of allegiance to him, (i. e. baptism,) is simply the recognition of this allegiance. Refusal is simply abusing the claims of the Saviour. But their abuse can never cancel our obligations to him, or diminish his claims upon us, or cease to be a guilty, treasonable course.

Treason is defined, in law, either a renunciation of allegiance to rightful sovereign, or a criminal neglect of duty to him. It is the *crimen læsæ majestatis*, (crime of abused majesty,) of the Romans. Hence, Blackstone tells us, that to refuse to take the oath of allegiance to the sovereign, that is, to recognize his just claims, is treason. So also, he says, to dissuade or hinder others from doing it, is treason. So also, to *alter the form*, or change the principles, of that oath, is treason. So also, to be joined with those who alter it,—to aid, abet, or assist, or to be in any way concerned, in such alteration of it, is treason. Of course, to administer such altered oath, or a *corrupt substitute*, is treason. Of course, to administer it to improper persons,—such as are not recognized in the realm as subjects, is treason. To subject such improper persons, or any persons, by such altered or vitiated oath, either ostensibly to the sovereign in full, or partly to the sovereign, and partly to other and rival lords, is treason.

So also, if we know any ill, either done or intended, against our rightful sovereign, or against his realm, if we neglect to hinder it when we can, or neglect to give information, it is treason. Believing these things, as I do, it would be treason in me to forbear the course I have taken. Also any direct attack on the right of the sovereign to rule, and any countenance of such attack in others, as also any and every possible attack upon him, as ruler, is *high treason*,—the greatest crime that can possibly be committed. Hence, Montesquieu tells us, that if the rights of the sovereign are not generally recognized, and if the crime of high treason is not well understood among the subjects, whereby the crime becomes vague and indefinite, the government soon degenerates into arbitrary power; because usurpers will, in such a case, make gradual encroachments upon him,—and anarchy, or the rise of petty governments under others, will, in such case, soon follow.

Hence, the great need of clearly understanding the crime of treason, and of high treason against the king of Zion, in order to prevent such crimes. So also to usurp any part of the power of the rightful sovereign, or to obstruct in any possible way his government, or to build up *imperiums in imperio*, (other governments within the realm,) has always been considered either high treason, or treason, according to the degree of the offence, and the part taken in it. So also, according to Blackstone, to adhere to the king's rivals, or be joined with them, or to aid, comfort, or assist them, while engaged in such a crime, or to be in any way concerned in it, is high treason, or treason against him, according to the part taken. Even to maintain in words, that any other person than the sovereign has any right to the government, or to any part of it; and over the whole or over any part of the subjects, is treason. And so strict is the law, that even the secret thought of doing any of these things, if it could be proven, would be punished as treason.

In worldly matters, the *people* rule. But in religion we are the subjects, exclusively under the King; and therefore we have no right to rule, or make laws at all; and for us to presume to do it, would be treason. It is presuming to do all this, which has produced all the divisions that exist in Christendom. To assume the reins of government, as many have done,—to contrive new folds,—to form new constitutions —to appoint new rulers, and to mislead the subjects into them, is certainly an insult to the rightful King, and is evidently high treason against him. All efforts to increase numbers in such treasonable folds, by stratagem or otherwise, is, of course, high treason.

Even to go wrongfully away from our rightful Sovereign, and to join another, even a lawful government, is felony. And even to refuse to aid the rightful sovereign in any employment within his kingdom, is a high misdemeanor.

Principals in all such crimes are those who do the deeds, and also those who are present, and either counsel, aid, advise, or in any way assist, in them; and also those who refuse to hinder the crime when they can. Accessories are those who are in any way concerned in the offence, or who in the least degree countenance or approve it, either before or after the commission; or who refuse to hinder it as far as possible. And so strict is the civil law, that even to receive, relieve, comfort, or assist, the offender, when so employed, or after it, if we know it, is to be partakers of his guilt, as an accessary, and to expose ourselves to the penalty. Ignorance is the only possible palliation that can be urged in mitigation of all this treason and high treason against the King of Zion.

Accessories are generally punished in the same way, in civil governments, as principals. It is high time, therefore, that the crimes of high treason, and treason, against the King of Zion, be clearly and definitely understood, in order to prevent its frequency, and the degeneracy into arbitrary governments, under other lords, so prevalent at present in Christendom. For Christians and ministers to assume the axiom, that they may contrive and form new folds at pleasure, and may rule and govern Christians as to them seems right, and may enter on a course of competition for numbers against the organization of Christ, is unquestionably high treason against him.

We are placed, therefore, in awfully solemn circumstances, in relation to the kingdom and dominion of Christ, and in relation to the oath of allegiance to him, as well as the part we are to take in relation to these rival kingdoms of men. We cannot plead ignorance any longer as an excuse for being joined with the King's rivals. If we go on under them, it must be hereafter wilful treason. We cannot swerve to the right hand, or to the left, from the laws of our King. Fearful indeed, is the responsibility resting upon the conscience of every Christian, in deciding whether he will support the King in Zion—his kingdom, the oath of allegiance to him, the majesty of his laws, and his constitution; or the usurpers of his power,—their other folds, the corrupted aud vitiated oath of allegiance to them, their laws, and their constitutions; and whether we will hereafter exert our influence, and build under them. We cannot be excused from disclosing his oath of allegiance, which has so long been covered over by these perversions of scripture. If we forbear to do that, we are partakers in the treasonable crime.

The amount of wickedness that accompanies the present treasonable state of the Christian world, against the kingdom and majesty of Christ, in all the several grades of principals and accessories, usurping his power, as it does, building up so many petty folds and dominions, within his realm, and trampling his rights in the dust, as it does, the day of judgment and the blaze of eternity alone will fully unfold. Oh! what an awful amount of treason, of high treason, and of rebellion against the King of Zion, is now in constant and daily progress, and in the open face of day. Those who profess to be his friends, tear down and oppose his real kingdom—trample in the dust the oath of allegiance he has established—build up other and rival kingdoms, according to their own caprice —mislead the people into them, and babes by stratagem, and thus treasonably build up his rivals, the usurpers of his power, and their rival kingdoms. Alas! what a wound to his bleeding cause—what a ruin of souls—what a disgrace to the Christian name—and what a hindrance thus interposed in the way of the conversion of the world.

In this point of view, we cannot but see that pædo-*rantism*, (i. e., the sprinkling of babes,) joining them, as it does, in their helpless state, to these folds of men, and being, as it is, the main subsidary in building them up, and in thus promoting this treasonable state,—must be, and is, a treasonable offence.

Parents and ministers cannot be guilty of baby sprinkling, without being either principals and accessories in this treasonable course. The framers of these treasonable folds *intended* it as a device whereby to build them up. The administration of a corrupted oath of allegiance to improper subjects, to build up *imperiums in imperio*, within the realm, and in a state of rivalship against the realm, must be treason, It is the main channel by which people are misled from infancy, without knowing it, into this treasonable state.

In a retrospective view of the epitome of ecclesiastical history we have given, we cannot but see, that if the imposture of baby immersion could have been prevented, popery could never have been built up, and church and state establishments never could have existed. All those horrors, and all that ruin of souls, during a thousand or more years, and all that long amount of treason against our dear Saviour, would have been prevented. And if baby sprinkling could have been prevented, none of these other modern kingdoms, the devices of men under the usurpers of Christ's power, could ever have been built up. These things are all a state of treason against Christ. This imposition upon parents, and through them upon babes, is the main support of all this treason. To practice it, therefore, is to promote treason, or to be accessary to treason. It tends to prevent the children, when converted, from taking the real oath of allegiance to Christ, and for this reason, also, is treasonable. It prepares the children to lead others into the same treasonable course; and on this account, is treasonable.

It is a cheat. Many falsehoods are uttered in its performance; is a modern hoax—and is treasonable for these reasons, in its nature, and therefore must be a great loathing and abhorrence in the sight of heaven. It enslaves the child to an usurped dominion. The sin of baby sprinkling, therefore, ought to be removed from our land.

The church, according to the Presbyterian confession of faith, consists of "all those that profess religion, *together with their children*, p. 111; of all "those persons, together with their children, who make profession," &c. p. 346; of "professing Christians, with their offspring," p. 347; of "infants descending from parents, either both, or but one of them professing faith in Christ, who are baptized," pp. 287, 121. "Baptism is not to be administered to any who are out of the visible church; but the infants being members, are to be baptized," p. 336. "The sacraments are instituted to put a visible difference between those that belong to the church, and the rest of the world," p. 117. "The visible church is a society of professors and their children," p. 176. "Children are federally holy, and therefore ought to be baptized," p. 430. All this is the device of the original contrivers of that fold, for the sake of securing numbers.

According to the Saybrook Platform, the church consists of professors, and "*their children with them*," p. 82. "Baptism is a sign of ingrafting into Christ," (i. e. into his church,) p. 87. Not only believers, but "the infants of one or both believing parents, can be baptized," and thus ingrafted into Christ, p. 87.

According to the Cambridge Platform, the infant seed of confederate visible believers, are members of the church with their parents, and when grown up are personally under the watch, discipline, and government of the church."

So also those who "owned the government," even though not converted, were to have their babes baptized into the church as church members. See Mather's Magnalia, II. 240. This plan was adopted in 1662, by the messengers and ministers of the churches of Massachusetts. It was also then decided, "In the administration of church power, it belongs to the pastors and other elders of each church," p. 234.

The troubles in Connecticut and Massachusetts about the "church care" of members, made such by sprinkling, in babyhood, caused the General Court of Massachusetts to call a convention at Boston, in 1691, in order to deliberate how to manage and discipline these "*baby members*," and how to keep them distinct from the "*pagans*" (i. e. unsprinkled persons) in their midst. And it was carefully provided by that convention, that such members when grown up, though unconverted, should have their babes baptized (rantized) into subjection to the same "church power" of the clergy. All other persons were denounced as pagans, by the language of that convention. Idem pp. 238—9. A fine system this for monopoly under self created rulers. These principles were adopted by the original contrivers of Congregationalism, so as to secure members, and compete against Episcopalians, and Pesbyterians.

According to the "Brief account of the Associated Presbyteries," the children are to be considered as "included within the covenant, and as belonging to God, and consequently to be baptized," p. 52. "If the children of believers are to be baptized, they must be considered and treated as subjects of the care and *discipline* of the churches to which their parents belong," p. 82. "No other supposition is consistent with the nature and design of baptism,—for nothing is more evident than that this ordinance is the mark of introduction into the church." Therefore "they must be subjects of discipline, according to their age and capacity," p. 82.

According to the Episcopal constitution, the baptism of a babe, makes it a "member of Christ, a child of God, and an inheritor of the kingdom of heaven;" and by it he is received "into Christ's body, the church." Book of Com. Prayer, p. 149.

According to the Methodist Discipline, Art. 17, "The baptism of children is to be retained in the church," and after the Episcopal principles, in general terms.

We have here the devices of the original contrivers of these Pædobaptist sects. All these constitutions are the contrivance of men, and all has been done within three hundred years past. If it be treason against the only rightful Sovereign, for men to form such folds, and to gather and control his subjects within them, then such projects about babes, in order to increase numbers, must be treasonable, of course.

The above quotations show the plans of the original contrivers. Not to carry out those principles, is to rebel against their own governments. If to contrive such folds,—such petty governments within the realm of Christ, is treason,—and if to build them up is treason,—and if to join and help in building them up, is treason, so also if there can be any binding force in such contrivances of men, not to carry them out, while one lives under them, is to commit treason under these contrivances. It is all treason, from first to last. Altering or patching the contrivance, leaves it, after all, a mere human device.

It is evident that no person can avoid the guilt of treason, only by returning to his allegiance to the King of Zion. If other lords have had dominion over us, and if we have lived under their constitutions, it should be so no more. No person can hold up these Christian kingdoms of men, and their human constitutions, these rivals against the kingdom and constitution of Christ, and this deception of baby sprinkling, their main subsidary, without being guilty of treason or high treason against the king in Zion, according to the part taken. No possible plea but that of ignorance that it was treason, can possibly be interposed, in mitigation of guilt before the throne of God.

I write as one who expects soon to die, and to meet what I say in the judgment. My natural feelings have uniformly pleaded to be excused from this task. In my eager pursuit, during more than twenty years, for fundamental principles of Christian union, and meeting with a repulse at every point; and in my efforts afterwards to refute the sermons of an intelligent Baptist minister, which he had, as I thought obtruded upon us, I was ultimately brought in my long train of investigations to this basis. I rebelled against becoming a Baptist, as long as I dared. I arrived, ultimately, at the conclusion that it would be treason in me, against the King in Zion, longer to forbear.

Having been misled from infancy into a treasonable course, and ignorantly, too; not to give information to others now, and take sides against it, would be *treason consciously and intentionally persisted in.* But few, perhaps, had become as familiar with both sides. I felt, therefore, that I could not meet it at the bar of God, should I forbear. It has been to me no small sacrifice, and no small trial. But the consciousness of pleading the cause of the King of Zion, and of meeting his approbation, has by far counterbalanced all these trials.

It was no small mortification to find I had been in such a treasonable course, and done so much injury for so long a time, even while I was enduring so many sacrifices with the honest intention in all things to serve and obey Christ. Yes, my brethren, I feel that my own baby sprinkling, by misleading and deceiving me, has blotted out in a great measure, the usefulness of my life. For it is difficult to tell whether the wrongs it has, by its delusive influence, led me to do, are not full equal to all the good I have done, notwithstanding I have been blessed in my ministry.

Brethren, *every babe* you sprinkle, may have *his* usefulness blotted out by that very transaction. Parents, if you have any "bowels of mercies" upon your children, forbear to mislead them—forbear to deceive them—forbear thus to build up a treasonable state of things against the King of Zion. Ministers, forbear to imbue your hands in this treasonable transaction, as you value your souls, and as you would meet it at the bar of God. I pity the deluded: and my regard for the rising generation, and for the honor of Christ, leads me to urge and beseech the deluded not to delude others. If you continue the delusion, it will be a tremendous thing for you to appear before the judgment seat of Christ.

Some of you have said you would never sprinkle another babe if it were not the custom of the denomination. Has this profane custom more force upon your consciences than the evident rights of Christ? I know some of your consciences trouble you. The conscience of the public is awaking. It will not, in my opinion, be ten years before it will be a shame and a disgrace, in the public estimation, to be guilty of the treasonable, profane crime of baby sprinkling, and its concomitant falsehoods. The pretended arguments for it are a mere sham. Its position on the map of history demonstrates it. Will you continue it? Rather rise, like men; follow truth, and return to the original fold of Christ. Once, a little *ardent spirits* was viewed as no evil. Behold the change! Baby sprinkling will soon be treated by an intelligent public with equal indignation.

LETTER XXI.

CONTRAST.

To show that our views of the real kingdom of Christ are correct, we propose to point out a number of strong points of contrast.

The kingdom of Christ was organized A. D. 29. Then John began to say, " The kingdom of God is come." The kingdom of the Pope, A. D. 606. The church and state ornanizations began in the days of Constantine. The kingdom of the Episcopalians, A. D. 1634. That of the Congregationalists, about the year 1545. The aristocracy of Presbyterianism, Nov. 20, 1541. The Methodist kingdom was never fairly organized with a bishop, till 1784.

In the kingdom of Christ, He is sole monarch. In the jurisdictions of those who seized the reins of government, from the third to the seventh centuries, usurpers and intruders governed. In the fold of the Pope, he was ruler and despot; in the fold of the church of England, the King or Queen, Parliament, and Bishops, were rulers; in the church and state organizations, the civil governments rule; in the Presbyterian fold, Calvin, his aristocracies, and their successors; and in the Methodist fold, Wesley's bishops, and those whom they appoint to officiate under them.

In the kingdom of Christ, the Eternal God appoints the King. "I have set my King upon my holy hill Zion."—"I will give thee the heathen for thine inheritance." But the aspiring and selfish clergy, in the early centuries, seized the reins of government over their folds, by rapacity. The Pope did the like. The civil governments did the like. The king, parliament, and bishops, did the like. Calvin did the like. The Presbyterian aristocracies were authorized by the "famous, learned, godly man, John Calvin," as he styled himself, to rule the Presbyterian fold. Wesley's bishops derived their power to rule, from Wesley. The General Courts in New-England, authorized the clergy, in some measure, to rule there; and the General Courts there, derived their power from the King of England, and the Parliament.

The kingdom of Christ is arranged and contrived by the infinite wisdom of God, as to King, subjects, initiating ordinance, outlines, privileges, discipline, and uniformity. Each of the other folds was contrived by the individuals who formed them, at the times and places specified; and they decided who should rule; what should be the offices over the people; the initiating ordinance from time to time; who should be the subjects; what the privileges, what the outlines, and what the discipline.

The kingdom of Christ accords with the infinite purity, and holy feelings of God. These other folds accords only with the mixed, imperfect, selfish, sectarian, and ambitious feelings of those men who contrived them.

The kingdom of Christ was formed for the best interest of all Christians, to put them in the best possible condition for their own good, and in such a way that they may do the greatest possible amount of good to each other, and to the world, and that God may be glorified. Each of these other folds, formed exclusively for the benefit of the sect, in each case, and those that will consent to go under the rulers, and government of the sect, and for the gratification of those rulers.

The kingdom of Christ was so organized, as to have all the people of Christ one. These folds provide for them to be divided into numberless subdivisons, and each of them is based upon a principle that leads to endless divisons.

The kingdom of Christ provides for Christians to enjoy the greatest possible amount of holy happiness in this world, by all being joined together in one fold under Him. These other folds greatly mar the happiness of Christians; stir up jealousy, selfishness, and sectarian feelings, whereby their happiness is exceedingly diminished, and they are most painfully annoyed by these divisions.

The kingdom of Christ is so arranged, as to enable us to see where the difficulty is, amid all these divisions. But those blinded with the delusions prevalent among the sects, cannot divine where the difficulty is, or wade through the mystery of iniquity, as long as they confide in their delusion.

The kingdom of Christ provides a way whereby all Christians can have free course, and labor for souls, without any hindrance except from a wicked world. But by the building up of these other folds, sectarianism has interwoven itself so extensively into all the affairs of saints, as to present thousands of obstacles in the way of the successful labors of Christians.

The kingdom of Christ presents an easy basis of Christian union. But one bred under the prejudices and delusions of sectarianism, cannot possibly discover any feasible basis of Christian union, as long as he remains under the delusion.

In the kingdom of Christ, God makes the constitution. In the other folds, men make the constitutions.

In the kingdom of Christ, free communion is established on the principle of one fold and one shepherd; free baptism to all converts, and free privileges to all who become members, and a law requiring all converts to go into his fold. By the establishment of these other folds, close communion is made, by shutting up Christians under human beings, and hindering them from being joined together under Christ.

The kingdom of Christ in all respects accords with the will of God; these other folds, in just so far as they differ, are contrary to the will of God.

The kingdom of Christ, therfore, is emphatically legitimate. But these other folds are illegitimate.

The kingdom of Christ affords every possible facility for Christian union. Its motto is, " Take the will of Christ—obey him in all things, and we are one. Admit no jurisdictions, but his; cease to teach for doctrines the commandments of men; lay aside human constitutions, for the sake of adopting that of Christ; dismiss your rulers, and take no ruler but Christ; let those persons only be church members, whom he has authorized, and let them be initiated in the way he has appointed,—and we are all one."

But these other folds present insurmountable barriers in the way of Christian union. They render Christian union impossible. Whenever all things in which they differ from the fold of Christ are laid aside, then they will become the fold of Christ, and of course all will be one. But as long as they continue as they are, either Christ must alter his kingdom, and follow after them for the sake of union, or the divisions will continue. Is it a desirable posture to demand of the Saviour to change the laws of his kingdom, for the sake of uniting our delusions and caprices? If Christ's kingdom stands, (and the gates of hell will never prevail against it,) then until these folds are discontinued, they will perpetuate these divisions.

In the kingdom of Christ there is but one Ruler, and he is a lawful ruler. In all these other folds, the rulers are illegitimate. Certainly no ruler can be lawful that adds to or takes from the regulations of the kingdom of Christ.

The kingdom of Christ is the invention of God. But these other folds are the inventions of men.

The kingdom of Christ is such as to keep itself united and harmonious. Strict obedience to all the laws is all that is necessary to keep every thing in harmonious order. But these other folds have the seeds of discord in every movement from the first separation.

Every law in the kingdom of God is holy, emanating, as it does, from the heart of the infinitely holy God. But the laws of these folds, in just so far as they are human, are unholy, and emanate from the hearts of unholy men. In most cases, they are such as are adapted to carry out their crooked, selfish, and sectarian purposes.

The kingdom of Christ is anti-sectarian. Sectarianism is from *seco*, to cut up. Certainly the kingdom of Christ does not cut itself up, when the King so ardently prayed that they all might be one. It is the rulers of these other folds of men, then, that cut up the Zion of God, and make all the sectarianism that exists.

The kingdom of Christ is adapted to gather all Christians under the exclusive jurisdiction of Christ, and the shadow of his kind wing. These other folds are adapted to hinder a result so desirable; to gather, restrict, and confine, large portions of Christians under rulers, who have usurped the dominion.

The kingdom of Christ is free in its ordinances, and if they were all obeyed by all Christians, would produce free communion among all Christians. To be baptized into the kingdom of Christ, in principle, precisely according to his command, is as free a privilege as the air we breathe. But these other folds restrict and confine Christians, and prejudice them against this course, hinder them from going into the kingdom of Christ, and in this way produce all the close communion there is. Those within the kingdom of Christ cannot repeal the law of that kingdom, requiring baptism in order to membership, nor the law requiring membership in order to privileges. Their hands are tied, and they are helpless. Those, then, who disregard these laws of the kingdom, breed and perpetuate all the divisions that exist, and make all the close communion there is.

The kingdom of Christ, being holy, just, and good, is the only right fold. But these folds of men are contrary to it.

The kingdom of Christ demands that all Christians obey the will of Christ. But the rulers of these folds seduce them away from Christ.

In the kingdom of Christ no laws but his prevail, and are all found in the sacred scriptures. But in the Roman Catholic fold, the laws of the Pope, and the traditions of mother church. In the Episcopal fold, the laws of the Parliament and bishops. In the national churches, the laws of the civil government. In the Presbyterian fold, the laws of Calvin, of the General Assemblies, and subordinate aristocracies. In the Methodist fold, the laws of Wesley his bishops, and the General Conference, and the circuit preachers prevail. If their laws perfectly coincide with the laws of Christ, then they are unnecessary, because we have them in the Bible. But in just so far as they differ, they are an addition to his laws, and expose men to " all the plagues," according to Rev. xxii. 18.

In the kingdom of Christ, he has all the power over the church. But the deceitful and aspiring hearts of these rulers are leading them to encroach upon this prerogative of his, in every way they can, and to worm themselves into the jurisdiction in every way they can. They have already done it so far as to breed all the disturbances that exist

In the kingdom of Christ he is exclusive ruler. These are so full of the love of rule, as to breed these separations for the sake of ruling.

In his kingdom, he forms the constitution. In this mass of sectarianism, men form the constitutions.

In his case, all are required to defend his constitution. With the seceders, the rulers seduce and prejudice the people against his constitution, as much as possible.

In the kingdom of Christ, the principle is recognized, that

O

no human being has the right to *alter an ordinance* of Christ. But in each of these other folds, the ordinance of baptism has been grossly altered. In the earlier periods of those folds, the people believed that rulers had the right to alter the ordinance of baptism. Calvin says, "The church hath granted to herself the privilege of somewhat altering it." The bishops of the church of England uniformly taught, from 1558 down to 1644, and forward, that the rulers had a *right to alter* that ordinance. Calvin's Presbytery, in 1643, in Geneva, and the Westminster Assembly acted on that principle, as well as the British Parliament. It was this belief that led to the alteration.

But in this country the people are too much enlightened to recognize such a principle. Since the ordinance was altered, therefore, some makers of dictionaries have, within a few years past, added this alteration, as a remote definition of baptizo. This fact, and the prevalence of sprinkling for baptism, have led the defenders of late, through delusion, to contend that this is valid baptism, and not an alteration, notwithstanding its unprincipled nature and effect in subjecting people to other rulers than Christ, and in other folds than His, and notwithstanding, in form, it is, in fact, the mere " substitute of a substitute." Although some are so well informed as to reject the principle that the people have the right to alter the ordinances of Christ, still they censure the Baptists severely because they can not conscientiously admit any transaction, however different in form, and unprincipled in its effect, to be baptism; or that people are properly in gospel order, who neglect to join the kingdom of Christ, and on the gospel principle of Christian union.

In the kingdom of Christ, the principle is recognized, that none but Christ has the right to establish regulations for the church, and the terms of Christian union. In these revolted folds, the idea seems very generally to prevail, that *men* may meet together, and form such regulations, and establish such principles as they please, just as if the power to make such regulations, was not in Christ, but in the people, and as if they had the jurisdiction.

In the kingdom of Christ, the principle prevails that all Christians must join where Christ pleases; as he knows better what is for our good, than we possibly can. In the other kingdoms, the principle prevails that Christians may all scatter wherever the leaders of sectarianism can seduce them.

Another important principle in the kingdom of Christ, is, that none but apparent believers, and apparent Christians, are to be admitted as members. In each of these other kingdoms of men, babes are admitted as members, and by stratagems. In the Episcopal church, the child is taught to call his sprinkling "baptism, whereby he was made a child of God, an heir of Christ, and an inheritor of the kingdom of heaven." "The church," according to the Presbyterian Confession of Faith, p. 111, "consists of those who profess religion, together with their children."

In the Methodist Episcopal church, the rule of infant baptism is the same as in the church of England. In all these folds of men, either baptism or the substitute are applied to babes as a stratagem.

It is a principle in the kingdom of Jesus Christ, that *immersion* only is baptism. John immersed in Jordan; and if the word had been translated, it would have read so. Jesus was immersed; and said, "Thus it becometh us (as the Presbyterian Campbell's translation is,) to ratify every ordinance." Christ never speaks of himself in the plural number. By "us," he must mean all those associated with him. Immersed, and immersion; and *in* water, not *with* water, would have been the translation, if these self-created rulers over the people, had not wished, and been determined, to mislead the people away from the kingdom of Jesus Christ, into subjection to themselves. The apostles immersed Christians in water. There were great conveniences for immersion in those times. The Jews were so superstitious in cleansing themselves from ceremonial defilements, that as Maimonides, a Jew, informs us, nearly every family had a convenient place in or near the house for bathing; and if a Jew went to the market, or touched a Gentile, he laid his *tunic*, or cloak aside, and bathed; and if a Gentile touched his couch, or his table, his dishes, or kettle, these were bathed; and their beds, and pillows, and garments, if a Gentile had been near them, were bathed; and in bathing their beds and pillows, he says, they dipped them a second time, where a part was held by the hand or between the thumb and finger, for fear that part would not be cleansed.

These superstitious customs are alluded to, in Mark vii. This state of things among the Jews, removes all difficulties about conveniences for the jailer, and the converts in his house to be *bathed* or *baptized* at midnight; and all difficulties about the baptism, within reasonable time, of so many of the three thousand, on the day of Pentecost, as had not previously been converted and baptized by John. Three thousand "were added." All the new converts were baptized as soon as circumstances permitted. The churches of Collosse and Rome, were *buried* in their baptism, and raised again, from whence an important argument to holiness of life is deduced. (Col. ii. and Rom. vi.) It is preposterous to suppose there was more than "one baptism," established by Christ.

St. Barnabas, of those early times, says, "It is all one whether we are *washed* in the sea, or in a pond; in a fountain or in a river; in standing or in running water. Nor is there any difference between those that John baptized in Jordan, and those that Peter baptized in the Tiber."

John Calvin, on John iii. 23, says: "It may be inferred from this, that baptism was administered by John and by Christ, by plunging the whole body under water." Here we perceive how baptism was performed among the ancients; for they immersed the whole body in water. Mosheim informs us, that during the first centuries, all Christians were buried under water in their baptism. Dr. Chambers' Cyclopædia says, " In the primitive times, this ceremony was performed by immersion, as it is to this day in the oriental churches, according to the original signification of the word." The apostolical constitutions, say, " Immersion is the dying with Christ. Emersion, or the coming from under the water, represents the resurrection." Chrysostom observes, " To be dipped and plunged into the water, and then ato rise out of it, is a symbol," &c. Therefore, Paul calls it a " burial," &c. St. Barnabas says, " We descend into the water full of sins and defilement, and come up out of it," &c. Here we have the only initiating ordinance under Christ in his kingdom. But the initiating ordinance under human rulers, into their folds, which they have organized, is s*prinkling* or *anything*, just as suits the caprice, if the candidate will only forsake Christ, and come under them. Babes they sprinkle into subjection to themselves, so as to make sure of them, when the babes cannot help themselves, and so as to secure them by stratagem, and secure them away from the kingdom of Christ, and in a state of permanent subjection to themselves if possible.

LETTER XXII.

CONTRAST.

It is a prominent law of Christ's kingdom, that all Christians, as soon as converted, subject themselves to the exclusive jurisdiction of Christ. But the leaders of all these sects do all they can to hinder it, and with the sectarian spirit of popery, try to manage them into their own folds.

In the one case, Christ alone makes all the laws. In the other folds, men become legislators, to a great extent.

In the one case, the law is, "no divisions." With the sectarians, the rule is, Hold up all the divisions and sectarianism that exists, and go on with it just as it is.

In the one case, under Christ all Christians are on equality. In the other cases, the few govern the many.

In the one case, it is a law that it is base ingratitude to forsake the kingdom of Christ. In the sects the converse of this is the rule of action.

Under Christ, the rule is, that all things written in the Bible are to remain. With the sects, the rule is, change to suit convenience, and for the interest of the party; and if the rulers so decide, let it be law.

Under Christ, Christian union and the terms are prescribed. But these render Christian union impossible, in the nature of things.

Under Christ, the law is, that as Christ is clothed with infinite knowledge, wisdom, goodness, and benevolence, all Christians should join where HE prescribes. With these, the rule is, to please self; to suffer self to be deluded, and to become subjected in some one of the sects, as if we were our own, and not Christ's.

With Christ the rule is, that church discipline be performed in the kingdom for the interest of Christ, whose will as expressed, is that "not one of these little ones should perish." With these, the discipline, in many cases, is more like suits, summonses, citations, law-suits, contentions, and a war of passions.

With Christ, church discipline is an agency to be done by us in behalf of Christ; to please him, and save his sheep from being lost.

1. Go in Christ's name, with his spirit, with humility, and meekness, and love to Christ, and out of regard to his interest, and because he has commanded,—and tell the offender his fault, with a view to reclaim him, and save him, and with a view to stop when Christ's end is answered. 2. If this fails, take one or two others, for the same purpose. 3. If this fails, tell it to the church. 4. If he will not hear the church, so as to be reclaimed, let him be as an heathen.

How different this, from the superciliousness of a citation

from a session, or from a circuit preacher, and the usual war of passions, where the purpose is to have those in power gratified, and the selfish ends of the sect advanced.

With Christ, the law is, that that the gospel of the kingdom be preached to all the world. With these, the rule is to preach the gospel, and the outlines of the sect, and subjection to rulers conjointly.

The kingdom of Christ is not Protestant. As Jesus Christ and those who have been in his kingdom, and under his exclusive jurisdiction, were never under the Pope, they of course were never in a condition to protest and secede from the pope, on a partial reformation.

"A protest is a solemn dissent on part of the minority, from the acts of the majority, or from those in power. Such a declaration was entered into by certain princes and deputies of imperial towns, against the celebrated decree of the diet of Spires, April 10, 1550. Those who protested were called Protestants."* Afterwards all who separated from the church or see of Rome, who became organized into the several protestant folds, differing from that of the pope, were called Protestants.†

Those who have *always* been against the wickedness of the Pope, from A. D. 29, till now, cannot legitimately be said to enter a protest as a ground of separation.

"The denomination called Baptists, (says Wycoff,) trace their origin from Christ and his apostles. The nature of their tenets is such, as not only to distinguish them from all others, but must necessarily prevent them from acknowledging any ecclesiastical authority on the part of those who differ from them. *No Baptist Church* (says he) *admits the slightest degree of subjection to any spiritual power on earth*, and therefore, *every body* of the kind, is, and *must be*, from the nature of its organization, *perfectly independent* of the Pope. That churches of our order existed at the time of the Reformation, will hardly be denied. Robinson, in his preface to Claude's Essay, while tracing up to the times of the apostles, those whose followers have, of late ages, been known in England as Dissenters, says, 'One branch uniformly denied the baptism of infants—all allowed Christian liberty, and all were enemies to an established hierarchy, reigning over the consciences of their brethren."

The Waldenses were estimated by one of their own writers, at the commencement of the Reformation, at *eight hun-*

---

* Wycoff.   † Robertson's Charles V.

dred thousand. Their opinions upon the subject of baptism, are shown by the following extracts from Jones' Church History:

"Also that baptism by water administered by the church, was of no use to children, because the children, so far from giving assent to it, cried at it." (Book of Sentences of the Inquisition of Toulouse.) "These heretics say, moreover, that this sacrament can be of no use to any but those who seek it with their own mouth and heart. Hence drawing this erroneous conclusion, that baptism can be of no use to infants." *Ermengardi contra Waldensium sectam cap.* 12.

"When Louis XII. sent the Master of Requests, and a Doctor of the Sorbonne to inquire into the character and tenets of the Waldenses, who inhabited a part of Provence, he learned from these commissioners, among other things, that "they observed the ordinance of baptism, according to the primitive church." In the twelfth article of their Confession of Faith, dated A. D. 1120, four hundred and more years before the Reformation, they confine the ordinances of baptism and the Lord's supper to *believers*. At this time, sprinkling was never practised in any part of Christendom, and drenching was only administered to the sick. "They contended, that a Christian church is an assembly of believers,' faithful men,' and that of such a church the Lord Jesus Christ is the Head, and he alone; and that it is governed by his word, and guarded by the Holy Spirit; that it behooves all Christians to walk in fellowship; that the only ordinances Christ hath appointed for the use of his churches, are baptism and the Lord's supper; that they are both symbolical ordinances or signs of holy things, 'visible emblems of invisible blessings,' and that believers only are the proper participants of them." No wonder that Limborch, Professor of Divinity in the University of Amsterdam, declared concerning them and the Albigenses, of whom we have not time now to treat:

"To speak candidly what I think of all the modern sects of Christians, the Dutch Baptists most resemble both the Albigenses, and the Waldenses."

The pastors of some of the churches of this people, in their letter to Œcolampodius, in 1530, say, "We have sustained, *for above these four hundred years*, most severe and cruel persecutions, not without signal marks of Christ's favor, as all the faithful can testify."

A regular succession of Welsh Baptists can be traced from the year 63, down to this time. Multitudes of Baptists have been found in England, from time immemorial. All Christians during the first two centuries, were of the same description. Multitudes in all parts of Europe have been known, in all ages, of the same description.

"Many a careless thinker," continues Wycoff, "classing the Baptists with the Protestants, concludes that they sprung up with the sects that divide Christendom, at the time of the Reformation. But history, and the nature of the case, show, that the classification and the conclusion founded thereon, have as little claim to truth and propriety, as though applied to the Jews. The history of the latter commences in the Old Testament: that of the former, who were first called Christians, at Antioch, from the name of their Master; and afterwards Baptists, from adhering to his ordinance, is dwelt upon at considerable length in the New Testament. Claiming our origin from the Lord Jesus, and his apostles, we cannot submit to be classed with Protestants; who looking to Rome as their common mother, *protest* against their parents proceedings, and call themselves, in consequence, reformed churches, on account of removing part of her errors. We call not our churches *reformed*, because we believe them no better than their predecessors, established by the primitive disciples." Adhering to the simple rules of the original kingdom of Christ, how desirable that we should adorn the doctrine of God our Saviour in all things.

We see here what Sir Isaac Newton means when he says, "The Baptists are the only people who never symbolized with antichrist;" and were "one of the two witnesses of the Apocalypse." The distinguishing principles of Baptists are, to be from the first under the exclusive jurisdiction, laws, and government of Christ; to allow no other rulers over churches but Christ; to change no laws, and to alter nothing; but to obey all, however self denying; to justify no separation from the jurisdiction of Christ; to justify none in remaining in a separate state. If they do it, and establish their own communions, they are accountable for the evils of the division. We cannot fellowship it, or be partakers of it. We pronounce popery to be antichrist—its ministry to have become entirely illegitimate—its principles of pretended ministers, monopolizing the appointing power, as to successors,— a delusion, and a tyrannic principle adapted to rob Christ of the exclusive appointing power, and to recognize and sanction transactions out of the jurisdiction of the King, as if they were legitimate. As the protestants inherit their appointing power solely from such a succession, we pronounce the successions derived, whether in the Congregational, Presbyterian or the Episcopalian limbs, to be no more valid or legitimate than the original succession in popery during 1000 years.

We hold that Christ always retained the appointing power to the ministry, under his own jurisdiction, and that the church and ministry have simply the responsibility of decid- on the evidence that Christ has called the candidate to the ministry—approving and praying over the case. We perfectly repudiate the principle of an officer having the power to appoint successors, and above all things of carrying and monopolizing such a power in a revolt, and a war of a thousand years against the real government.

The Protestants are partially reformed from popery. They have reformed in doctrine, and some of them have put themselves in a posture to promote revivals of religion. The national churches are the exception.

The points in which they still differ from us are,

1. In holding the principle of the appointing power to the ministry to be in that succession, which has descended from popery. As in popery it was nothing, of course, nothing is derived. The pertinacious adherence to this principle, and the pride that holds it up, keeps those churches under the influence of such a ministry, prejudiced against the real principles of the kingdom, and in a state of continued separation from it.

2. In the legality of a separation from the original fold, and the refusal to return.

3. In allowing such a mass of rulers over them, which is but little better than popery itself, and is evidently making the state of the world worse and worse. A spurious class of officers ruling over them, is now doing most of the mischief, prejudicing the people, and hindering their return; and by their papers, is diffusing their sectarianism, and shutting the people away from the truth as far as possible. By adhering to such masses of spurious officers and rulers, the jurisdiction of Christ does not reach them, nor they reach it, but they remain under usurpers.

4. In having their churches so joined together, as that some by the rulers can be managed into a course of controlling the others, whereby the exclusve jurisdiction of Christ, is thus defeated.

5. In their remaining palpably in this alienated state, from the kingdom of Christ, in a line of succession ever since the first separation in the third, fourth, and fifth centuries, and in succession, including popery itself; and even though reformed somewhat, still refusing to return to Christ.

6. In admitting the laws of these spurious rulers to be commingled with those of the Bible, and to become their rules of action.

7. In their refusal to be baptized into the exclusive jurisdiction of Christ, as soon as converted; thus disobeying a positive law of Christ.

8. In their sprinkling of babes; falsely calling it baptism —thereby mocking the sacred Trinity—binding out their babes as slaves to spurious rulers, and hindering them when converted, from going under the exclusive jurisdiction of Christ, according to his command.

9. In suffering their delusions to become so thick upon them, as to believe in the wresting of the scriptures, to favor that mockery upon babes, so as to believe for a moment the Bible favors that modern hoax.

10. In slanderously and falsely reiterating the charge of close communion upon those who do go under the exclusive jurisdiction of Christ, solely because they do not sanction that alienated state away from the jurisdiction of Christ.

Those in the kingdom of Christ, do not make the close communion. Two principles, baptism under Christ's jurisdiction, essential to membership; and membership essential to privileges, are truly obeyed. But it is because they are the laws of Christ. Obedience to these laws does not make close communion.

Here are two points of difference that stand out prominently.

This separation leads to the taking of opposite sides on a number of other prominent principles, as well as these which are put side by side, that all may see them.

In the Kingdom of Christ are the following principles:	In the Sectarian folds, are the following principles:
1. No being in the universe, besides the great Jehovah, shall have liberty to make a fold, or a constitution of a fold, in which to gather the friends of the Saviour.	1. Human beings may build just as many folds, and form just as many constitutions as they please, and shut up all the friends of the Saviour they can.
2. Jesus Christ is to be sole King; exclusively to reign;	2. Human beings may be rulers according to such capricious constitutions which they may choose to form; may create as many rulers as they please; give just such ti-

have all the power, and the exclusive jurisdiction.

3. All legislative, judicial, and executive powers are vested in Christ.

4. All Christians, as soon as converted, must come into the fold, or kingdom of Christ, so as to be one, and enjoy free communion together.

5. The laws are all written in the Bible.

6. As people naturally are estranged, they must become the hearty friends of the King, in order properly to take the oath of allegiance.

7. Baptism is the voluntary subjection of himself, on the part of a believer, to the exclusive jurisdiction of Christ, within his kingdom.

8. This subjection to the exclusive jurisdiction of Christ in his way, is necessary to membership under him, and membership to privileges.

9. To alter either the form of that oath, or the principles of it, so as to recognize *other* jurisdictions, other *rulers*, or

tles as they please; may cause the churches to come under the jurisdiction of men, and so keep them away from Christ.

3. Men may assume legislative, judicial, and executive powers.

4. Christians and converts need not go under the jurisdiction of Christ, within his fold, but may follow their own caprice—go into the folds of men—and thus breed separations and alienations from the jurisdiction of Christ.

5. Other laws, which throw those of the Bible in the shade, may be enacted by men, and are just as good.

6. Conversion is not a necessary pre-requisite, in order to be committed in other folds by the substitute for baptism, whereby they become confined away from the fold of Christ. It may all be done in infancy.

7. Baptism is nothing—is a disgrace—a subject of ridicule—is indecent—is nothing but our substitute—a mere token of national circumcision.

8. The original oath of allegiance to Christ in his kingdom, is not necessary in order to enjoy Christian privileges within the folds of spurious rulers, as contrived by men. They allow persons to have their own way.

9. That oath may be altered by men at pleasure, both as to principle and form, and men may fritter it away to no-

other *folds*, or to build them up with other *subjects*, or with another *oath*,—as it would be in *all* governments, so *here*, is high treason against the King.

10. An opposition line of things, or *imperium in imperio*, or competing folds,—as in all other governments, so here, is high treason.

11. Church discipline is exclusively the exercise of delegated power from the rightful Sovereign; and in manner, form, spirit, and purpose, precisely as he has prescribed; and for his interest, and that of his kingdom.

12. To aid, abet, or assist, in building up any state of things, as in all other governments, so here, is treasonable rebellion; and more heinous, as the character of the King is infinitely more glorious than that of any other king.

13. Jesus Christ alone has the appointing power to the ministry.

14. All divisions must be nipt in the bud.

15. Jesus Christ is recogni-

thing—oppose it—counteract its binding force, and prevent people from taking it—may build up other and competing folds, under other rulers, at pleasure, and thus wash their hands in innocency, and repel with violence the foul charge of treason.

10. Men may establish just as many opposition lines against Christ, as they please, the more the better.

11. Church discipline is a controlling power, emanating from human rulers over the people, to be exercised for the good of the sect, and according to the caprice of the rulers.

12. That which would be rebellion against human governments, is not rebellion against the King of Zion; and the more we build up opposition lines against him, the more we do God service.

13. A succession from popery, through 12 or 1400 hundred years revolt, has the monopoly of the appointing power to the ministry, derived from thence by stealth through revolters from popery, though none in the succession have ever been baptized into the jurisdiction of Christ.

14. Divisions, as they exist are permanently to remain, and to be increased; the lapse of time has legalized them.

15. A spurious set of rulers,

zed as the only fountain of power, in all things.

16. None are within the kingdom of Christ, but those, who, after conversion, are baptized into the exclusive jurisdiction of Christ.

17. Free communion to all Christians, by keeping the avenues into that kingdom free and open to all real Christians.

18. No churches may be *so* joined together, as to control each other at all, in any way which will in the least interfere with the exclusive jurisdiction of Christ, as sole Monarch; and no rulers are ever to be admitted, who will interfere with his exclusive dominion, and jurisdiction, as sole King.

in each organization, is to be recognized as the dignified fountain of all power.

16. All the Jewish nation, and their circumcised children—all the revolters from the third to the seventh century—all of popedom, and the immersed babes—all the national churches under civil rulers, and all the new folds, since 1534, with their babes, are the legitimate, well organized kingdom of Christ.

17. After obstructing the avenues to the real kingdom of Christ, a demand for free communion is to be presented; based upon the principle, that all may do that which is right in their own eyes, and pleasing to themselves, in relation to the oath of allegiance to Christ—may go where they please—may stir up all the prejudices they can, against those who obey Christ—may hinder all they can from going into the kingdom of Christ, and then throw all the blame of the divisions over upon those who adhere to Christ's kingdom.

18. Churches may be so joined together, as to have a national government—a popish government—an Episcopal government—a Presbyterian government—a Wesleyan government, or any other government self-created rulers are disposed to assume, and the jurisdiction of Christ be thus totally discarded.

P

19. All action in relation to the ministry, is under the king, and within his kingdom. Membership, and piety, and qualifications to be judged of by those within the kingdom, according to the rules of Christ are indispensable.	19. All action in relation to the ministry, is within our folds, and derived from our spurious rulers. Membership, with us is all that is requisite. A succession of the appointing power derived from popery, is a good enough authority.

It is easy to see that this world of iniquity, in fact, grows out of the influence of rulers; who blind the people, and prevent their return to the jurisdiction of Christ, through a selfish love of rule, and sectarian feelings.

From infancy up, people become blinded by tradition, delusion, and the whole course of education. The rulers having been blinded in this way, are not conscious of the injury they are doing.

There is every reason to have full confidence in the piety of those who give evidence of it, and to ascribe all the wrong to their delusion.

Whenever the people will leave these usurped jurisdictions, and come under the exclusive jurisdiction of Christ, divisions will cease.

These rulers exercise a power, in a vast many cases, not much inferior to popery itself.

LETTER XXIII.

CONTRAST (*continued.*)

Christ says, "Strait is the gate, and pressed or fenced is the way that leadeth unto life,"—into holy enjoyments, into the spiritual life of the soul. But " wide is the gate, and broad is the way that leads into an absolved or scattered state." These ideas are the true image of the original. This is preceded by intimations of the readiness of God to give the Holy Spirit, and of the advantages of being within the kingdom. This is followed by a caution to "beware of false prophets, coming in sheep's clothing,"—inwardly of an hungry, wolfish spirit. Who dare deny that the Saviour here cautions the world against this sectarian state, and that this was the just aim of this instruction?

Christ prepared a " strait" course under his own jurisdiction, into which all his disciples were baptized, under him as their Leader.

In the third century, a portion of the clergy through the love of power, misled many from it, into another channel. The civil governments soon misled others directly away from Christ. Popery soon misled multitudes away from the fold of Christ. The rulers of the Church of England misled the nation not only away from popery, but also still away from the fold of Christ. The rulers over Presbyterianism misled the people not only away from popery, but still away from the jurisdiction of Christ. The same remarks are true of the leaders of the Lutheran, and all other churches that are shaped differently from the organized kingdom of Christ. Episcopacy in the United States, is a detachment from the church of England; pursuing a course similar to mother Church, with some emendations. And Wesleyan Methodism is a revolt from the church of England. It is under rulers created by Wesley. It is truly an improvement on their condition as Episcopalians. But still the regulations lead the people away from the organized fold of Christ, and keep them under leaders who are as "ravening wolves," in their love of power. All the rulers over churches, usurping the dominion, answers the same description.

The following figure will help to illustrate this state of things. The longitude and departure from the strait course of Jesus Christ, is, in proportion to the influence of human rulers, and the power they presume to exercise—the effect of infant baptism and other stratagems in producing an impenitent church—the general course in which the leaders presume to lead the people—together with all the other causes in tne train. In this, our judgment must be our guide. In all other respects, it presents the view with accuracy as to the time and place, of the origin, and the general course in which the leaders have conducted the people.

The lines in the cut represent the fences. The spaces between represent the general course in which the rulers, severally have led the people.

Let AB from the year 29, to the year 1841, represent the "strait way," fenced on the right hand and on the left, by the principles and laws of the kingdom, and the course, to wit: under the exclusive jurisdiction of Christ—repudiating all human rulers,—all the devices of men,—all innovations—all changes of ordinances,—all substitutions,—all human laws, —all invasions of the outlines of the kingdom,— and carefully observing the original oath of allegiance, as established at

1841.   29

A — Jurisdiction of Christ.
C
D — Ambitious Clergy.
F
E — Popery.
G — Episcopacy.
H 15 L. Presbyterianism. I
J Congreg'n'm. K
L Episcopacy in U. S. M
N 1/3 L. Methodism. O
B

the first by the King, in becoming members after conversion, and not before,—and all retaining the position of scholars or disciples, obeying his will, and utterly refusing to admit intruders to dictate or rule in any thing.

CD then, will represent the course in which the ambitious clergy, who seized the reins of government, from the third to the sixth century, led the people away from the jurisdiction of Christ, establishing infant baptism in 418, in order to build up their own power and jurisdiction, by this stratagem, making new laws, and misdirecting the people by *their* control.

DE will represent the course in which the Popes in succession, misled the people, under their despotic sway, directly away from the course Christ had established. All the national jurisdictions, misled the people, in courses which might be represented by lines nearly parallel.

FG will represent the course in which Henry VIII., who assumed to be Head of the Church, in 1534, his Parliament, and the bishops; in the form of the national church of England,—misdirected the people away from popery, but still away from the direction of the only rightful King in Zion.

HI will represent the course in which the people have been led by the jurisdiction of Presbyterianism, as established by John Calvin, Nov. 20, 1541. Its several offices, he enacted; such as Ruling Elders, Bishops,—its enlarged and extended powers—its Sessions, Presbyteries, Synods, and General Assemblies,—its courts, and litigious bodies—its vexatious lawsuits, and doctrine of endless appeals,—its legislative, judicial, and executive powers,—its law-suits, as a substitute for Gospel discipline, and the establishment of it as a national religion in Scotland, in 1560, as a matter of course, from the nature of things, would still mislead the people under its control, away from the exclusive jurisdiction of Christ, and from the course which he pointed out,—being that of scholars exclusively under Him, as their King and Leader.

JK will represent Congregationalism, first started in 1590. In Europe, this community were called Independents. They were a detachment from Presbyterians, and from others. They have scarcely flourished except in New England. The establishment of them by law in Massachusetts and Connecticut, the jurisdiction over them by the civil governments in New England, and the making of church members while babes by sprinkling, and the cruel persecutions of all others,—of course, misled the people still away from the jurisdiction of Christ.

LM will represent the course in which the Episcopal rulers in the United States, have led those people who were under their jurisdiction, much improved from the national church —relying mostly on the sprinkling stratagem upon babes, for the enlargement of their jurisdiction, and the increase of numbers.

NO will represent the course which Wesley's bishops, and subordinate clergy have led the people, who through the stratagem of the class paper, and of infant sprinkling, and other means have been subjected to their jurisdiction. As all Wesley's movements were substantially under the jurisdiction of the church of England, till 1784, the time Wesley created a bishop, (as he pretended,) I give that period as the *real* origin of Methodism, especially its government.

I stop here to remark, once more, that I do not blame the people who have been so misled away from the jurisdiction of the King, by the rulers. I know not as they could have avoided the course, or done better under the circumstances in which they were from time to time placed. Nor do I blame the rulers in gross. Many of them, being deluded, no doubt, have been, and are still, actuated by honest motives, Nor do I dash away all these several folds, so far as to say, they have been of no use. Many of them, certainly, were useful for the times. Presbyterianism, Congregationalism, and Wesleyanism, were then exceedingly useful, and perhaps the best that could be in those times, considering the comparative darkness, the general ignorance concerning the rights of conscience, and the general impression that every church must have rulers who might make laws, and change ordinances, and that the people must obey them. These all might have served as school-masters, to lead the people back from popery, into the real kingdom of Christ.

But what I *do* say, is, that times have changed, the rights of conscience are more generally understood, and the rights of Jesus Christ, as King in his real kingdom, are seen now, and these separate folds, now, are worse than useless. Their utility has gone by. The darkness which made them necessary is past, and the true light shines. The people, now, are qualified to guide themselves according to the real laws of the real kingdom. The millenium can never take place till the regulations of the real kingdom prevail. And efforts in heathen lands can never be very useful, except in the shape of the real kingdom of Christ. It is cruelty to the heathen, to carry this sectarianism amongst them.

And I do say, that to give up attachments to former views, usages of youth, and denominational rules, for the sake of moulding ourselves into subordination to the real rules and regulations of the real kingdom of Christ, is a sacrifice which every minister, and every Christian, who has fallen into those folds, is now called upon to make. The value of union among Christians, the evils of disunion, and the palpable rights of Jesus Christ the King; as well as the tendency of it on a perishing world, loudly call on all to take that course, and to magnanimously make the sacrifice, in their own predilection, and private feelings, which are necessary in order to so glorious a result. We cannot longer refuse without sinning against light and against knowledge.

We do remonstrate, affectionately, with those who through the love of party, seem determined to sustain this sectarianism, and perpetuate these evils. It certainly must give way. The emulation, therefore, should be, who will be first to give way, and let the kingdom of Christ come, in lieu of these dominions of men. Pertinacious adherence to a sect, may keep off the happy results some longer, but cannot prevent that result from ultimately occurring. What is the sacrifice of giving up early predilections, usages, and biasses, delusions, mistakes, and errors, when contrasted with the advantages of Christian union—of having the real kingdom of Christ prevail—of setting a right example, and of united effort on a perishing world? The price is small for objects so noble. All changes by some are reprobated as if we must certainly be right in infancy. But nothing is more honorable than to change, if, in doing it, we relinquish error, and yield to divine truth. Covenant engagements, with some, are an obstacle. But covenants, if they hold us to a wrong course, or prevent us from a right course before God, or if they were blindly made by us in infancy, cannot be binding; because we had no right so to bind or restrict ourselves, or others to bind us; and such an obligation is void, *ab initio*, on the same principles as masonic obligations, blindly taken, were void. Things that are wrong, remain wrong, and obligating ourselves to them, cannot make them right, or justify us in such obligation, or in carrying it out. To bind ourselves to a wrong, may be blindly, and therefore, honestly done. But when we see the wrong, to fulfil that obligation, when we have the power of rescinding, is criminal. Firmness in cleaving to divine truth as fast as we learn it, is a noble trait of character. But to adhere to the wrong, because we have always been so, and because of a pride in being consistent with our former selves, is base stubbornness.

To show where the truth lies, I would reason on the first

principles of government. On the above figure, then, it is clear that an office conferred under the jurisdiction of Christ, AB, if the officer leaves, and goes into another jurisdiction, CD, he cannot hold his office as legitimate in CD. As well might an office conferred in one kingdom, be legitimate when carried into another. It is impossible, in the nature of things, to get a legitimate office, into the illegitimate jurisdiction. Christ has never made provision for carrying an office out of of his own jurisdiction, into that, or any other, and therefore, it cannot be carried. So also if there were a legitimate office in CD, still if the person goes into the jurisdiction DE, he cannot carry his office. So also if an office were legitimate under the popish jurisdiction, DE, yet as it was conferred for the exclusive purposes of popery, it could not, legitimately, be carried into the revolted folds, FG, and HI, the Episcopalian, and the Presbyterian. Those bishops, therefore, when they left the popish fold, held no offices. And Calvin, when he left the popish fold, held no office. It is not only preposterous to suppose any office was legitimate in popery; but it is preposterous even supposing it was legitimate to think it could legitimately be carried into the revolted Episcopalian, and the Presbyterian folds. As well might an office conferred in Great Britain, be brought to the United States, and be legitimate here. Of course no legitimate offices can be derived from the Presbyterian folds, into the Congregational, Episcopalian, and the Methodist Episcopal folds, the sprouts of those others.

The people, certainly, cannot make a Christian office legitimate. The idea has ever been scouted by Episcopalians, and Presbyterians, that the people can ordain or confer a Christian office. The people do not hold the jurisdiction here, as they do in civil matters, of course they cannot make the offices. Who then does hold the jurisdiction and offices within his gift? None but Christ. And He of course confers all the offices exclusively under his own jurisdiction, as his law requires all converts to come there. Every thing therefore, becomes entirely illegitimate out of his jurisdiction. The people have the jurisdiction over their worldly matters. But Christ, as King, holds firmly the jurisdiction over all matters of religion. The tail must not become the head, nor the head be treated as if it were the tail. The scholar must not govern the teacher.

As Christ declared there must be but "one fold, and one shepherd," of course the building of other folds, is illegitimate, because forbidden in that principle, and because they of course, cannot exist without an illegitimate jurisdiction, and illegitimate rulers. Consequently, every thing within them is illegitimate from the nature of the case.

Again, Christ never conferred offices under his own jurisdiction, AB, in such a sense as to give those officers the power of appointing all their own successors, even there. For this would be conferring the jurisdiction over offices upon men, which would be just as dangerous as to confer the whole jurisdiction of his church upon men at once. The passage, "Those things which thou hast heard of me, before many witnesses, the same commit thou to others also;" alludes to "WORDS," not to offices, as some have vainly supposed. Preaching and spreading the gospel is the duty enforced. But the right of calling men to the ministry, and of qualifying them, he has reserved to himself. The church and the ministry, as conservators, are to act on his behalf, in every case, and to decide on the evidence that he has so called the candidate to the work, and in doing it, to pray over the case. The imposition of hands does not confer the office; this is nothing but an expression of friendly feeling. The decision of the church, and of brethren in the ministry, does not confer the office. It simply decides first of all that Christ has called the person to officiate; they then proceed to set him apart, acting as Christ's agents. The whole jurisdiction, and calling, and ordination, is Christ's. We are merely his servants like scholars in a school, acting under the guidance of the Great Teacher. To suppose that *we* may run away with the jurisdiction, is preposterous. To claim the right even there, of appointing all the officers in the succession, would be gross usurpation, and an invasion of the prerogative of Christ. To claim the right, therefore, of carrying an office out of his jurisdiction, AB, into the usurped jurisdiction, CD, and there to appoint successors, is a still more gross usurpation, and invasion of his rights. As CD is illegitimate, it would be treason to do it. It is as if an officer under a government should presume to carry his office where a revolt from that government had established another jurisdiction, and then claim the right of appointing a succession of officers. The whole of it is entirely contrary to the first principles of government, and a violation of all legislative rights. On what principle, then, can the power of appointing such a succession of officers be carried into the revolt DE, under the Pope, and a line of succession be, in any possible sense, legitimate? And on what principle can such an appointing power, after popery has lasted nine hundred years, be taken thence, and be exercised legitimately, in the Episcopal course, FG. Moreover, officers, holding any sort of power in DE, received it, if at all, to be exercised there. Of course, they could not legitimately carry it into HI, the Presbyterian revolt. Where did Calvin then, get his power to appoint his officers, and where did Wesley get his? Officers have not the power of appointing successors, even under the jurisdiction of Christ. Of course, no officer can legitimately appoint such successors in a revolt. It would be claiming greater powers in a revolt, than exist under the rightful jurisdiction. Of course, no such appointing power can exist in JK, LM, and NO,—the Congregational, the Episcopalian, and the Methodist Episcopal course.

And further, no person was ever recognized as being even a member in the church or kingdom of Christ, until after they were converted, and until they were baptized into the exclusive jurisdiction of Christ. Though all the men in these other movements are Christians, still as they have never been so baptized, they are not yet even members. Every thing must be illegitimate, also, for this reason. Can offices be legitimate, where even a regular membership does not exist?

From all this, it results, of course, that the humble office of a teacher under Christ's jurisdiction, AB, cannot be carried into the illegitimate jurisdiction CD, and then be enlarged to the extent in which they usurped power in those times, and be a legitimate office, in that enlarged capacity. It cannot, then be carried into the illegitimate jurisdiction DE, and then be enlarged to the despotic powers of a Pope, and of Bishops under him, and be legitimate in those enlargements. It could not be legitimate, and be carried into FG,—the course of the church of England, with the retention of those enlarged powers. It could not be legitimate, in the Presbyterian course HI with all the changes, enlargements, and new shapes of its exercise, and for new and totally different purposes from any thing which had ever preceded it. Of course, in the person of Wesley, it could not be legitimate. And if it were, his conferring of a greater office than he even supposed himself possessed, of course, could not be legitimate. The same remarks apply every where, in the whole revolt.

There is nothing legitimate out of the jurisdiction of Christ. Of course, the mutual covenants to sustain the revolt, in each and every case, are illegitimate covenants; and to carry them out, and fulfil them must be wicked and awful sin against the King in Zion. The whole was also illegitimate, because it was an illegitimate succession, from Christ's fold from first to last. Christ blessed them while their minds were dark, and they knew not what they did, because they were honest, and meant no harm, as far as circumstances admitted. But if thay continue to sin against light and knowledge, they cannot expect to be blessed in it in future.

Sectarianism is in this whole succession, from first to last; comprehending all the several courses in which the leaders have led the people, and all the several acts from first to last, beginning on the map at C.

Close communion began at the same place. There was nothing of it before. In the fold AB, the humiliating ordinance of immersion, " the *test* of a good conscience," whereby the believer subjects himself to the exclusive jurisdiction of Christ, has, from the first been necessary in order to membership, and membership essential in order to privileges. This course, down to C, made no close communion. The continuance down to B, of course, has made none. For these principles which did not make it from A to C, could not make it from C to B. Of course, the revolt at C, and the whole movement away from the jurisdiction of Christ, in establishing a separate communion, has done it. It is all the result of misleading Christians into the wrong course. and thus establishing separate communions. "Open communion," as it is vulgarly, but falsely called, is fellowshiping this whole revolt, from the jurisdiction of Christ, from C to the utmost extremity. It is the fellowshiping of all these separate communions. Close communion, as it is vulgarly but falsely called, in the real organization of Christ, is nothing but adherence to the original principles of the kingdom; namely baptism essential to membership, and membership essential to privileges; it is, therefore no close communion at all. There is no close communion in this; it is false and slanderous to charge it over upon such. Non-intercourse with illegitimate separations, is not close communion. It is those who bring the charge, who make all the close communion there is, or even has been. Disfellowshiping these separate jurisdictions and these separate movements, and non-intercourse with it, is the whole of our offending, for which we have been slandered, held up to odium, and abused in public and private. Where the fault is, every candid person can see, and in the great reckoning day it will be seen by all.

It is mistaken views in those who have thus abused us, and therefore, we forgive it, and only ask in future that all will do us justice, in our honest adherence to the fundamental principles of the kingdom of Christ, from first to last.

As this whole succession from the first is illegitimate, of

course, all the alterations of ordinances, by the rulers, are illegitimate. The substitutes, of course, are nothing. Honest Christians, however, immersed there after conversion, can mend all the deficiency there is in their baptism, by returning to the jurisdiction of Christ, and thus leaving an illegitimate jurisdiction. Christians in these folds, need bring no letters of commendation from these illegitimate folds, to the fold of Christ. Yet, if perfectly convenient, a certificate of good character does no hurt. Where the church know the person, it does no good, except as a matter of courtesy to the feelings of the church that is left. Under the jurisdiction of Christ, no such letters of commendation are by any means essential. The Christian may be taken up precisely as a new convert, and be received in all respects as such.

LETTER XXIV.

PERSECUTIONS ENFORCING STRATAGEMS ON HELPLESS BABES.

The immersion of babes was first enforced, for the sake of building up an illegitimate government, in the year 418. It was soon enforced by Popery, for a similar purpose—soon by Charlemagne, and other earthly governments. It continued to be enforced by all illegitimate governmen, over nominal Christians, till substitutes were adopted. It was enforced by the church of England, and by Presbyterianism, when they first commenced.

Pouring water upon babes began to be enforced in the two latter organizations, after 1556.

The sprinkling of babes first began to be enforced, as such, about 1643, 1644, and 1648, by the Presbyterian, Episcopal, and the New-England Congregational governments. It was about an hundred years later, before it was enforced in Germany.

The *enforcements* by which these stratagems have been propagated, require a distinct Letter.

The Donatists were bitterly persecuted, soon after the stratagem was first enforced, because of their refusal to obey the dictation of illegitimate rulers. Austin says of them, "Ye permit babes to be saved without baptism. These things are very perverse, and against the catholic faith." It was this same Austin who had procured that law to be enacted, in 418.

In 590, a curse was denounced, in Spain, upon the opposers of infant baptism; and uniformity in it was enforced by the arm of civil power.

In 596, Austin, the monk, was sent among the pure church in England, to bring them over to the same practice. He gathered a council of them, and first proposed all the popish ceremonies to them. They refused to adopt them. Then said he, baptize babes, keep Easter, and preach as I have exhorted you. But these they refused. Then said he, I will bring an army upon you, and destroy you. Accordingly he did it. In Bangor, (England) were more than 2,000 devoted Christians in a college, and hundreds of faithful preachers were sent forth from it every year. Because they refused infant baptism, and other popish practices, they were all put to the sword, and their buildings were burnt.

In 610, the baptism of babes being held in low repute, it was ordained and decreed, that all babes must be baptized, as being necessary to salvation, and upon penalty of damnation, as against the parents.

In A. D. 700, a King of the West Saxons prescribed a penalty, in money, upon the parents for the omission of infant baptism even for the space of thirty days from their birth.

Charlemagne prescribed a penalty of 120 shillings in certain cases, 60 schillings in other cases, and 30 shillings in other cases for every omission of the baptism of a babe, for the space of a year; to be collected by distress of goods, and sales.

In 1050, a Pope passed another decree enforcing infant baptism.

In 1070, Pope Gregory passed a law that those children whose parents were dead, absent, or unknown, should be baptized into popery.

Deytingius tells us, about that time, "If parents will not have their children baptized, they are, by the authority of the magistrate, taken by force from their parents, and baptized. But when baptized, they are returned to their parents.

In 1022, fourteen persons were burnt to death, at Lyons, for opposing infant baptism.

In the time of Henry VIII., a large number of persons in England, were put to death for opposing infant baptism.

From the first establishment of the Episcopal religion in England, down to this time, the penalty for omitting infant baptism, is, that such persons when grown up, shall be treat ed as outlaws, they shall not inherit any estates, or be capable of holding them. Their marriages shall not be recognized as legal; their children shall be deemed as illegitimate; and shall be deprived of the benefit of the poor laws.

In 1095, a number of persons at Pepuza, in Italy, were condemned, and suffered death, because they opposed infant baptism.

Peter de Bruys, a zealous reformer, after laboring faithfully for twenty years, in promoting revivals, in gathering churches, and in promoting the real kingdom and jurisdiction of Jesus Christ, was in 1130, at St. Giles', burnt to death for opposing infant baptism.

Henry, another zealous reformer, who succeeded him, after whom were named the Henricians, was in 1148, imprisoned till he died, on account of his opposition to infant baptism.

During this century, the Waldenses and Albigenses were most cruelly persecuted, because of their opposition to infant baptism.

In 1179, the Pope *anathematized* the Waldenses, because they opposed infant baptism.

In 1181, the Albigenses were "DAMNED" by the Pope, for opposing infant baptism.

In 1182, many Waldenses in Flanders, suffered death because they opposed infant baptism.

In 1199, about two hundred thousand of the Albigenses were inhumanly butchered, because of this opposition to infant baptism.

In the year 1200, many Waldenses, in Germany, were inhumanly burnt to death, because they would not practice infant baptism, but opposed it.

In 1230, many of the Waldenses in Tryers, for the same reason.

In 1232, nineteen persons at Thoulouse, were inhumanly burnt to death, because they opposed infant baptism. Four converts, at Marseilles, were, the same year, burnt to death, for the same reason.

At Zickrixsee, in 1336, three men, and one woman, were seized, imprisoned, put upon the rack, and tortured, till the blood gushed out of their mouths, and then they were beheaded, and their bodies were publicly burnt, because they rejected infant baptism.

At Crena, in Austria, in 1315, many Waldenses were burnt to death, for opposing infant baptism.

In 1522, at Zurich, an edict was passed against the Baptists. A penalty of two guilders was set upon all who opposed infant baptism.

In 1527, one Skooner, a Baptist minister, was beheaded. Seventy others were put to death at the same time, for *speaking* against infant baptism.

In 1529, fourteen persons were put to death, for being what was called by civil governments, re-baptized; i. e. baptized according to the command of Christ, despite the stratagem played off upon them in infancy.

At Zurich, in 1526, Felix Mans, a faithful Baptist minister, was publicly drowned because he disapproved of infant baptism.

About the same time, another Baptist minister was imprisoned, condemned, and burnt to death without the town, for the same reason.

In 1528, at Vienna, the learned Pacimontanus, was publicly burnt to death, for preaching and writing against infant baptism.

In 1532, at Harlaem, a woman for being baptized by a Baptist minister, was, by a civil process thrown into the lake and drowned. Her husband and two others were publicly burnt to death, at the Hague, the same year, for the same offence against the government.

In 1533, at Leanwarden, one Snyder was publicly beheaded for being baptized by a Baptist minister.

In 1535, three men and two women were put to death for being baptized by a Baptist minister. The men were beheaded, and the women were drowned in the sea, with great stones fastened to their necks.

In 1530, an edict was passed at Zurich, making it death for any one to be baptized, who had been christened in infancy.

In this year, in Holland, the harboring of Baptist ministers was forbidden, and a reward of twelve guilders was offered for every Baptist minister that should be apprehended.

In 1539, a man, and his wife, and their son, were put to death, for being baptized by such a minister.

In 1536, John Calvin informed the civil magistrate against Servetus, as an opposer of infant baptism; for which he (Servetus) was arrested, condemned, and burnt on a slow fire of green wood. It is true, Calvin also accused him of being a Unitarian. But the civil law had nothing to do with this point. It was his opposition to infant baptism which procured his death, according to law.

In 1535, Charles V. passed a decree, dated June 10th, against the Ana-baptist and Waldensian Christians, commanding them to refrain from those practices, (immersing believers, and discarding infant baptism,) and to refrain from preaching or publishing the same, under the penalty of the forfeiture of *life and goods, without mercy.* The men to be burnt, the women to be drowned. And all that conceal, and harbor, or neglect to prosecute the law against them, to suffer the same penalty. Informants were to have one third part of the estates. In Queen Mary's time, thousands of Baptists were put to death, as such.

In 1556, Philip the second, King of Spain, renewed and extended this edict, from which time it continued in force for about 45 years; during which period thousands were burnt to death, or drowned.

George Wippe, at Dort, on the 4th Aug. 1558, for having presumed to be re-baptized; thereby reproaching infant baptism, was " condemned, to the honor of God, and for an example to others, to be drowned in a barrel, after which his body was to be publicly hanged, and his estate to be forfeited to the Town's Treasury."

In 1560, eighteen baptized persons were put to death at Antwerp.

On May 2, 1648, the cruel edict, or gag-law was passed by Parliament; requiring permanent imprisonment, if a person should *speak* against infant sprinkling. Soon after, all Baptists were required to depart out of the realm.

In France, within the space of thirty years, 39 Princes, 148 Counts, 234 Barons, 147,518 Gentlemen, and 760,000 persons of a lower rank,—making in all *nine hundred and seven thousand, nine hundred and thirty-nine persons*, in that short space, were put to death as heretics.

In 1648, a confession of faith, containing *sprinkling* as baptism; and requiring infant sprinkling, under the false name of "*infant baptism*," was established by law in Massachusetts, and in Connecticut. Congregationalism, it seems, first came into existence about 1590.

To show the spirit and design of the civil governments, in establishing it by law, we adduce the following persecutions against those who defended the exclusive jurisdiction of Christ, and the initiating ordinance under him, both before and after the establishment. The spirit in England, and in New-England, seemed to be very much the same. For in 1659, a Mr. Edwards, Lecturer in Christ-church, directed magistrates how to act in order to establish Presbyterianism, without liberty of conscience to any others. He advises the magistrates to execute some exemplary punishment upon all dippers. And if any, after being dipped, fall sick and die, the dippers should be indicted under the statute against *killing* the King's subjects, and be prosecuted accordingly. The Parliament should take some *severe cou se* with all the dippers, as they had done at Zurich, i. e. put them to death, and confiscate their goods.

In 1639, six Baptists, for attempting to organize a Baptist church, at Weymouth, Massachusetts, were arrested and tried before the General Court at Boston, on March 13, for an attempt to worship God contrary to law, and were fined 67 dollars, down to a less sum each.

On Nov. 13, 1644, the following law was passed, by the Legislature of Massachusetts, viz: "It is ordered and agreed, that if any person within this State, shall either openly condemn, or oppose the baptizing (rantizing) of infants, or go about secretly to seduce others from the approbation or use thereof, or shall purposely depart the congregation, at its administration; every such person shall be sentenced to *banishment.*"

On Oct. 17, 1643, four persons were tried by the General Court, for being Baptists, and were sentenced to be shut up in separate prisons,—to be there set to work, and to wear such *bolts and irons* as may hinder their escape. They were kept in prison till March 7, 1644, when they were sentenced by the General Court to banishment.

In 1644, at Hingham, Massachusetts, a man, for turning Baptist, and refusing to have his babe sprinkled, was, by the General Court, tied up to a whipping post, and publicly whipped upon his naked back.

In July, 1651, three Baptist ministers, viz. Clark, Holmes, and Moody, were arrested at Lynn, Massachusetts, on the Sabbath, while Clark was preaching, and were imprisoned in Boston, until they were tried. At the trial, Clark was fined a hundred dollars for preaching, Holmes sixty-six dollars and sixty-seven cents, for aiding, and Moody sixteen dollars and sixty-seven cents, for attending. They were sentenced to be publicly whipt, if payment were not made. Holmes refused to suffer his friends to pay the fine, and so he was publicly whipped at Boston. Two spectators, showing signs of sympathy at his bloody whipping, were suspected of entertaining Baptist sentiments, were arrested, tried, and condemned, and sentenced to pay twenty shillings each, and to be publicly whipped themselves, for their sympathy.

In 1655, nine persons, in Boston, were arrested, imprisoned, and sentenced to public whipping, and other sufferings, for denying infant baptism, and attempting to form a Baptist church in Boston, according to the organization of Christ. Three of these were banished, by sentence of the Court. But refusing to leave, they were imprisoned again. The Baptists obtained a House to worship in, and the General Court passed a law closing the doors, and inhibiting the holding of any meeting in the same.

Between 1727, and 1733, 28 Baptists were imprisoned at Bristol, Massachusetts, for refusing to pay taxes for the support of Pædorantist ministers.

In 1751, Rev. Mr. Moulton, for preaching Baptist sentiments, was arrested at Sturbridge, Mass. and imprisoned, and finally adjudged to be a vagrant and a vagabond, and as such sentenced to banishment. His deacon, and five brethren were imprisoned in Worcester Jail, for attending his ministry. In Ashfield, Mass. in 1770, 400 acres of land, belonging to Baptist members, were sold according to law, to pay taxes for the support of Pædorantist ministers.

In October, 1656, it was enacted by the General Court in Connecticut, "That no town within this jurisdiction, shall entertain any Quakers, Ranters, (a name of opprobrium given to Baptists,) Adamites, or such like notorious heretics, nor suffer them to continue above fourteen days, upon the penalty of five pounds.

In 1658, the General Court sitting at New Haven, passed a new law, increasing the penalties, and prohibiting the common people from *all conversation* with them, under the penalty of five pounds. ($16 67.) It was also enacted at that time, "that if any person, not being a lawfully allowed minister, shall pretend to profane the holy sacrements, (baptism and the Lord's supper,) by administering, or making a show of administering them, to any persons whatsoever, and being thereof convicted before a County Court, where the offence was committed, shall incur the penalty of ten pounds, ($33,34) and for every such offence suffer corporeal punishment by whipping, not exceeding thirty stripes for each offence." Such a government exalted itself above all that is called God; and of course assumed to be Head of the church.

In 1742, it was enacted, that "if any ordained minister, or any other person, shall enter into any parish, not immediately under his charge, and shall there preach and exhort the people, he shall be denied and excluded the benefit of any law of this colony, and shall be sent as a vagrant person by warrant from any assistant Justice of the Peace, from constable to constable out of the bounds of the colony."

In February, 1744, fourteen persons were arrested at Saybrook, (Ct.) on a charge of "holding a meeting contrary to law, on God's holy Sabbath-day," were arraigned, fined, driven on foot to the county jail, and were imprisoned, without food, fire, or beds; and would have perished but for the sympathies of people secretly affording relief.

On Nov. 19, 1744, two students were expelled from college, in Connecticut, for attending a meeting in Canterbury, not authorized by law. According to the laws of the State, the whole territory is divided into parishes. No Baptist church could possibly come up, except by special license of the General Court. No Baptist minister could possibly come up except by special license of the General Court. No Baptist minister could possibly preach in a parish, without incurring the penalty of $33, and thirty stripes besides. How does this look by the command of Christ, to preach the Gospel of the kingdom everywhere.

The Episcopal church of England has enforced infant immersion from its first establishment in 1534, down to 1644; and since that time infant sprinkling; thereby making the babe a church-member under that illegitimate goverment over Christians, on the penalty of the exclusion of the parent from the church, and of the child from all the privileges of a citizen, and all the benefits of any law whatsoever.

Presbyterianism, from its first organization, Nov. 20, 1541, enforced infant immersion by law, till infant sprinkling at Geneva, and in Scotland, was substituted; and in England till the act of the Westminster Assembly, by a majority of ONE, passed in 1643; and in the United States, till the General Courts, in 1648, substituted infant sprinkling for the Congregationalists: infant immersion was the law. Among the Catholics, until 1311, infant immersion had always been the law, since it was first established in 606. In Germany, infant immersion was the law, until about 75 or an 100 years ago. Since these periods it is found that infant sprinkling is just as good a stratagem, to secure the babes under illegitimate governors, and thus to defraud the Lord Jesus Christ. The parents are forced to be parties in betraying their own babes into this fraudulent state, by the selfish rulers in those several organizations, under the false pretence that it is giving them to Christ, when it is only giving them, and binding them out to his rivals. Until some fifteen or twenty years since, every member in the Presbyterian, Congregational, and other similar churches, were *forced* thus to bind out their babes to the illegitimate rulers, under that *swindling* pretence, or incur the penalty of excommunication.

We see, then, by what coercive measures this stratagem has been enforced in all ages, and in all its different forms, and what purposes it has been adapted and designated to subserve.

It is perfectly clear, it has been adapted to counteract the growth of the real kingdom of Christ, as organized by himself, and to build up the organizations of his rivals, and to subserve their selfish and ambitious projects.

The pretence that it comes in lieu of circumcision, and that it is to be applied to female babes, and also, the pretence, that the babes, when converted, are not to be baptized into Christ, while the circumcised babes, when converted, in the apostolic times, were baptized into Christ, are perfect proofs that it is a sheer delusion, and a profane mockery of the real ordinance of Jesus Christ. In the absence of all other proof, the means resorted to in order to enforce it, are " proofs as strong as holy writ," that it is an invention of men—a mere stratagem—a cheat upon Christ, and upon all the parties concerned, except the illegitimate rulers, and adapted solely to subserve *their* iniquitous, and selfish purposes. Every person who aids, or abets in it, or refuses to act against it, conduces to the same iniquitous end.

The Baptists have been persecuted in all ages, from the first, on two general reasons: 1. for strenuously maintaining all the laws of Christ, and recognizing Him as sole Monarch, and sole Ruler: 2. for opposing the laws and the government and the stratagems of all other rulers, in just so far as they counteract the rights and equities of Christ, the King over his own church.

It is evident, from this view, that infant baptism and infant rantism is a stratagem which has been used by the ambitious usurpers of dominion over the church, in the accomplishment of greater injury to the kingdom and cause of Christ, and to the world, than any other stratagem or delusion which has ever prevailed, and has been enforced in all ages, since it began, by persecution, by the arm of civil power, by the sword, by wars and slaughter, by menaces, threatning the excommunication of the parents who refused, and by the greatest conceiveable cruelties. By these means, the babes have been extorted from the Saviour, and from their parents, and by a solemn mockery have been secured by usurpers, and by tyrants.

LETTER XXV.

INFANT SPRINKLING AN IMMORALITY, AND POSITIVELY FORBIDDEN—POINTS OF DIFFERENCE.

According to the Presbyterian Directory, before the sprinkling of a babe, the minister is to say, " That it is instituted by Christ," [*one* falsehood,] "That it (the sprinkling of the babe) is a seal of the righteousness of faith," [a *second* falsehood,]— " That the seed of the faithful have as good a right to this ordinance, (baby sprinkling) as the seed of Abraham had to circumcision," [a *third* falsehood,]—" That Christ commanded all nations to be baptized,"[a *fourth* falsehood. He commanded his apostles to *disciple* them first, and then to *baptize*, not rantize, them,]—" That of the seed of such is the kingdom of heaven," [a *fifth* falsehood; " Of such," i. e. those who are like them—those who are " converted, and are become as little children, is the kingdom of heaven ;"]—" That the children are federally holy, and therefore ought to be baptized," [a *sixth* falsehood;] after which he is to sprinkle or pour water on the face of the child, and to say " I baptize thee," [a *seventh* falsehood,]—" In the name of the Father, of the Son, and of the Holy Ghost." If *by authority of the triune God*, be the intention, this is an *eighth falsehood*. If *into subjection to the triune God*, be intended, this is a *ninth* falsehood. For the stratagem is only used in such cases as subjects the babe to illegitimate rulers. " The whole should be concluded with prayers,"—if the minister prays over it, and calls it a " dedication to God," although the parents may mean so, yet it is not so, in fact, but is a *tenth* falsehood, it is only giving them to that church. If the minister tells God in prayer, that all has been done according to divine command, this is an *eleventh* falsehood. If, after the child becomes an adult, and a convert, he is told that he has been *baptized*, this is a *twelfth* falsehood. Did Free-masonry ever require its officers to utter so many falsehoods, in any one of its ceremonies? It is therefore a palpable IMMORALITY, not only because of the frauds, but also because of the falsehoods accompanying it.

It is, therefore, positively forbidden in the word of God. I

In all the passages forbidding the taking of the name of God in vain. 2. In all those which prohibit all fraud, false pretensions, and deceptions. 3. In all those that enforce the utterance of the truth. 4. In all those which prohibit the utterance of falsehoods. 5. In the command requiring all believers to be baptized, this hindrance is forbidden. 6. In all the commands prohibiting all additions to the word of God. 7. In all the prohibitions from taking away from God's Book. This takes away Christian baptism. 8. The command, requiring that there be but "one fold," prohibits the building up of illegitimate folds by such means. 9. In all the prohibitions from 'teaching for doctrines the commandments of men,' Mark vii. 7, 8. 10. In the prohibitions of all divisions; this great cause of divisions is positively forbidden. 11. In the command to Christians "not to be unequally yoked together with unbelievers." 12. In the command daily to pray "Thy kingdom come," is prohibited this hindrance of its prevalence in Gospel form. We might name many other similar principles and passages which prohibit this ceremony. Of course, those on whom it has been performed, are forbidden in all these principles, from confiding in it, or carrying out its inconsistencies.

A review of all the evils which this and its predecessors, infant immersion, and infant pouring, have produced in building up Popery—national churches—spiritual wickednesses in high places,—persecuting usurpers, and rivals against the dominion of Christ, clearly shows, also, that it is substantially forbidden as a positive immorality. Free-masonry, as such, Mormonism, by name, and gambling, dancing, and the use of alcohol, are not prohibited by being expressly named in so many words. Yet the plain principles of the Bible prohibits them all. And yet these latter are no more plainly forbidden than that. As we would avoid partaking of other people's sins, then let us renounce that fraud with disdain.

The sprinkling of adults, for baptism, is also positively forbidden. 1. In the command, enforcing immersion, according to the primary definition of the prominent words of the law of Christ, and the plain understanding, and practice of the inspired apostles, and primitive Christians. A law that is so plain, prohibits a substitute which defeats it. 2. In the passages forbidding all diminutions, or taking away from the laws of Christ. 3. In the passages forbidding all additions. 4. In the passages prohibiting all substitutes, and all teaching for doctrines the commandments of men. 5. In all the passages that prohibit the utterance of falsehood, as is done whenever it is called baptism. 6. In all the passages which prohibit all divsions, and of course all *causes* of divisions. 7. In the passages forbidding the taking away from the word. This removes Christian baptism. When Naaman was commanded to go and wash seven times in Jordan, he was prohibited from every substitute that would evade, in the least, the compliance with that positive command. The command of Christ requiring all believers to be immersed into the exclusive jurisdiction of Christ, forbids all evasions of that command. All rules of regular subordination to the proper authorities, teach the duty of entire obedience to all the laws of such authorities, without the least equivocation.

We differ from all who differ from us in the following important points.

1. In our definition of the kingdom of Christ. We believe the King is absolute Monarch—that believers are the only proper subjects to be admitted, because he has said so—and that immersion (a humiliating transaction, whereby we subject ourselves to His jurisdiction, within his kingdom) is essential in order to membership, and because he has made it necessary by positive command. No converts, until they were thus initiated were ever considered as visible members in form, within that kingdom. "In one spirit they were all baptized into one body;" (1 Cor. xii. 13,) i. e. the body consisted of those who had one spirit, and baptism made them members.

2. We differ from all others in the whole question about rulers over the church. But one is our Master, even Christ. We deny the legitimacy of any office whatever, in any person, that gives him any power at all over the church, or any right to interfere at all against the exclusive dominion of Christ.

3. We insist on the independence of each church, whereby no other church or human being can interfere at all against the exclusive dominion of Christ. The joining of churches together, thereby affording facilities to usurpers of dominion, and thus countervailing the exclusive jurisdiction of Christ, is rebellion against the King. We insist that each church is subject exclusively to the King, as sole Ruler and sole lawmaker.

4. We insist that Christian baptism, is the oath of allegiance to the King.

5. We insist that regular membership, under the King, is indispensible in order to communion at the table; and that membership, so formed under him, is indispensible not only in order to partake of the supper, but also in order to a legit-

imate ministry. The ministry, and the membership, and the communions, every where else, are out of the visible and regular kingdom and jurisdiction of Christ.

6. We differ entirely as to the question who causes the divisions. We insist it is those who disobey the regulations of the kingdom, and wander into other folds, that cause the divisions.

7. We differ entirely in the question, who causes the close communion. We insist it is effected by building up distant communions separate and apart from the regular kingdom of Christ. As there was no close communion during the 250 years, at the beginning of the Christian era, when the kingdom alone prevailed. The same principles, continued, cannot produce it. It must, therefore be movements out of the kingdom, which have produced it. These movements are the building up of separate communions.

8. We differ, by insisting that the whole Bible should be literally translated out of the original languages, in which they were first written by the Spirit of inspiration, without covering over anything by the transfer of barbarous Greek, or by mistranslation. As all the versions for more than 1300 years, translated *baptizo*, and *baptisma*, precisely alike, and precisely according to the apostolic practice, we insist that all versions should have continued so to translate them, and so to have prevented the divisions.

9. We insist that infant sprinkling is nothing; not only because it is an invention of men, but even supposing it to be a substitute for circumcision, its friends are totally inconsistent with themselves in applying it to females; and in so using it as to cause it to hinder the subject from being baptized into Christ, after conversion, just as the circumcised were in the times of the apostles; and that such an inconsistent use of it defeats the rights of Christ, and the growth of his real kingdom, and is unprincipled in its nature.

10. We insist, that to call popery the kingdom of Christ, after its existence, the national churches after their existence; Episcopacy, with its governments, after its commencement in 1534, Presbyterianism, with its governments, after 1541, the New-England churches, under that national establishment, after 1648, and Methodism with its government, after its establishment, in 1784,—is to call the inventions and governments of men, at so late periods, *as a mass*, the kingdom of Christ; and governments, too, that are perfectly illegitimate, and that entirely counteract the government and dominion of Christ. We cannot have intercourse with, or fellow-

ship such innovations of men, and such interferences against Christ. We should be traitors to our King, and his rights should we do it.

11. We insist that church discipline in every church is to be performed in the name of the King, and precisely according to the benevolent rules laid down in the 18th of Matthew.

12. We insist that it is the indispensible duty of all converts to be one, under the exclusive jurisdiction of the King, and that there should be but " one fold and one Shepherd," —" one Lord, one faith, and one baptism."

13. We insist that we do not make close communion, but are the aggrieved and injured party. When our dear Christian friends leave us and go into other communions, with which we cannot have any intercourse, by reason of the laws of Christ; they make the close communion. As it is wrong for us to have interconrse with such a separation, it is wrong, of course, for them to separate themselves from the kingdom of Christ. We, as the party aggrieved and injured, in our tenderest love to them as Christians, have just cause to remonstrate with them, on account of their secession, and *their* close communion. We by the written laws of Christ, are shut up to the faith that baptized believers alone are proper communicants. They *can* alter and return to the laws of the King. But *we cannot* violate his laws and follow after them, and be honest. For those, therefore, to charge us with making close communion, and of being the close communion party, is contrary to truth. As they are the only party who *can*, in the nature of things, restore union, they surely ought to do it: the laws of Christ require it.

So far are we from causing close communion and divisions, that our love of Christian union is deeply pained by these things. So also the tenderest feelings of the King, and those of all heaven must be wounded for the same cause. The enemy blasphemes, the infidel exults, and the grand Adversary rejoices to have it so. We dissent entirely from the charge of causing any close communion, or any divisions.

We have been the persecuted in all ages, since the divisions began. It is cruel, in addition to all the persecutions, to charge the innocent with all the guilt of close communion, when we have done nothing to make it. Obedience to Christ is all our offending. Close communion does not belong to us, but to the other side of the House.

The commission of Christ commands his ministers 1. to disciple (*matheteusate*) all nations; 2. to baptize them. Jesus

R

made and baptized more disciples than John. John, then, made and baptized disciples. The conversation of Christ with Nicodemus, with the woman of Samaria, and others, and the specimens of his calling disciples, show how he discipled them. John's efforts in teaching the people *repentance* and *faith* in "Him who should come after," show us how John made disciples. To "disciple," is to teach them the doctrine of Christ, their duties to Him, the readiness of the Holy Spirit to help and to show them how to practice the spirit of Christ. In a word, their *conversion* is their being *discipled.* This half of the commission, then, requires us to labor for the conversion of the world.

The other half of the commission, baptizing them into the name, &c. "Baptizing them into Christ," (Gal. vi. 27.)—"baptizing them into one body," (1 Cor. xii. 13.)—"washing their bodies in pure water," on the "profession of their faith," (Heb. x. 22, 23,) is the same as gathering them under the King, by this oath of allegiance to him. "Thus it becometh us to fulfil all righteousness." Except a man be born of water as well as of the Spirit, he cannot become a member of his visible kingdom.

Large portions of ministers, since the divisions and the lording by illegitimate rulers sprung up, have utterly refused to obey the last half of the commission. Yea, through their delusion they have counteracted it by the lying ceremony upon babes, first above named. They will, therefore, have a tremendous account to give at the bar of God.

If that ceremony were universally to prevail, and be confided in, it would totally prostrate the real kingdom of Christ, and all would be illegitimate governments; just in proportion as it does prevail, it now prostrates the real organized kingdom of Christ.

Those ministers incur a fearful amount of crime, who thus totally neglect and counteract the last half of the commission of the King, and devote all their lives in building up **treason** and rebellion in Israel. May the Lord arrest them in this their criminal, their mad career, and restore them to their right reason. Through strange infatuation, some of old took away the key of knowledge,—taught for doctrines the commandments of men—refused to enter the organized kingdom of God themselves, and "them that were entering they hindered." Matt. xxiii. 13. Mark vii. 7, 8.

The whole drift of sectarianism, from the first, with its illegitimate rulers, its stratagem upon babes, and all its **persecutions**, has been to hinder people from entering the organized kingdom of God, by the regular oath of allegiance to the King, and to extend in lieu of it the folds and dominions of usurpers, and allegiance to them. Will a man rob God, the Redeemer, the King in Zion? Ye, even this whole mass, have robbed the rightful King, have invaded his prerogative, robbed him of his subjects, kept them away from his kingdom by stratagems, and devoted your lives too much to the interests of other and rival lords, to the enlisting of helpless babes and of men under them, thus hindering the union of Christians, and the extension of the kingdom of Christ.

LETTER XXVI.

LITERAL VERSIONS.

All versions of the Bible that were ever made, previous to the times before given, when men altered the ordinance of baptism in form, uniformly rendered *Baptizo*, and its cognates, in all languages, according to the renderings hereafter given; i. e. by words in all cases, signifying immersion. Among these are, 1. the Syriac version, the oldest existing translation out of the original Greek, in the world, 2. The Armenian version. 3. The Georgian. 4. The Coptic. 5. The Sahidic. 6. The Arabic. 7. The Ethiopic. 8. The Amharic. 9. The Gothic. 10. The German. 11. The Danish. 12. The Dutch. 13. The Swedish. 14. The Russian. 15. That of Sabat. 16. The Peshito Syriac, and a great many others, with the exception, since those times of the Catholic versions, and of those circulated by the Episcopalians, the Presbyterians, the Congregationalists, and the Methodists in modern times. All others, it is believed, without an exception, have continued to translate it in the same way. The Baptists, in all their versions, during the last fifty years, in heathen lands, which now extend to the languages spoken by probably *six hundred millions of souls*, have also uniformly translated in the same way; i. e. they have given literal versions of every word, praying that they might know the mind of the Holy Ghost; and also, that they might give the heathen the mind of the Holy Ghost, in every word. This is right. Still the slanderous charge, from the last mentioned denominations, of "sectarianism," of "bigotry," of "blind zeal," &c., is continued against them for this righteous course.

"We are content," says the Committee of the Baptist

Union, "to leave the defence of Baptist translators, in the hands of that late eminently gifted servant of the British and Foreign Bible Society, to whom we have before referred." "Bigotry," says Mr. Greenfield, "that is, blind zeal, aud prejudice, the Baptists cannot justly be accused of, while they have the primitive sense of the term, and the rendering of so many ancient and modern translations, as the foundation upon which they have grounded their version; nor can they, consistently, be charged with sectarianism, while they are found in company with the churches of Syria, Arabia, Ethiopia, Egypt, Germany, Holland, Sweden, Denmark, and others, together with the Church of England itself. If they be bigots, I know not what name the advocates for pouring or sprinkling, who have no such basis to rest on, merit; and if theirs be a sect, it must be confessed to be a very ancient, and a very extensive one."

"But there is another point of view," he continues, (and while he writes these memorable words, he says, as a preface to them, 'I wish it to be distinctly understood, that I am neither a Baptist, nor the son of a Baptist') "there is another point of view in which the opponents of the Serampore Missionaries should consider the subject: and one which involves the most important consequences. Before they arraign the British and Foreign Bible Society as guilty of gross and unpardonable dereliction of duty, in aiding the Serampore translators, and prefer a recommendation for them to withdraw that aid, they should be fully prepared to carry their censure, as well as their recommendation, to a much greater extent. In consistency, if that aid be withdrawn from the Serampore Missionaries because they have rendered $\beta\alpha\pi\tau\iota\zeta\omega$ to *immerse*, then must it be also withdrawn from the churches of Syria, of Arabia, of Abyssinia, of Egypt, of Germany, of Holland, of Denmark, &c.; and the venerable Peshito Syriac Version, the Arabic versions of the Propaganda, of Sabat, &c.; the Ethiopic, the Coptic, and other versions must all be suppressed. If, however, they are not thus prepared to carry their recommendation to its fullest extent, then must they close their mouths for ever against their Baptist brethren. But should a faction so far prevail over the good sense of the Committee, and the sound catholic principles upon which the Society is founded, and which have ever been its boast and glory, as well as the most powerful means of its extraordinary success, 'then its honor will be laid in the dust:' and from a splendid temple, in the service of which the whole Christian world would cordially unite, it will dwindle into a contemptible edifice, dedicated to party feelings, motives, and views. The broad basis upon which it is founded, is its strength and security; contract this within narrower limits, and it falls into ruins."

If such would be the consequence of such a course, in the British and Foreign Bible Society, as intimated by that learned Episcopalian, then what is the fact with the American Bible Society, in the war it has waged against literal versions, during the last five years; and in successively resolving that such are "false versions," that they will not aid in the circulation of such, and that they will not aid in the circulation of any except "such as conform, in the principles of their translation, to the common English version." Is not the verdict pronounced by Mr. Greenfield, upon such a course, a correct verdict?

The above small portions of Christendom, since the periods above alluded to, have attempted to blot out the real oath of allegiance to Christ, and to propagate their "substitute;" and finally, since 1640, to propagate their "*substitute* of a substitute." They have done it by warring against literal versions, and by continuing to insert the Greek words untranslated,* and by fraudulently adding new definitions in some Greek Lexicons, to *baptizo*, which never in fact, belonged to it. How many of them are sinning *ignorantly* in this matter, and how many *consciously*, is known only to the Searcher of hearts. The fact that all this has been done, is known to the world. Of late, they have, in their Bible Societies, attempted to propagate some very corrupt versions on these points, in *foreign* lands.†

Had they not been thus guilty of "corrupting the word of God," and of "handling it deceitfully," literal translations like the following, would have always appeared, and been *continued* in the Bible everywhere. This would have prevent-

---

* The first English version was made in 1290; Wickliff's in 1380; Tindall's in 1526; Coverdale's in 1535; Matthew's in 1537; Cranmer's in 1539; the Geneva Bible, in 1560; the Bishop's Bible, in 1568; and King James' in 1611. The Roman Hierarchy first introduced *baptize* and *baptism* into the English language, to favor their projects; and these words have since been introduced into some versions of the English Bible, in order to obscure that ordinance, and to afford a pretence for their substitutes, and continued for that purpose.

† In a Seneca version, they have translated *baptizo* by *sprinkle*; in an Icelandic, by *wash*; in a Chinese, by *wash*; and in a Russian, by *cross*. They have prepared a modern Greek Testament, in which they have taken out many words, and substituted others. They have also corrupted a Strasburgh, a Lausanne, a Turkish, and a Hebrew Bible; and all this within a very few years past, to favor their subtleties.

ed these painful divisions on a point so vital to Christian union. And had they kept themselves free from illegitimate rulers, which always corrupt a church; from infant baptism; and from baby sprinkling, its substitute, and from such a use of it as to counteract Christian baptism; and had they been of the number that subjected themselves to the jurisdiction of Christ, according to his regulations within his kingdom, how much better it would have been for the world. What an immense amount of injury, then, have they done by thus cleaving to those inventions of men, and consequently, by opposing the simplicity of the Gospel.

In addition to all we have said concerning the meaning of *baptizo*, we appeal not only to the primary definition of it, in all Greek Lexicons; which according to every legal principle of construction is to be taken as the *meaning*, but to the Greek church, in all ages—to the profane Greek authors—to Josephus and Philo, as Jewish writers to the Septuagint—to the most learned Greek scholars—and to all who are unbiassed,—to the most learned commentators, and to the most eminent scholars of our own times, even in other ranks, such as George Campbell, Professor Porson, Dr. Chalmers, Bishop Smith. Mr. Goodell and others. Porson, the Professor of Greek in the University of Cambridge, and considered now as the first Greek scholar in England, when asked the meaning of *baptizo*, replied, that "it was absurd to imagine that it had any other meaning than to *dip entirely*, or *plunge*, or *immerse*." He is in the Pædobaptist ranks.

Wherefore laying aside the barbarous Greek words, introduced as above, for the obscuration of the subject, and taking the real translation; and after correcting the mistranslations otherwise, the following is the literal translation of the passages referred to, viz:

Matthew iii. 5. And were immersed in the Jordan confessing their sins.

Matt. iii. 11. I immerse you in water, unto repentance,—He shall immerse you in the Holy Ghost and fire. [fulfilled, Acts ii. 2—4.]

Matt. iii. 13. Then went Jesus to Galilee to Jordan to John to be immersed by him.—v. 14. I have need to be immersed of thee,—

Matt. iii. 16. And Jesus being immersed, ascended up quickly out of the water, and behold the heavens were opened unto him, and he saw the Spirit of God descending as a dove, and coming upon him.

Matt. xx. 22. Are ye able to drink the cup which I will to drink, and to undergo the immersion which I undergo?

Verse 23. Ye shall indeed drink the cup which I will to drink, and undergo the immersion which I undergo.

Matt. xxviii. 19. Having gone forth disciple all nations, immersing them in the name of the Father, and of the Son, and of the Holy Ghost.

Mark i. 4. John went forth immersing in the wilderness, and preaching the immersion of repentance for the remission of sins.

Verse 5. —and were all immersed in the river Jordan, by him, confessing their sins.

Verse 8. I have indeed immersed you in water, but He shall immerse you in the Holy Ghost. (See Acts ii. 2—4,)

Verse 9. And it happened in those days, that Jesus went from Nazareth of Galilee, and was immersed by John into the Jordan.

Mark vii. 4. —and from the markets, except they are immersed, they eat not. And many other things have they received to hold; the immersions of cups and pots and brazen vessels, and of tables.*

---

* Scaliger tells us, the superstitious part of the Jews every day dipped the whole body before they ate, and that a *laver* or convenient place for it as an appendage to every house, was as necessary, in their opinion, as the house itself. They dipped also their couches, tables, beds, pillows, pots, cups, &c., as purifications. Always after touching a Gentile, or going to market, they were thus purified; and if a Gentile had touched any of their things, it was thus immersed and purified. *See Maimonides.*

The foundation of this superstition was in such passages as these: Levit. xi. 32, —must be put into water,—verse 40, —clothes to be washed,—verses 44, 45. Ye shall, therefore, sanctify yourselves, and ye shall be holy, &c. Levit. xiii. 6, —for the plague he shall wash his clothes;—verse 54, —shall wash the thing wherein the plague is,—verse 58, —the garment shall be washed a second time to be clean :—Chap. xiv. 9, —shall wash his clothes and his flesh.—Verse 47, He that lieth in the house shall wash his clothes, and he that eateth in the house shall wash his clothes :—Chron. xv. 6. He that sitteth &c. shall bathe himself in water, &c.—verse 7, And he that toucheth the flesh of him that is unclean shall wash his clothes and bathe himself in water. In verses 8, 10, 11, the same washing of clothes, and bathing of himself in water is enforced. Verse 12. Every vessel that has been touched by an impure person, must be rinsed in water; verse 13, —shall wash his clothes, and bathe his flesh in water; verse 18, —bathe themselves in water; verse 21, —wash clothes, and bathe himself in water. The same is commanded in verses 22, 27, 31; in Chap. xvi. 4, 26, and xvii. 15, 16, and also in Num. xix. 7, 8, 19. In Deut. xxiii. 11, "Lavers to wash in," are mentioned. Hence, we read, Heb. ix. 10, of things which stood in meats and drinks, and divers immersions. We have here these immersions. The Jews, as Wall and others tell us, when Gentile families joined them as proselytes, were all of them required to be immersed or purified. Yet that those children born after were not immersed. This was often called Proselyte Baptism. It was the mere purification of them in water, when they left their

Mark vii. 8. For laying aside the commandments of God, ye hold the traditions of men; the immersions of pots and cups, and many other similar things ye do.

[The remarks in verse 9, about rejecting the commandment of God, that ye may keep your own traditions, are in point, in the rejection of Christian baptism in order that ye may keep your own substitutes, and infant sprinkling.]

Mark x. 38. Can ye drink the cup that I drink, and undergo the immersion that I undergo?

Verse 39. Ye shall truly drink the cup that I drink, and undergo the immersion that I undergo.

Mark xi. 30. The immersion of John; was it from heaven or of men? (In John i. 33, it is intimated that God sent John to immerse. It was, therefore, from heaven.)

Mark xvi. 15, 16. Go ye into all the world, preach the Gospel to every creature. He that believeth and is immersed shall be saved. (Saved may mean *shielded* and protected under the King, within his fold, and be thus conducted to heaven under his guidance.)

Luke iii. 7. Then said he to the multitude that came to be immersed of him, &c.

Verse 12. And there came publicans also to be immersed of him, and said, Sir, what shall we do?

Verse 16. I indeed immerse you in water; he shall immerse in the Holy Ghost and fire.

Verse 21. And it came to pass in the time that all the people were immersed; and Jesus being immersed, and praying, that the heaven was opened, &c. (Christ prayed after coming up out of the water, and God there answered prayer miraculously.)

Luke vii. 29. And all the people that heard, and the publicans justified God, having undergone the immersion of John.

Verse 30. But the Pharisees and lawyers rejected the counsel of God unto themselves, not having been immersed of him.

Luke xi. 38. But the Pharisee seeing it, marvelled, because he had not immersed before dinner. (See note on Mark vii. 4.)

Luke xii. 50. But I have an immersion to undergo, and how am I straitened till it be accomplished.

Luke xx. 4. The immersion of John; was it from heaven or from men?

John i. 25. Why then do ye immerse if you are not the Christ, &c.

Gentile associates. It was this same purification above alluded to. Those born after were not required to be purified in that way.

Verse 25. John replied, saying, I immerse in water,—
—— 28. —where John was immersing.
—— 31. But that he might become manifest to Israel, for this reason I have come immersing in water.

Verse 33. But he who sent me to immerse in water, He said unto me, Upon whomsoever thou shalt see the Spirit descending and remaining upon him, this is he who immerses in the Holy Ghost. (See Acts ii. 2—4.)

John iii. 22. —and there he remained and immersed.

—— 23. And John was immersing in Ænon, near to Salem, because there was much water. And they came and were immersed.

Verse 26. He who was with thee beyond Jordan, behold he immerses, and all come to him.

John iv. 1. —heard that Jesus makes and immerses more disciples than John,—ver. 2,—though Jesus himself did not immerse but his disciples did it. (He discipled them, his disciples immersed them, and into his name.)

John x. 4. —beyond Jordan into the place where John was immersing.

Act i. 5. For John truly immersed in water, but ye shall be immersed in the Holy Ghost, not many days hence. (fulfilled, Acts ii. 2—4. Of this last passage Bishop Tillotson says, "They were all immersed in the Holy Ghost.")

Acts ii. 38. Repent and be immersed each one of you in the name of Jesus Christ, for the remission of sins. And ye shall receive the gift of the Holy Ghost; because the promise (of the Holy Ghost, Joel ii. 28—32, quoted Acts ii. 17—21; the miracles, the signs and wonders he wrought being the things promised,) is to you, and to the children of you, and to all those who are at a great distance, as many of them as the Lord our God shall call.

Verse 41. Therefore, indeed, those who gladly received his word, were immersed. And on that day about three thousand souls were placed to them.

Acts viii. 12. And when they confided in Philip preaching the things concerning the kingdom of God, and the name of Jesus Christ, they were immersed, both men and women.

Verse 13. And Simon also himself believing. And continuing with Philip, and seeing the signs and great miracles that were done, he was astonished.

Verse 15, 16. —prayed for them, that they might receive the Holy Ghost, (the miraculous operations.) For as yet he was fallen on none of them, and it only existed that they were immersed into the name of the Lord Jesus.

Verse 36. —Behold the water, what hindereth me to be immersed?

Verse 38. And they both descended into the water, to wit, both Philip and the Eunuch; and he immersed him.

Verse 39. And when they come up out of the water, the Spirit of the Lord caught away Philip.

Acts ix. 18. And immediately there fell from his eyes something like scales, and immediately he saw. And having arisen up he was immersed.

Acts x. 47. Whether any one can prohibit water that these should not be immersed who have received the Holy Ghost as also we? (This inquiry is based in the fact that the converts were Gentiles.)

Verse 48. And he in the name of the Lord commanded them to be immersed. (The authority is in Matt. xxviii. 19. The fact that they were converted, is assigned, v. 47, as the basis and ground of it.)

Acts xi. 16. And I remembered the word of the Lord, as he said, John indeed immersed you in water, but ye shall be immersed in the Holy Ghost not many days hence.

Acts xvi. 15. And when she was immersed, and the household of her, (in verse 40, this household is called "the brethren.")

Verse 33. —and was immersed, he, and all those of him, immediately. (The word had been spoken to them all, v. 32, and all were converts, v. 24.)

Acts xviii. 8. And Crispus, a ruler of the synagogue, confided in the Lord, with all the house of him. (Another whole family converted.) And many of the Corinthians, hearing, believed, and were immersed.

Acts xix. 1—6. And finding some of his disciples, he said unto them, Have ye who believe received the Holy Ghost? (his miraculous powers.) And they said unto him, But we have not heard if there is the Holy Ghost, (the miraculous powers.) And he said unto them, Into what were ye immersed? And they said, into John's immersion. And Paul said, John truly immersed with the immersion of repentance, saying unto the people (that he immersed,) that they must believe on (confide in) Him who was coming after him; that is, on Christ Jesus. And they hearing it were immersed (in fact,) into the name of the Lord Jesus. (We here are taught, in a literal version, that John in reality immersed into subjection to Christ, and that it was so understood. In John iii. 26—36, we see particularly, how John exalted Christ, and instructed the disciples to trust in him.) And Paul placing his hands upon them, the Holy Ghost (in his miraculous powers) came upon them. And they spake with tongues, and spake forth.

Acts xxii. 16. And now what willest thou? Arise be immersed and wash away thy sins, calling on the name of the Lord. (Paul as well as well as Jesus, prayed as soon as he came out of the water.)

Rom. vi. 3. Or are ye ignorant that as many of us as were immersed into Christ, were immersed into the death of Him.

Verse 4. Therefore we are buried together with him, by the immersion into the death; that as Christ was raised from death by the glory of the Father, so also we will walk in newness of life.

Verse 5. For if planted together, we have been conformed to the resemblance of the death of Him, so also we will be, of the resurrection.

Verse 6. This knowing, that the old man of us, was cotemporaneously crucified, that the body of sin might be destroyed, to the intent that we should no longer serve sin.

Verse 7. For he who is thus dead, has been delivered from sin. 8. And if we died with Christ, we trust that also we shall live with him.

1 Cor. i. 13. —or were ye immersed into the name of Paul.
—— 14. I thank my God that I immersed no one of you except Crispus and Gaius,—15.—that no one should say I immersed into my own name. And I immersed also the household of Stephanus. (they were adults addicting themselves to the ministry of the saints, &c. chap. xvi. 15.) Otherwise I know not that I immersed any other. For Christ sent me not to immerse, but to evangelize. (i. e. when Christ appeared to me, his language was not about immersion, but about evangelizing the Gentiles. Acts ch. ix.)

1 Cor. x. 2. And all into Moses, (into subjection to him as a leader,) were immersed in the cloud and in the sea.

1 Cor. xii. 13. For also in one spirit, we all were immersed into one body. (The body it is here said, consisted of those who had one spirit, and were immersed, and immersion made them members.)

Verse 14. For the body also is not one member but many.
—— 27. But ye are the body of Christ, and members consisting of parts. (i. e. consisting of separate churches.)

1 Cor. xv. 29. Because what will those do who are immersed for those that are dead. If the dead are not raised at all, why also are they immersed for those that are dead?

Gal. iii. 27. For as many of us as were immersed into Christ, have come under Christ.

Verse 28. There is not the Jew nor the Greek, there is not the servant nor the free. There is not the masculine and the feminine; for all are one under Christ Jesus.

Verse 29. And if ye are (the property) of Christ, then are ye the posterity of Abraham, and inheritors (of Christ) according to the promise.

Luke iii. 2, 3. The word of the Lord came upon John the son of Zechariah, in the wilderness. And he came into all the circumjacent country of the Jordan, preaching the immersion of repentance for the remission of sins.

Acts x. 37. After the immersion which John preached:

—— xii. 54. John, preached, before his coming the immersion of repentance to all the people.

Acts xviii. 25. —being experienced only as to the immersion of John.

Eph. iv. 5. One Lord, one faith, one immersion,—6.—One God and Father of all, who is over all and through all, and in you all.

Col. ii. 12. Jointly buried with him in the immersion in which also we were jointly raised by the faith of the energy of God, who raised Him from the dead.

Heb. vi. 1. Therefore leaving the account—v. 2,—of the instruction about immersions, and of the imposition of hands, and of the resurrection of the dead, and of the permanent sentence.

Heb. ix. 10. —stood in divers immersions. (See Note on Mark vii. 4.)

Heb. x. 22, 23. And having our bodies washed in pure water, let us hold fast the profession of our faith firmly.

Titus iii. 5. But according to his mercy hath he saved (protected) us by the washing of regeneration, and the renewing of the Holy Ghost. (The washing here spoken of, is that which pertains to the second birth, in contradistinction from that of the first birth. It is, therefore the immersion. We are saved or protected through this instrumentality, as it puts us into the fold of Christ, under the shadow of his wing, and under his protection. By this means, and the constant renewing of the Holy Ghost, we are helped onward toward heaven itself.)

1 Pet. iii. 21. The antitype to which immersion, according to the resurrection of Christ, doth now save us, (not the putting away of the filth of the flesh, but the test of a good conscience.) [Immersion, by putting us into the fold of Christ, the ark of safety, and under his protection, saves us from ma-

ny evils in this world, and help us along on the road to heaven.]

John iii. 5. Verily, verily, I say unto you, unless any one be born of water and of the Spirit, he cannot enter into the kingdom of God. (It is absolutely essential, according to this language of Christ, to have a birth of water, in order to enter that visible kingdom of God, as it was organized on earth.)

John xiii. 10. He who is washed (is immersed) needeth not save to wash his feet.

Eph. vi. 11. But ye are washed, (immersed) but ye are sanctified, but ye are justified, in the name of the Lord Jesus, and by the Spirit of our God.

These are all literal translations, with suggestions between the parenthesis. Had it not been for the tricks of the Roman Catholic priests, in relation to the initiating Christian ordinance, and their desire to conceal them, by the use of heathen Greek—their anglicising of Greek words to conceal their tricks,—the knavery of those who introduced the Greek words into the English Bible—the corrupt course of those bishops, of 1568, who made a version to favor the national church of England—the corruption of James, in retaining so many of them, and the corruption of the rulers and bishops of the church of England, and that of others who have directly or indirectly aided in these things,—we should always have enjoyed the privilege of literal versions. How, I ask, can we avoid the guilt of adding to or taking from the word of God, if we continue to circulate such obscure versions? Those who undertake to defend sprinkling for baptism, from the Bible, might just as well undertake to defend free-masonry from the Bible.

The following passages, literally translated, express the time of the commencement of the kingdom of Christ.

Matt. iii. 2. Repent, for the kingdom of heaven has come.

—— iv. 17. From that time, began Jesus to preach, and to say, Repent, for the kingdom of heaven has come.

—— x. 7. And as ye go, preach, saying, The kingdom of heaven has come.

—— xii. 28. —then is the kingdom of heaven come unto you.

Luke xi. 20. The kingdom of heaven has come upon you.

Mark i. 15. The time is fulfilled, the kingdom of God has come.

Luke xvi. 16. The law and the prophets were until John. Since that time, the kingdom of God is preached.

Matt. xi. 12. From the days of John the Baptist, until now,

the kingdom of God suffereth violence, and the violent rapaciously seize it.

Matt. xii. 28. And if I by the Spirit of God cast out devils, then the kingdom of God hath come unto you.

—— xxi. 43. The kingdom of God shall be taken from you, and given to a nation bringing forth the fruits of it.

—— vi. 33. But seek ye first the kingdom of God and His righteousness.

The following literal versions express the qualifications requisite, at that time, for membership in the kingdom:

Luke ix. 62. No one putting his hand to the plough, and looking back, is well placed for (or towards) the kingdom of God.

Matt. iii. 7—9. The Pharisees and Sadducees were rejected because they brought not forth the fruits of repentance, and because they relied on the fact that they had Abraham for a father.

Matt. v. 20. I say unto you that unless your righteousness abound more than that of the Scribes and Pharisees, ye shall by no means enter into the kingdom of heaven. (It was the kingdom of heaven, because the kingdom of heaven extended to earth.)

Matt. v. 3. Blessed are the poor in spirit for of them is the kingdom of heaven.

Matt. v. 10. Blessed are those who are persecuted for righteousness sake, for of them is the kingdom of heaven.

—— v. 19. Those (members) who break the least commandments, and shall teach men so, shall be called the leas in the kingdom of heaven.

—— vii. 11. Not every one that saith unto me, Lord, Lord, shall enter into the kingdom of heaven, but he that doeth the will of my Father in heaven.

Matt. xviii. 3. Except ye be converted, and become as little children, ye shall in no case enter into the kingdom of heaven.

—— xix. 23. —hardly will a rich (worldly) man enter into the kingdom of heaven.

—— xxi. 31. —The publicans and harlots precede you towards the kingdom of God.

Mark iii. 35. Whosoever shall do the will of my Father, the same is my brother, and sister, and mother.

—— x. 15. Whosoever shall not receive the kingdom of God as a child, shall not enter into it.

Luke vii. 29, 30. And all the people that heard, and the publicans, justified God, having undergone the immersion o

John. But the Pharisees and lawyers rejected the counsel of God towards them, not being immersed of him, (not being qualified for becoming members of the kingdom.)

Matt. xii. 30. He that is not with me is against me; and he that gathereth not with me, scattereth abroad. (All who gather not into his kingdom, scatter abroad.)

John iii. 5. Except a man be born of water and of the Spirit, he cannot enter into the kingdom of God

———— xviii. 36. My kingdom is not of this world.

Verse 37. Thou sayest that I am a King: to this end was I born, and for this purpose came I into the world, that I should bear witness unto the truth. Every one that is of the truth heareth my voice.

We see here the qualifications for membership in Christ's time. We have before shown who were baptized into the kingdom by the apostles.

I here add the literal version of two other passages, as relating to the equality and unity of those within the church.

The one is, 1 Cor. xiv. 32—34. Let the spirits of the prophets be in subjection to the prophets. For God is not the God of confusion, but of peace as in all the meetings of the saints. Let your wives in these meetings (meetings for speaking in tongues, &c. ver. 27—31.) be silent, because it is not permitted to them to speak, but to be in subjection, as also the law says. And if they desire to learn any thing, let them ask their husbands in the house; for it is unbecoming to wives to speak in this meeting.

As these meetings have long since passed away, the regulations about them, of course, cannot apply to other meetings, but have passed away also. It related to *wives*, pertained to that class of meetings, and was, perhaps, the result of some *law*, alluded to in verse 34, unknown to us.

The other is, 1 Tim. ii. 11, 12. Let the wife learn in quietness, in all subordination. And I suffer not the wife to teach or to authenticate the husband, but to be in quietness.

The old translators must have had much of the love of rule over females, and felt much self-importance, or they would not have strained their version to the utmost verge, as they have done here, in order to justify such a course. That *all things be done decently and in order*, is all the regulation there is concerning the female portion of the church; speaking in conferences, and prayer meetings. The first of the above passages has no allusion to ordinary Christian meetings. The other simply prohibits the usurpation by the wife, of authority over the husband. If those ministers who love to rule, and to stretch their gag-law, would think of the prohibitions from the King, against lording it over His church, and cease their own dogmatical construction of the above passages, Christians would feel greatly relieved of a tyrannic obstruction to religious freedom.

LETTER XXVII.
CLOSE COMMUNION.

This offence, from the nature of things, must be the establishment of a communion under human regulations, and in such a way as closes and fences that communion against a portion of their fellow Christians, wherever it exists.

As *we* have not made *our* regulations and we only obey those of the King, from the nature of the case with us, neither the initiating ordinance into the kingdom, nor the privileges within it, nor the freedom of ingress is closed up by *us*. All things are free precisely as the Lord made them, so far as we are concerned: we are not guilty of close communion therefore.

To establish a separate communion, under other rulers, without gospel baptism, and to make church members by infant sprinkling, is to establish a communion to which we cannot approach, by reason of the laws and regulations of our King. We, therefore, are the sinned against, not the sinners in this thing. If a church were to be organized in some place without any water, or any baptism, this would make close communion between those and all others. And it would be false and cruel to blame the churches who believe baptism (or what they call such) is necessary before communion, as causing that close communion. It would be those who organize without any baptism, that would make that close communion. The others would be the injured party.

The substitutes for Christian baptism to us, when examined in the light of the Bible, are no baptism at all. They are the mere inventions of men. Such churches, to us, are as if they had no baptism. They stand in the same relation to us as a church would to them, who should discard all water. Being aggrieved and injured in our feelings of love to them, and in our love of Christian union, as they would be in the other supposed case, we have reason affectionately to remonstrate, therefore, with our Christian friends, against this close communion. We feel injured, that they should shut themselves away from our fellowship, and from the regulations of Christ, and adhere to a communion to which they know we cannot come. We are shut up by the laws of Christ to the regulations of his kingdom, and cannot help ourselves by following after them if we would, without trampling down the laws of the kingdom. But *they can* help the case—*can* obey the rules of the kingdom—*can* return to the original regulations of Christ. *They can* remove the close communion, but we cannot. They have made it, we have not. With all the tenderness of Christian affection, therefore, we urge them to cease to perpetuate close communion between themselves and us. We are pained and aggrieved with it. Christ and all Heaven, no doubt, are aggrieved with it.

In Scotland, the established Presbyterian Church—the Covenanters,—the Relief Church—the Church of England—the Bergers—the Anti-Bergers—the Independents—the Wesleyan Methodists, and the Independent Methodists, all hold close communion in the strict sense of the word; no one of these churches communing with another. As they all make their own regulations, they could avoid this if they would.

When the Congregational churches were established in New England, they continued in the same way, until about twenty or thirty years since. The Presbyterians held strict communion in the United States, for a long time, except with the Congregationalists. Both still continue an arbitrary close communion against a large proportion of their own church members. For all sprinkled babes are considered in their books, as church members. No one can commune with the national church of England, without a certificate of his birth, and of baptism, as performed by an Episcopal minister there, and without proof that he has been also confirmed there. Dr. Milner, and Dr. Hawks, who visited England in 1836, and 1837, were neither of them permitted to preach in Episcopal pulpits there, because not rantized, confirmed, or ordained there. Nor could they have been admitted, for the same reason, to the communion there. A Presbyterian, Congregational, Methodist, or Baptist minister could not be admitted into the pulpit with an Episcopal minister, either there or here, or take any part with him, or exchange with him. In the Methodist Discipline, ch. i. § 22, it reads " Let no person, that is not a member of our church, be admitted to the communion, without examination, and some token given by an Elder or a deacon." In ch. ii. § 6.—" Give no tickets to any till they have left off superfluous ornaments. Give no tickets to any that wear high heads, enormous bonnets, ruffles, or rings." In ch. i. § 1 8, 2, 3.—" those who hold doctrines, privately, or publicly, contrary to *our* articles of religion," are to be proceeded against " as in cases of gross immorailty." Can we consistently be admitted by them who hold to views for which their own members would be excluded? Most of the forms of Scotch Presbyterianism hold close communion in the strict sense.

These are all the contrivances of men. The only fault of us Baptists is, that we obey the regulations of Christ, and of his kingdom. We make no close communion, we make no laws about it, but simply obey the laws of Christ. This view is introduced in order to show what a vast amount of close communion is actually made by the regulations of human beings. It is cruel, as against us, in our fellow Christians thus to separate themselves from us into close communions. We feel it most keenly. But in addition to all this, for them to charge us with *making* close communion, as between them and us; no charge was ever more false or cruel! It is adding insult to injury. We are the most averse to close communion of any portion of Christians that can be found. We have the laws of the kingdom, the rules of admission, and all other things where Christ left them, and simply obey them. By all the sincere and warm affection we have, therefore, for our fellow Christians—by our mutual love of each other, as Christians—by the regard we all ought to have for the prayer of Christ, " that all his people might be one," and for his law that there should be but " one fold," and for his law requiring all Christians to be baptized into subjection to himself; and by the great advantages to us all, and to the world, that would result from Christian union; by the great wants of the perishing heathen, and their need of Christian union among us, in exertions for their welfare, and by a review of all the advantages the church might have enjoyed, if they had continued to be one, and by a candid view of the evtls that have resulted from divisions, we most earnestly and affectionately *beseech* our fellow Christians in the other ranks, to relinquish and totally to discontinue their close commuion. It is a departure from the regulations of the kingdom of Christ, and a pertinacious adherence to the inventions of men—to the new folds which men have made in modern times—to illegitimate rulers, and initiations under them, which makes all the close communion, and all the divisions that exist.

NOTE.

In confirmation of the main statement about the change of the ordinance, I here add an attestation of the Catholics; being a note found in a Rhenish Testament, published in 1582, on Matt. iii. 6, —"baptized in Jordan," &c. The note is in these words, "The word baptism signifies a washing: particularly when it is done by immersion, or by dipping, or plunging a thing under water, *which* WAS FORMERLY *the ordinary way of administering the ordinance of baptism.*

"But the Church, which cannot change the least article of the Christian Faith, is not so tied up to matters of discipline and ceremonies. Not only the Catholic church, but also the PRETENDED REFORMED CHURCHES HAVE ALTERED *this primitive custom*, in giving the sacrament of baptism. They now allow of baptism by pouring or sprinkling on the person baptized. Nay, many of their ministers do it now-a-days, by fillipping a wet finger and thumb over the child's head, or by shaking a wet finger or two over the child, which it *is hard enough to call baptism in any sense.*"

A copy of the Testament and the Note, is in the hands of J. M'Gowan of New York.

THE END.

A
Biographical Sketch
of
John Flavel Bliss
(1787-1873)
by
John Franklin Jones

A
Biographical Sketch
John Flavel Bliss
(1787-1873)

John Flavel Bliss was born 8 June 1787 in Hebron, Connecticut. His father was Ellis Bliss (born 25 September 1733 in Hebron, Tolland, Connecticut). His mother was Grace Ford Bliss (born 29 November 1747) (Rootsweb, 8/30/06).

Bliss married Ann Elizabeth Hosmer (born 12 April 1789 in Farmington, Connecticut.). They were married 12 April 1812 and parented William Hosmer Bliss (born 10 June 1813 in Avon, New York, Livingston County); Effie E. Bliss (born 2 February 1815 in Avon, New York); and Fanny W. Bliss (born 23 March 1817 in Avon, New York) (Rootsweb, 8/30/06).

He was ordained and installed as the pastor of the Congregational Church, Farmington, Connecticut 25 February 1812 and served there until February 1818 (*Rochester Presbytery*, 129). It is interesting to note that Bliss became the pastor of this church just two months prior to his marriage in the same church.

On 11 February 1819, Bliss was installed as the first pastor of the church at Clarkson, Connecticut (Thornton County). The church began as a Congregation church 1 April 1816 and came under the care of the Presbytery of Ontario 10 February, 1819, just one day prior to Bliss's being installed as its pastor. The church changed its name to "The First Congregational Church of Clarkson" 6 May 1823 (*Rochester Presbytery*, 155).

Bliss was in the General Assembly of the Presbyterian Church in 1829 when the Assembly addressed the question, "Are the baptisms of Popish priests to be accepted by our [Presbyterian] Churches as valid baptisms?" (Bliss in *Graves*).

He was the second pastor of the First Congregational Church of Friendship (Allegany County, New York), organized 14 August 1835. The specific dates and length of his service in this church are unknown (*Friendship Village*, 718).

The church at Henrietta, New York (Monroe County) was spawned as a 1810-preaching point of the Pittsford Presbyterian church and its pastor, Solomon Allen. It organized as the Congregational Church of Henrietta 20 May 1816. John F. Bliss actively furthered the organization and preached occasionally for the fledgling organization in its meetings in the school house (*Rochester Presbytery*, 193-94).

Bliss preached at the first meeting of the Rochester-Genesee Presbytery, newly-organized by dividing the Presbyteries of Ontario and Niagara. At the 6 April 1819 meeting, held in the building–the same house of worship occupied at that time by the First church--on State Street in Rochesterville (early name for Rochester)--he took his text from 2 Corinthians 11:16 (*Rochester Presbytery*, 28).

Bliss was one of five licensed to preach by the Henrietta church, which became the United Henrietta Baptist Church, and one of three ordained by that church to the ministry (*Henrietta Baptist Church*). While no extant details have come to light, this ordination in this Baptist church is significant. It marked his formal transition into Baptist views. He had previously been ordained a Congregational pastor in 1812 and preach at the Presbyterian Presbytery in 1819.

A BIOGRAPHICAL SKETCH OF JOHN FLAVEL BLISS

The Henrietta church listed Bliss among its pastors (1839-?, with the next listed pastor beginning his tenure in 1841) (*Henrietta Baptist Church*).

The only extant work authored by Bliss is his *Letters on Christian Baptism as the Initiating Ordinance into the Real Kingdom of Christ* (Lexington, NY: Levi L. Hill, 1841).

Rev. Bliss was listed as an ordained minister in 1842 by the Monroe (New York) Baptist Association, but not as a pastor at that time. He was a member of the Ogden Baptist Church (Monroe County) and the Churchville Baptist Church (Monroe County). He appears to have been a founding member of the latter and served as its church clerk for several years (*1842 Monroe Baptist Association*).

J. F. Bliss was listed as clerk of the Chautauque No. 2 Association (Chautaugua County, New York) in 1845 (*Benedict*).

In 1852, he wrote the Circular Letter for the Monroe Association on the theme, "The importance of the revival of religion in all our churches, and in all our members" (*1852 Monroe Baptist Association*). He also belonged to the Sweden Baptist Church and the Bergen Baptist Church (Genesee County) and served both as pastor in 1860, while still living in Churchville (*1860 Monroe Baptist Association*).

The 1860 US Census listed him as a "Baptist clergyperson" (*1860 US Census*). The 1870 US Census listed him as a "Farmer" (*1870 US Census*).

Bliss died December 11, 1873 in Churchville, New York (Monroe County) *(Rootsweb, 8/30/06)*.

BIBLIOGRAPHY

1842 Annual of the Monroe Baptist Association, Monroe New York. Monroe, NY: Monroe Baptist Association, 1842, cited in Betsy Dunbar, email to the writer, 29 August 2006. Cited as *1842 Monroe Baptist Association*.

1852 Annual of the Monroe Baptist Association, Monroe New York. Monroe, NY: Monroe Baptist Association, 1852, cited in

Betsy Dunbar, email to the writer, 29 August 2006. Cited as *1852 Monroe Baptist Association.*

1860 US Census. Cited in Betsy Dunbar, email to the writer, 29 August 2006.

1860 Annual of the Monroe Baptist Association, Monroe New York. Monroe, NY: Monroe Baptist Association, 1860, cited in Betsy Dunbar, email to the writer, Tuesday, 29 August 2006 4:08 PM. Cited as *1860 Monroe Baptist Association.*

1870 US Census. Cited in Betsy Dunbar, email to the writer, 29 August 2006.

Andrews, Georgia Drew, ed. "History of Friendship Village, New York." In *A Centennial Memorial: History of Allegany County, New York.* Alfred, NY: W. A. Fergusson & Co., 1896. Available at http://history.rays-place.com/ny/friendship-v-ny1.htm. Accessed 30 August 2006. Cited as *Friendship Village.*
Benedict, David. *History of the Baptists,* 949, cited in Betsy Dunbar, email to the writer, 29 August 2006

Bliss J. F., in "Popery and Protestantism Compared." Cited in J. R. Graves, *The Tri-lemma; OR, Death by Three Horns.* Accessible at http://www.pbministries.org/Theology/J.%20R.%20Graves/Tri-lemma/tri-lemma_02.htm. Accessed 30 August 2006. Cited as *Bliss in Graves.*

Bliss, John Flavel. *Letters on Christian Baptism As the Initiating Ordinances.* Lexington, NY: Levi L. Hill, 1841.

Commemorative Biographical Record of Tolland and Windham Counties Connecticut. Biographical Sketches of Prominent and Representative Citizens and of Many of the Early Settled Families. Chicago: J. H. Beers & Co., 1903.

Dunbar, Betsy. Email to the writer, 29 August 2006.

ftp://ftp.rootsweb.com/pub/usgenweb/ct/ctstate/books/beer001a.txt. Accessed 27 August 2006.

Graves, J. R. *The Tri-lemma; OR, Death by Three Horns.*

A Biographical Sketch of John Flavel Bliss

Accessible at http://www.pbministries.org/Theology/J.%20R.%20Graves/Tri-lemma/tri-lemma_02.htm. Accessed 30 August 2006.

History of Rochester Presbytery from the earliest settlement of the country : embracing original records of Ontario Association, and the presbyteries of Ontario, Rochester (former), Genesee River and Rochester City, to which are appended biographical sketches of deceased ministers and brief histories of individual churches. Rochester. New York, NY: Democrat-Chronicle Press, 1889. Cited as *Rochester Presbytery*.

http://genforum.genealogy.com/bliss/messages/1333.html.

http://www.pbministries.org/Theology/J.%20R.%20Graves/Tri-lemma/tri-lemma_02.htm. Accessed 30 August 2006.

http://www.rootsweb.com/~nymonroe/vr/newspaper-marriages-1.htm. Accessed 30 August 2006. Cited as *Rootsweb 8/30/06*.

http://www.rootsweb.com/~nyrgs/hearye/v073Fa1986.htm. Accessed 26 August 2006. Cited as *Rootsweb 8/26/06*.

Monroe Baptist Association, "Sketch of the United Henrietta Baptist Church. Monroe." In *1866 Annual of the Monroe Baptist Association.* Monroe, New York. Monroe, New York: Monroe Baptist Assocation, 1866, 21-23, cited in Betsy Dunbar, email to the writer, 29 August 2006. Cited as *Henrietta Baptist Church*.

The Monroe Republican, 17, 1824, cited in http://www.rootsweb.com/~nymonroe/vr/newspaper-marriages-1.htm. Accessed 30 August 2006.

THE BAPTIST STANDARD BEARER, INC.

a non-profit, tax-exempt corporation
committed to the Publication & Preservation
of the Baptist Heritage.

CURRENT TITLES AVAILABLE IN
THE BAPTIST *DISTINCTIVES* SERIES

KIFFIN, WILLIAM   A Sober Discourse of Right to Church-Communion. Wherein is proved by Scripture, the Example of the Primitive Times, and the Practice of All that have Professed the Christian Religion: That no Unbaptized person may be Regularly admitted to the Lord's Supper. (London: George Larkin, 1681).

KINGHORN, JOSEPH   Baptism, A Term of Communion. (Norwich: Bacon, Kinnebrook, and Co., 1816)

KINGHORN, JOSEPH   A Defense of "Baptism, A Term of Communion". In Answer To Robert Hall's Reply. (Norwich: Wilkin and Youngman, 1820).

GILL, JOHN   Gospel Baptism. A Collection of Sermons, Tracts, etc., on Scriptural Authority, the Nature of the New Testament Church and the Ordinance of Baptism by John Gill. (Paris, AR: The Baptist Standard Bearer, Inc., 2006).

CARSON, ALEXANDER	Ecclesiastical Polity of the New Testament. (Dublin: William Carson, 1856).
BOOTH, ABRAHAM	A Defense of the Baptists. A Declaration and Vindication of Three Historically Distinctive Baptist Principles. Compiled and Set Forth in the Republication of Three Books. Revised edition. (Paris, AR: The Baptist Standard Bearer, Inc., 2006).
BOOTH, ABRAHAM	Paedobaptism Examined on the Principles, Concessions, and Reasonings of the Most Learned Paedobaptists. With Replies to the Arguments and Objections of Dr. Williams and Mr. Peter Edwards. 3 volumes. (London: Ebenezer Palmer, 1829).
CARROLL, B. H.	*Ecclesia* - The Church. With an Appendix. (Louisville: Baptist Book Concern, 1903).
CHRISTIAN, JOHN T.	Immersion, The Act of Christian Baptism. (Louisville: Baptist Book Concern, 1891).
FROST, J. M.	Pedobaptism: Is It From Heaven Or Of Men? (Philadelphia: American Baptist Publication Society, 1875).
FULLER, RICHARD	Baptism, and the Terms of Communion; An Argument. (Charleston, SC: Southern Baptist Publication Society, 1854).
GRAVES, J. R.	Tri-Lemma: or, Death By Three Horns. The Presbyterian General Assembly Not Able To Decide This Question: "Is Baptism In The Romish Church Valid?" 1st Edition.

(Nashville: Southwestern Publishing House, 1861).

MELL, P.H.   Baptism In Its Mode and Subjects. (Charleston, SC: Southern Baptist Publications Society, 1853).

JETER, JEREMIAH B.   Baptist Principles Reset. Consisting of Articles on Distinctive Baptist Principles by Various Authors. With an Appendix. (Richmond: The Religious Herald Co., 1902).

PENDLETON, J.M.   Distinctive Principles of Baptists. (Philadelphia: American Baptist Publication Society, 1882).

THOMAS, JESSE B.   The Church and the Kingdom. A New Testament Study. (Louisville: Baptist Book Concern, 1914).

WALLER, JOHN L.   Open Communion Shown to be Unscriptural & Deleterious. With an introductory essay by Dr. D. R. Campbell and an Appendix. (Louisville: Baptist Book Concern, 1859).

For a complete list of current authors/titles, visit our internet site at:
www.standardbearer.org
or write us at:

he Baptist Standard Bearer, Inc.

NUMBER ONE IRON OAKS DRIVE • PARIS, ARKANSAS 72855

TEL # 479-963-3831   FAX # 479-963-8083
EMAIL: Baptist@centurytel.net   http://www.standardbearer.org

Thou hast given a standard to them that fear thee; that it may be displayed because of the truth. — Psalm 60:4

www.ingramcontent.com/pod-product-compliance
Lightning Source LLC
Chambersburg PA
CBHW020752160426

43192CB00006B/322